Chapter & Verse(Chorus Verse)
or
(Another Dickhead) On The Road

By Tony Wright

Jack

I ♡ YA

Tony x

THANK YOU!

For my Mother, my Family

&

the memories of Scott Hutchison & Stevie "Rainy Boy Sleep" Martin

Published 2018 by Tony Wright
©2018 Tony Wright
ISBN 978-1-5272-3074-3

Edited by Steven Rainey
Cover artwork by Serena Quinn
Rear cover photograph by Colm Laverty
Twitter – @Toeknee_Wright
Rock &/or Roll.

Interior design by April Sky Design, Newtownards www.aprilsky.co.uk
Printed by GPS Colour Graphics Limited, Belfast

When the light surrounding is dying
& darkness overcomes all you survey
Fret not, for the night shall turn
At the Dawning of your new day.

& when your hope feels like its drowning
Succumbing, to the burden of fears
Travel slow, but travel forward
You'll see, all is rarely how it appears

Head up, & toward your horizon
Move steady, onto your promise so great
Freed from the shackles of excuses
Guided, by the reason of your fate

For only you, can let that light in
Only you, can embark upon that way
Only you, can cast out your demon
& begin the Dawning of your new day.

Me, just then.

Part One

1

"...he lives a pretty weird life..."

These words – uttered by my good friend and associate, jazz musician David Lyttle, during a performance by the two of us at the Belfast Metropolitan Arts Centre during his time as Artist in Residence (it's a gig in most other places, but in a theatre, a performance) – have been echoing in my mind ever since.

We'd been playing for roughly an hour to an enraptured, engaged, and encaged audience, and we were coming towards the end of our set. I had to retune my guitar so David took the baton and spoke to the gathered listeners about his residency, our recent album, and how we had come to work together, having only been aware of each other through reputation a few months previous.

He was doing a great job, even I was interested.

Of course I was, he was full of praise for me. As he enthused about what a fantastic songwriter I was, I found myself thinking, "David has always been very astute. The man has a PhD in Musicology, he knows the mark of the greats when he hears them."

I stood there, finely tuning my guitar, one ear on the tuner, the other ear absorbing the lavish praise being bestowed upon me, as well as the platitudes of thanks to our wholly contented audience. He urged the audience to support musicians like ourselves, again citing myself as an example due to the time and dedication I had put in over the years to being a full-time songwriter and musician.

I readied myself for the penultimate song of the gig...sorry, performance.

Then, at the tail end of David's expertly executed and entirely accurate monologue, he said those words.

"...he lives a pretty weird life..."

I quietly laughed, and the gaze of the audience briefly but immediately switched from David to me. They weren't laughing. A few smiles peppered throughout, sure, and they were in no way judging me I hasten to add, merely responding to the sudden burst of amusement from the other musician on stage who was providing their night's cultural fulfilment in Belfast's gloriously overpriced Cathedral Quarter.

"...he lives a pretty weird life..."

We played our final two songs and the audience bayed for more. Which we couldn't provide as we simply didn't have any more to play. Unless we went down the improvisational route. We'd performed our album in its entirety – plus a new song we hadn't sufficiently rehearsed, which I hadn't played as well as I would've liked – so an improvised encore was a no-go for the evening.

We said our thank-you's, and reminded the audience we had our own respective solo albums for sale, and that our collaborative effort was available for purchase online. I shook some hands and told a few attendees that we'd see them in bar downstairs for a quick drink, if they were interested.

I shouldn't have said this.

I was in a rush to get the last train north at 2253 from the inappropriately named Belfast Central Station (I mean, it's not very 'central'. 'Central-ish'? Yes.). But the shameful truth was that the attendees I asked were three women. One of whom had immediately caught my eye upon her entering the building, and I wanted to at least get her name. I mean, she knew mine, why shouldn't I ask hers? I was attempting to get better and more confident at doing such things, having spent the bulk of the preceding years as a solo musician. In every sense of the word.

They had been sat in the front row of the gig...sorry...performance, and I had to use a substantial amount of will power to stop my eyes wandering toward her – a sure-fire way to forget lyrics, chord progressions, and quite possibly, myself. I was determined to get her name. For all I knew, she could be the fabled, "One".

But there was that line, echoing in my mind...

"...he lives a pretty weird life..."

I packed my equipment away. One of the perks of being an acoustic guitar player, is that gear is lightweight, and there isn't a whole lot of it. I made some brief small talk with the remaining audience members, and sold a few CDs. I gave David a warm congratulatory handshake, exchanged good byes, and walked to the elevator.

"...he lives a pretty weird life..."

I walked to the bar and ordered a half of Devil's Backbone, allowing myself a smirk at the name. Glancing at the time, I saw I only had about 5 minutes before my taxi to the train station, and I intended to at least get this lady's name. As long as I could remember how to speak, I guessed I'd be okay.

Looking around me, I saw that she was sitting with her back to the bar, accompanied by one of her friends, while the other was nowhere to be seen. It alleviated my nerves a little, as approaching two people is much less terrifying than approaching three.

As I approached they both welcomed me with smiles and thanks for the show, which I politely accepted, and thanked them for coming. I formally introduced myself, as did they. Alexa and Deborah...dear sweet Deborah. I made a joke about my stage-name, VerseChorusVerse (I'll come to that later), and we were smiles all round. My nerves dropped to about 50%. Fantastic.

I asked them about themselves, and her friend began to lead the conversation. All the while she kept quiet, but we kept exchanging glances and smiles intermittently. She was beautiful. Her friend did some genuinely worthwhile work for a charity, and whilst I should've been more interested in her gallant career, the shameful truth is all I wanted to do was to turn conversation back to the lady I had forbade my eyes from earlier that evening, Deborah.

Just as an opportunity to do that arose, her other friend returned. Again I introduced myself, her name was Ciara. I quickly checked the time, then stole another smile from the Deborah, before readjusting my view to Ciara, who asked me about my plans for the evening, and whether I was really heading back to Portstewart (David had mentioned that I was based there, and that I'd be heading back that direction, post-performance).

Now, most humans above the age of 13 would probably be able to interpret such a question as a time to possibly reappraise ones plans, given the current company.

Not I.

I am savagely unaware of such possibilities, the concept, entirely alien.

"Well, I gotta split in a few minutes actually," I responded, whilst finishing off my clearly slow acting Devils Backbone. A silence from the three ladies ensued, their heads slightly tilted to one side in an intrigued manner, urging extrapolation.

With all the charm of an ashtray left in the rain on a back step, I filled the silence with a white lie. "Yeah, there's a chance the toilet may flood again, and I'm just house sitting on a long term basis. Technically, I'm homeless. It's not my place, I gotta go back to make sure it's okay – it's a big ol' town house that I potter about, and I'm a little worried about the pipes".

As I spoke these words – and I have no idea why I did – I was puzzled as to why I had mentioned a flooding toilet. That *had* happened, but about a year ago, and the problem had long been taken care of. The three exchanged glances with one another before dear sweet Deborah said, "Wow, yeah, ok! Well that sucks."

"Yeeeah," I replied whilst picking up my guitar, blissfully unaware – for the time being – of just how pathetic my encounter had been with them.

I smiled and shook hands with each of them, thanking them by name for coming along, and that I really hoped to see them again. That was one third of the truth any way; as cool as they had been, and as nice as it would be to see two of them again, I only wanted to definitely see one of them again.

I then left the building and my taxi promptly arrived bang on time. We made our way to Central(ish) Station, where I paid the man and said thanks. After exiting the vehicle, I made my way to train platform and boarded the train north, when it suddenly dawned on me as I took my seat, like a regretful Archimedes...

What the hell was I doing going back to Portstewart?

2

David had spoken the truth. I do live a pretty weird life.

Nothing worryingly weird – I hope – but weird, upon reflection, nonetheless.

I guess it was just odd for me to hear it being said out loud to a room full of strangers, by a friend who hasn't known me for a very long time, but long enough to establish that there is something weird about my life, and how it continues to unfold. It's like I had been suspicious of the slightly out of the ordinary way my life was, but hadn't genuinely accepted until I heard it said, from someone whose opinion I value.

It sat with me, as it still does, as both a comfort of acknowledgement, and a blight of reason.

I'm 35 years old, and I've been a songwriter and musician, to some extent, for 27 of those years. I started gigging my own material 21 years ago in 1995, and 20 years ago had my first flirtation with the behemoth that is the Music Industry, when BMG, then one of the world's biggest music groups, considered signing my band, PepperBook (comprised of my buddies Adrian Rowe, Graeme Harbinson, Delwyn Kane – later replaced by Johnny Adger – and I).

This process was strung out for nearly two years before they changed their minds, devastating my hopes and ambitions for a time. When others of my age were studying for GCSEs, I was being flown back and forth to London, being told how great I was. My exam results didn't agree with this forecast of greatness.

After a little while I began to dust myself down and rebuild those hopes and ambitions from the beating they'd taken at the hands of the industry. Slowly, but surely, I was getting back on my feet and music was leading me back on to the path from which I'd briefly strayed.

Then, 16 years ago, my Mother passed away.

My Mother, who had taught me how to play guitar in the first place. She had been ill for a while – diagnosed shortly after BMG had first shown an interest – but her wishes were for my Dad, Nana, Auntie, and Uncle, to keep the severity and advanced nature of the sickness from me and my brother Dario, so that we wouldn't worry.

It's taken a long time for me to understand why she did this, and honestly I still don't know if I really do. Dario and I knew she had been ill, but thought the cancer was in remission, and then suddenly...our Mother was gone.

Everything was jarred and nothing seemed to matter anymore.

The people I was in a band with, my best friends, started to go to university, and my playmates and confidants of old continued rightfully on their own paths. Whether I liked it or not, we were growing up.

After a little bit of forgetting about the world and everyone else in it, I fell in love with a girl. She actively encouraged me to get back into making music, as it was what I loved so much. She was right. Or so I've thought.

13 years ago, I joined a covers band on the North Coast, on the premise that they stopped doing covers and concentrated on doing our own material. They agreed.

Nearing our second anniversary of being together, the girl I had fallen for had to leave Northern Ireland – for a year – to do her work placement across the water in Cambridge. This terrified her greatly, and she didn't want us to be so far apart. Neither did I, so I found a year long music course I could attend in Liverpool. Whilst it was obviously not a neighbouring town to Cambridge, it was at least in the same country, and we could spend our weekends together. We were deeply in love after all, and we were bound to marry and have a family. We had discussed it a few times with wide eyed excitement and genuine happiness – or so I thought.

She left for Cambridge two months before I was due to leave for Liverpool. We spoke on the phone, emailed, sent texts, and wrote letters to each other in the interim two months, keeping the candle burning.

In this time, I rehearsed as often as I could with my new band (the monstrously named, Zombie Safari Park – made up of Stephen Donaghy, Andy Hasson, Rory Friers, Darren Johnston, and Chris Wee). We picked up gigs when we could, wrote songs, and began to build a bit of a fan base, in an area where bands performing their own material had been thin on the ground since the slow dispersal of my last band, PepperBook. Chris, the drummer, was also heading to England, but we promised to gig whenever we returned for weekends or holidays. We were committed to our preposterously named band.

I laboured on building sites.

I helped to build a gym.

I worked as a janitor at a chip board factory.

I was a removal man.

I did what I could to earn money, like we all do.

I worked any job I could to build up some more cash for my impending relocation to England.

Throughout this, music was there as a vent. Using the back-burning sadness as fuel to a deeply set, melodic furnace that burned within, both sustaining and aiding me.

Two days before I was due to leave for Liverpool, my beloved girlfriend told me from out of the blue she was coming home for the weekend. This may be the oldest cliché I use in these writings, but the news was music to my ears, and music meant a great deal to me. We met at her family home and made love whilst her parents watched television in the room below us.

The next day she came to see me in Portstewart just as I was finishing my packing for Liverpool, and she broke up with me.

Why, I'm still not 100% sure, but to say I was heartbroken would be putting it lightly.

The following day, me and my dad left for Liverpool. We got a ferry from Belfast to Scotland, and drove south towards the home of The Beatles, and the two footballing giants of Liverpool FC & Liverpool FC Reserves. I can't remember too much about that drive, but I'm sure I wasn't the best company.

I remember when my Dad left me at my new home on Myrtle Street (or Mehrrr-til Street as the locals called it), I stood amidst all my worldly, boxed possessions, having a distinct feeling of, "What the fuck am I doing here?" I'd come to Liverpool to be close to my now ex-girlfriend, left my family and band, and was now feeling pretty close to a Neil Young lyric.

The rest of my new flatmates began to arrive as I hid in my room, trying to conceal my confusion and bewilderment at the whirlwind that had taken place in the preceding 72 hours.

Finally I built the courage to go and introduce myself; I rolled a joint from some crappy hash I had smuggled over with me, picked up the box of beer my dad had bought me before he left, and made my way up to the communal living area of my new home to meet my new accomplices in the art of survival. I was about to find out that they were all 18, while they were all about to discover that I was an old timer at the age of 22.

I confidently, yet foolishly, bestrode amongst them. I laid my slab of beer on the table and lit my joint, boisterously introducing myself to their collectively horrified fresh faces (five females and two other males). "Hello! I'm Tony & I'm Irish," I said whilst cracking open a can of beer with a 5 inch spliff dangling from my mouth, putting my Irish Brothers and Sisters back several decades. My introduction was met with looks of shock and a hint of disgust, as one of the girls pointed out the 'No Smoking' sign.

Hurriedly & bravely, I retreated to my room.

This would be a recurring act during my time in Liverpool.

As I struggled to get to grips with what I was actually doing there, I figured I might as well make the most of it. I made new friends, whilst keeping in constant touch with my friends and bandmates back home.

I started to discover new styles of music, and connected with more people than I thought possible through our shared love of it – collectively broadening our horizons. My friend, Matt Thomason, played me a great deal of new bands that began to change the way I listened to music, and soon these new sounds would irreversibly alter my emotional connection with it.

In keeping with my ridiculous band names of the past, I fell for a genre of music with just as absurd a title. Post-Rock. It was at this time I joined my first instrumental band with Matt, our whiskey loving Norwegian buddy Chris, and my sometime smoking associate and all round great Scot, Nathan. We were called, "My Kin Variant", and would play all night long using the college facilities, never deeming the outside world worthy of hearing our twisted and ethereal strung-out jams.

I began mailing the guys in Zombie Safari Park the names of these bands and urging them to check them out. I later found out that they didn't. That was cool though, as it meant I got to play them to them whenever I went home, and getting to see the looks on their faces, knowing that my buddy Matt had seen the exact same look of wonder on my own face a few months previous.

Back in Liverpool, little dramas took place and quickly disappeared again. I began to feel genuinely at home in my adopted city. The possibility of staying on and doing a degree there began to interest me. But what of ZSP?

A few months before my course was due to end, I got an email from an old friend, Paul Clegg, who was finding success as a tour manger. He asked me if I wanted to be a guitar tech on a European tour with a couple of American metal bands, Godhead, and Society 1. I'd earn no money, but I wouldn't lose any either, AND I got to stay on a proper tour-bus. Clearly, having an affinity for ludicrously named bands, I accepted, and was given two and a half weeks leave from college by my Tutors.

The things I saw on that first European tour would be enough to merit their own book. The depths of depravity that I witnessed on that run led me to abstain from any sort of alcohol for the then foresee-able future. I made that decision halfway through the tour.

When I returned, I had made up my mind that University was not right for me at that time. I was now 23, and if I was serious about being a musician, I'd need to be out amongst it. Had I been 18, I'm sure my thoughts would've been different, but it really felt like it was now, or never.

I graduated with a Merit from LIPA (Liverpool Institute of Performing Arts), and Sir Paul McCartney, Tony Wilson, Willy Russell, and Susanna Hoffs waved me on with luck in all my future endeavours at our Graduation ceremony. I even gave Macca a Zombie Safari Park CD, which I'm sure he appreciated.

I returned to the land of my forefathers with a new found vigour and appetite. Music and I, we were gonna do just fine.

3

At an abandoned band practice – through lack of personnel – I suggested we try some instrumental "jams", as we, annoyingly, would say. Johnny Adger, PepperBook's old bassist (and more than that, a close friend) was there at my invitation, as he often was, along with a blue bag full of beer. He plugged himself in, as did two newer friends: Rory Friers and Chris Wee of Zombie Safari Park.

In that first jam, we worked on the bones of three tracks, one of which was two simple progressions I had written in Liverpool, some months previously. The first version was nearly 14 minutes long. It was named, in the preposterously post-rock fashion, 'And The Voiceless Were Never Heard As They Never Learnt To Speak'. In time, after a few gigs, I mercifully shortened it to 'The Voiceless'. This helped cut down our considerable set length at shows. It went on to become the first anthem from my newly formed band. The four of us playing together felt perfect; like a completed puzzle, we made each other better musicians. In keeping with the preposterously post-rock names, we called ourselves And So I Watch You From Afar. I was, and remain, the only crossover member.

Zombie Safari Park continued to gig, and we'd started to get a bit of recognition from further afield. The gigs were becoming notoriously rambunctious, and locally, we were racking up the miles. All the while, I was on my lonely, self-imposed perch of sobriety, even going to a gym several times a week. A far cry from my sarcastic, grunge/punk rock beginnings.

One evening – mid 2004 – Zombie Safari Park were booked to play The Hoot, in Downpatrick. We started off as energetically as had come to be expected, so much so that I soon felt a bit of a stitch in my abdomen. By the time we launched into our second song, the stitch had become a bit more pronounced, so I stopped jumping off anything and everything I could. By the time the third song started I was crouching down. Looking every bit the clichéd, tortured, pained singer.

The audience were lapping it up and going nuts. At the third song's conclusion, I sheepishly said into the microphone, "I need an ambulance". The crowd loved this and whooped and hollered some more, and all of a sudden I found tremendous empathy with the late Tommy Cooper.

Barely able to move or breathe, I said it again.

Same reaction.

Slowly, when they realised I wasn't getting up and that I wasn't balled into the foetal position for the sake of entertainment, the band started to gather round me. A minor commotion broke out. People were shouting for help, asking me what was wrong. All I could muster was a grimace and a faint, "Help". One of the guys picked me up, and they carried me towards our car. They carefully placed me on a ledge outside the bar as they opened the car and made room for me. I fell from it onto the cold pavement, balled into the foetal position again.

I watched in horror as my skin began to change colour. Chameleon-like, my entire body shifted to a lifeless, dead grey, mirroring the footpath beneath me. I shut my eyes as tight as I could. I didn't want to see what was happening to me. The pain had shifted from my abdomen to my heart, and I was convinced I was having a heart attack.

23 years old, in the best shape of my life, and having a heart attack.

Wonderful.

At the Medical Centre in Downpatrick, placed on a stretcher, I was brought into a private room where they proceeded to cut my clothes from me. I opened my eyes for the first time in 10 minutes, and made brief eye-contact with a passing nurse. She started to cry. Further cementing my belief that I was surely a goner. They then proceeded to cut my stupidly baggy trousers off (as opposed to the stupidly skinny ones I may have been wearing had this been a few years later).

As they cut off my jeans, the Doctor loudly proclaimed, "Good God! How... Mr Wright...How long has your scrotum been like that?"

I remember thinking, "Odd question...what the hell has that got to do with me having a heart attack?"

Several months earlier, whilst still living in Liverpool, I had found a small skin lesion on the afore mentioned scrotum. I went to the student doctor to get it checked out, and I was assured that it was nothing to worry about, and that it should disappear in due course. So, naturally, I thought that was what the good Doctor was referring to, a reasonable assumption, given the circumstances, no? I summoned the strength to answer her query, "A few months..." "A FEW MONTHS?!" she exclaimed, with a combination of horror and disgust. It was at this moment I realised I'd have to open my eyes again, if only to discover why there was such an undue commotion about my scrotum. I was, understandably, curious.

Only this commotion was most certainly not undue. Not by a long shot.

This commotion was a richly deserved one, something that I, and the other poor unfortunate witnesses in the room, could agree on.

What I had seen as I had opened my eyes for only the third time in fifteen minutes, was that the contents of my scrotal sac, whatever they may have been, had caused my sac to swell up to such a size that it was just above my knees and solid to the touch. I would describe it as a flesh coloured appendage, roughly the same dimensions of a prize winning grapefruit. Only it wasn't flesh coloured. Like the rest of my skin it was a dull, pavement hue of grey.

I could only be described, at that time, as a one handled human space-hopper.

It's obvious to me now that the reason I thought I was having a heart attack was because it was valiantly taking all the strain. There was no pain down there, for now. My heart was taking one for the team. This lasted a few more minutes, until my brain had processed what I had just saw.

"No!" I meekly bellowed, before tailing off. "Uh, I dunno...I dunno how long..." Which I'm certain brought some relief to the gathered medical staff, knowing that I hadn't been waddling around with this monstrosity for months. Maybe they thought that it explained the excessively baggy jeans? Who knows? Not I, and I didn't care to ask them at the time, while they certainly didn't care to ask again.

In the corner, glancing over towards me with combined looks of medical interest, pity, and disgust, they quietly but frantically discussed what may be going on.

What was the cause of this freakish growth?

One of the doctors began to calmly explain that an ambulance was on its way to take me to the nearest hospital, Lagan Valley, about 20 minutes away. I wanted to ask for something for the pain when the doctor, sensing a young man who has turned a deathly, impossible grey, who is the process of experiencing a severe body-shock due to the sudden freakish expansion in size to an area best treated with gentle tenderness, explained to me that they couldn't give me anything for the pain, as I was being rushed for surgery.

I'll leave it to your hugely capable imagination with regards as to what I thought of that assertion.

The ambulance arrived with remarkable speed, all things considered. It certainly didn't seem like it was going that fast whenever we were on our way back to the hospital, feeling more like we were on a casual Sunday drive to Alpha Centauri at the time.

I would've given anything for greater velocity right then.

I was alone in the back of that ambulance and my panicked thoughts were moving at a greater speed than the emergency vehicle ever could.

Surely, this was it.

My heart felt like it was about to burst out of my chest in flames, if only to give some space to whatever it was that was vastly over occupying my nethers.

The siren wasn't even sounding.

"What on God's green earth could have warranted a siren blast more than the freak of nature that had become my ball bag?" I recall reasoning, both rationally and lucidly, at the time.

When we got to the hospital, the paramedics were wholly forgiven for the lack of siren by me. They had me out of that thing and in an operating theatre in double quick time. By this stage, the pain had begun to make things seem more warped than I ever thought possible. I could have sworn I was hallucinating through pain.

Finally, I was on the operating table, and the surgeon entered the theatre. He was a tall, older man. A shock of white hair and a beard that somehow made him look like a hybrid of Santa Claus, Harold Shipman, and the classic personification of God. That either boded very well, or very, very poorly for me.

He briefly explained that they thought I'd suffered a strangled testicle, whilst he affixed a mask to me telling me to breathe deeply, and that I'd soon be unconscious.

As I huffed on the gas provided, I momentarily felt a wave of relief.

This reprieve wasn't long lived.

The very last thing I remember as he stood over me, was a brief but deliriously extreme panic after he said, "We may have to remove your testicles completely."

I awoke some hours later, and with my eyes still closed, I started to piece together the preceding evening's chain of events.

Gig.

Downpatrick.

Load-in.

Soundcheck.

Food.

Gig.

Pain.

Grey.

Pain.

Scrotum.

Pain.

Terror.

Pain.

Ambulance.

Pain.

Hospital...

It was then I remembered the surgeon's final words to me.

My eyes have never opened so wide and so quickly. "A blink of an eye", is commonly accepted as pretty quick, and this was half the speed.

I was still alive, unless heaven, hell or purgatory resembled a curtained-off hospital bed. I was thankful. Thankful yet terrified.

Terrified to put my hands down to where my testicles might not be anymore.

Terrified to look beside me in case there was a little jar sitting there with my testicles bobbing in some liquid, the same way I'd received my adenoids all those years ago, like some weird trophy of condolences.

It was then that a nurse pulled back my curtain to check on me.

Upon seeing that I was awake, she warmly smiled and was about to speak when I rudely, but understandably, I feel – given the circumstances – interrupted her.

"Have I still got balls?" I urgently enquired, a question I hope I never have to ask again.

She laughed uproariously and replied, "Oh no, no, no..."

"W-what!?" I again, rudely, but once again understandably, interrupted her. "Let me finish", she continued. "It was nothing to do with your testicles, you're still all in one piece."

The sigh and thankful profanity I let out is probably still reverberating around the Lagan Valley, spooking wild life to this very day. She went on to tell me that I'd had a dramatic, inguinal hernia, explaining in medical detail what had happened, and that once the consultant said so, I'd be free to go. I'd have a bit of a recovery period, but, ultimately, I'd be right as rain in a month or two.

I was greeted by some of the guys in the band, who were almost as relieved as I was. They'd tried to notify my father and brother, but my Dad was in Australia, and I had – of course – put my brother's name in my phone under a nickname I'd never once referred to him as in front of other humans. Who would think to phone Guru George when looking for Dario Wright? Only me, or possibly the Guru himself.

So I thank them, my former bandmates – and all of the medical team – implicitly, for staying with me and saving me on a truly bizarre night.

It would not be the last time that I would be admitted to hospital in the ensuing seven years.

4

Right now, at the very moment of writing this, my pretty weird life has taken me to the tiny seaside village of Cushendun, County Antrim, Northern Ireland. The Mull of Kintyre – favoured Mull of my old buddy McCartney – is only 15 miles or so from the shore, and clearly visible on days equal to said clarity.

I am in a rather beautiful 200 year old Big House, built in 1813, and appropriately called, "Rockport". It sits on Murloch Bay, a mere stone's throw from the ocean, and from the window directly in front of me, I can see the village's modest and beautiful beach. A fence and a little bit of grassland separates the sand from the Gaelic Football and Hurling pitch. I can see the heart of the town from here, little over half a mile from me. We are tucked away from the maddening crowd, where the stunning Glens of Antrim tumble down, and the Glendun River meets the Atlantic Ocean.

The local legend of how the river got its name is typically both sweet and violent, a familiar trait of Irish folklore around these parts. The legend goes that one day, hundreds and hundreds of years ago, a beautiful young lady was strolling from glen to glen. At the peak of one, she came across an older lady, dutifully washing hundreds of tiny white shirts. When the younger of the two ladies enquired as to why on earth the other was washing these minuscule white overalls, she was greeted with the grim forewarning that the following day The Irish Fairies were due to go to war with their nearby Scottish counterparts. Since, like most people, the younger lady had never borne witness to the Fairies, she wondered how she would know who would triumph in this petite but savage battle? The older lady informed her that if the Scottish Fairies were to win, the river in which she was washing the battle regalia would run brown from the Irish Fairy blood. 'Dun', is Irish for brown. Hence the Glendun River. The brown tinge of the water that flows down the Glens to meet with the sea suggests that the Scots overturned the Irish little people. It also suggests that, unless brown blood coursed through their veins, they had some severe type of blood poisoning that would have done them in eventually.

Out of the window to my right, and the first thing I've seen these past few mornings, is what's left of Carras Castle, dated back to around the early 14th Century. The place is steeped in history, and like all places so deeply entrenched in the past, it's also mired in – you guessed it – death.

To say there's a macabre history to the grounds is somewhat of an understatement. Once, it was occupied by the Irish King, Shane O'Neill. In 1565 he held the exquisitely named Sorley Boy McDonnell, a local clan leader and potential blues musician, captive. Two years later (in 1567, number fans) the McDonnell clan had taken over residency of the castle, and after a defeat at the hands of O'Neill, they invited him to his former residence to show there were no hard feelings, and to party for two days in the time honoured tradition of hunting and feasting. O'Neill graciously accepted the invitation, and had a whale of a time at his old stomping ground with the apparently thoroughly decent and magnanimous McDonnells, never once having to ask where the toilet was. Marvellous.

Unfortunately, on the third day – when house parties tend to get out of control – they stabbed him to death, and sent his severed head to the representatives of Queen Elizabeth (to whom O'Neill had sworn an allegiance to, in Irish), who were then lording it up in Dublin Castle.

Even grimmer than all of this is that in medieval times, the grounds served as a mass grave for ill children, the remains of which were moved to the consecrated grounds of the local Church a few years ago.

The poet Moira O'Neill (no relation to the unfortunate afore mentioned Shane) lived here, and penned *The Songs of The Glens* within its walls. The house also holds some ties to Sir Roger Casement, and I've been told that George Bernard Shaw and Patrick Pearse were frequent guests, most likely through the Casement connection. Whether or not Bernard Shaw and Pearse were guests at the same time, I have no idea. Parties tend to go awry around here it seems.

In 1941 it was purchased by the former Town Clerk of Belfast, John Archer, whose wife (I regret I couldn't find her name) was known to hold many séances and, according to local folklore, upset a great many of the roaming, unsettled souls that densely populate such a historical site. One of the evenings when I first stayed at the house a few years ago, they decided to make their presence known to lucky old me.

I was tidying up some edits on a demo recording I had made earlier, when a visible and audible spike appeared on a track from out of nowhere. Visible, in that the waveform on the screen had spiked, and audible, in that my headphones made such a momentary whelp that I felt as if my eardrums had been perforated with a hot needle. At any other time I would have put this down to a glitch in the software, or perhaps a sudden power surge. Believe me, a paranormal intervention would be pretty much the last thing I would reason for such interference. But at the exact moment that this recorded anomaly happened, out of the corner of my eye, the D string broke on my acoustic guitar which was propped against the nearest wall.

The exact moment.

My guitar was not connected to the recording interface.

Needless to say, I bravely whimpered in cowering fear.

Shaken, I rose from my seat and made my way downstairs to the kitchen to get a glass of water, and try to figure out a reasonable explanation for the bizarre grouping of events that had just taken place. I stood in the kitchen, hopelessly foraging through memories for any time in my guitar playing life when a string has broken when I haven't been playing or even holding the instrument. This was most certainly new to me. As I stood there, I noticed that something was missing. *It was silent.*

Anytime I had left my room and descended to the ground floor, the big ol' nasty guard dog, a beautifully ugly big Boxer called Tor (short for Victoria), barked like crazy. She didn't like me much, and thus was an excellent guard dog since I was, for all intents and purposes, a total stranger to her and her domain, which was hers to guard.

She was silent.

Not a peep out of her from outside, where the moaning winds were leading my thoughts further and further from a rational explanation. A sane man would have thought that she was probably asleep. I am clearly not a sane man.

Whenever I hear dogs going crazy, I immediately think a Terminator is about to appear from the future. So when I was greeted with this discordant void of sound, and the potentially supernatural occurrence that I had just been privy to, naturally I assumed some terrible fate had befallen Tor.

Or she, like me, was way too shit scared to sound a peep.

This being the 21st century, I did what any self-depreciating anxiety ridden Millennial would do whilst temporarily housed in a 200 year old Manor – I asked the Internet what the hell was going on and what should I do, by way of a Facebook status update. I hadn't forgotten my deep seated need to brag, despite my terrified and confused condition. I wanted people to know I was scared, but I was in really nice place too.

A pagan friend who was well read, and more experienced in the paranormal than I, got back to me. She told me that, from what I had shared, they didn't sound that they were malevolent spirits, but rather that they were just saying 'hello', and had probably never seen a home studio set up before.

She encouraged me to talk to them, but not in the clichéd and patronising manner of, "Oooooh is there anybody there?", but rather more a polite introduction and a 'thank you' for letting me stay in their house.

I thought, sure, why not?

I started in the kitchen, and continued as I walked up the stairs, towards and into my room, like a gushing houseguest in the residence of the Invisible Man, who has forsaken his bandages and is proudly swinging it in the nip, silently accepting my lavish praise for permitting me to reside for a few days in his beautifully restored and historic home.

That night, I slept sounder than I have done since I was a child. A full, uninterrupted eight and a half hours, with no troubling dreams or disturbances.

I awoke feeling like a new man, full of optimism and promise.

The following morning I told Patrick, who looks after the place, and had returned at an early hour, about my experiences. He laughed and basically said, "I warned ya!" when, from behind him, mercifully, emerged Tor. After cocking her head from side to side in that inquisitive way that dogs do, she opened her mouth, let out her tongue, started to wag her stump of a tail, and ran towards me with all the love, warmth and enthusiasm of a pet welcoming home her master.

I don't always get to stay I places like this I must stress. Very rarely in fact. This is my third time, having been lucky enough to enjoy the good graces of the owner to record an album here, that, at the time of writing, is still unreleased.

I have been thinking with great regularity that it may be my last album.

5

In January 2014, I moved out of Belfast, after nearly ten years of calling it home. For nearly four of those years, I had lived with two supremely inspirational talents in their respective fields; my good friends and creative sparks, Will McConnell – a videographer/film maker/camera operator with an unwavering eye and vision; a true artist – and Katie Richardson, a musician/songwriter/artist/actor with such myriad talent and drive that she would effortlessly make the most hard-working person feel like a sloth.

We had to move out of our shared home, as the landlady had decided to sell, but at least we'd been given plenty of warning. As Will and Katie made independent plans about the location of their next residence, I decided it was perhaps time to stretch my legs. I didn't feel as welcome in the city as I had done pre-2011.

Belfast, where I had come of age musically, and knew more people than my hazy memory could ever deal with. It had seemed like the centre of the universe only a few years previously, when my band was doing well, and nothing could stop our rapid ascent. Not even getting hit by a speeding black taxi.

Late 2007 was a wonderful time to be in Northern Ireland's capital. There was a tremendous sense of optimism, which permeated throughout my bandmates and I. Myself and three others (two bandmates) lived in a terraced house just off the Lisburn Road, where so many of the city's young student population, and other blow-ins of a similar age resided.

I had a full-time job as a supervisor in Auntie Annies – a pub/music venue on the Dublin Road – and when I wasn't there, I was at rehearsals with the long-named band I'd formed. We were quickly building a reputation as the most exciting new band that the city and province had seen in years; energetic, passionate, and inventive.

When I returned home from work in the small hours, they would often be awake and waiting for me in the tiny living room, and from there we would smoke way too many cigarettes, and commence scheming for the future, about how we would realise our promise and try to establish ourselves as the most important band since The Clash.

Well, you've got to dream big don't you?

Working in a bar like Auntie Annies, one of the best small live venues in the city, meant that I very quickly got to know pretty much everyone in our burgeoning music scene, and I politely, but incessantly, pushed my band on them. I was always amused at people's bemusement when I told them our preposterous name, and that we didn't have any vocals.

There was a vibrant social life connected with all of this, and putting yourself out there was nearly as important as the hours you put in writing and rehearsing. A night out to a gig or a club was basically an exercise in self-promotion and getting like-minded souls to commit to coming to your gigs when they came around. As a young, occasionally single man, I stepped up to this perilous but vital part of being in an up and coming band. We all did, brave, intrepid souls that we were.

As the end of the year approached I had ceased working in the bar for good. It came after a few months of sick leave when, after two unfortunate shifts, I'd managed to have two more hernias. I remember complaining to my manager about discomfort for the second time in a week, when he justifiably enough declared, "For Christ's sake Tony, you can't have two hernias in a week!" It was a strange duality of painful elation when upon visiting my GP and being examined, he exclaimed, "Good God man, you appear to have had two hernias in week!"

I'd never been as happy, or smug, handing over a sick note.

Mercifully, no nut flooding this time but, annoyingly, these hernias were three and four (I'd had another in late 2004 when I thought I'd recovered sufficiently, but went back to waiting tables too soon). Enough was enough. I accepted Statutory Sick Pay from my employers, and then quit when it had run its course. It was time – 2007 was the year I became a full-time musician.

One weekend in December, we were booked as main support to the sensational Fighting With Wire at their album launch at the Nerve Centre, in their home city of Derry. Fighting With Wire were, along with a group called LaFaro, the best band on the island, as far as I was concerned. I was, and remain, close friends with singer and guitarist, Cahir O'Doherty. We had toured together in our previous bands (PepperBook and Clearshot, respectively), and when my musical activities had dwindled a little in the years between then, Cahir's had flourished as he got out and did the all-important, and often forgotten, work. The guy is an inspiration. He worked as a guitar tech for bigger bands on the road. Wrote with up and coming musicians both locally and internationally. Most wisely and successfully however, he joined up with a band called JetPlane

Landing, took on the joint mantle of the band's main writer and lead guitarist, and together with a well-earned reputation for incendiary live shows, in a few short years he'd helped them establish a rapidly expanding cult fan-base that lapped up their every move.

Cahir wanted his own creative outlet and the opportunity to sing lead vocals again, and thus Fighting With Wire were born. They almost instantly had a strong following, due to his pedigree and the quality of his previous work, which was well deserved. Fighting With Wire were a hook heavy, monster of a rock trio. The NME described their then impending debut album as, "A train wreck of unrivalled shite". In 2007, a fierce rock band getting a review like that from the sadly, even then, fast declining music weekly was a badge of honour to be proudly displayed.

We were pretty excited to be playing with these guys, on a big stage, in a 600 capacity venue that they would no doubt sell out. Which made it, at that time, the most people my new band would have performed in front of.

The gig was on a Saturday in Derry, but this was a Friday in Belfast, and there was socialising to be done.

Nothing too monumental, we were wannabe professionals after all.

A few drinks were had at the home of a friend; another richly talented musician, Niall Kennedy, who had just started gigging with his fantastic new band, Panama Kings. They were a rabble rousing pop quartet and sonically they were a world away from my band. Many people felt that they would be the band to follow where great Northern Irish bands like Therapy?, Ash, and Snow Patrol had led, achieving that elusive crossover chart success. Turns out we were all wrong on that account, and a (mostly) mild-mannered trio from Bangor called Two Door Cinema Club would take that honour, eclipsing all the bands they had previously opened up for – ourselves included – in Northern Ireland.

Other than what was to happen later on that night, there was nothing else to mark this night out as remarkable. It was a standard Belfast Friday for young people: drink enough at home so you didn't have to spend too much on alcohol when you actually made it out of the door and into the pub, club or venue. You could always continue your battle with sobriety by having a smoke of an elicit, exotic, jazz cigarette. Ways and means at remaining inebriated were never far away, and never harder than booze and a little marijuana. It was a good, innocent time.

We went to Laverys on Shaftesbury Square. Or at least I think we did. As I said, the night was, until a point, quite unremarkable.

I have foggy memories of several of us walking up the Lisburn Road, with the intention of going back to Niall's place. As we began to pass the City Hospital, I decided I was going to quickly stop off at my place to pick up some more drink.

I loudly slurred my noble intentions to the group, and in a flagrant disregard for all common sense, I stumbled off of the pedestrian sanctuary of the pavement with my thoughts focused only on the alcohol transit mission I had elected to go on, not on the speeding Black Taxi bringing up the rear.

The Black Taxi that I was about to become accidentally yet forcibly familiar with.

From the accounts of my fellow imbibers, he was doing about 40mph, and for a short amount of time, I was too, as I soared through the night air, until I crashed back down to the road, some 10ft away from the initial impact.

A twisted, but breathing, human heap on the road.

The taxi driver promptly stopped the cab (I had a slight hand in it though, I like to think), and was understandably furious with me. He left both vehicle and passenger, rushed toward me and gave me a weakened, but firm kick as he unloaded his favourite couplings of insults and swear words, one by one, at my incumbent, unresponsive and unconscious body.

My friends were screaming and panicking – the velocity at which I'd been hit was enough to kill someone, and the distance and speed with which I had arched into the air before plummeting back to the cold, hard road was forceful enough that the impact to the surface could have theoretically finished the job, if the initial hit had only served to soften me up. Not to mention I was doing my best impression of a dead guy. My fellow pedestrians ran over to restrain the driver and stop him from kicking me anymore, whilst another one of our party phoned for an ambulance.

I remember briefly waking up on the way to the hospital.

"Where are we going? What happened?" I uttered.

"You're going to Hospital, Mr Wright, you were hit by a Black Cab. You're lucky to be alive", came the response from the paramedic. And I was, very lucky. Exceedingly so, and thankful, and sore. So very sore.

My mind must've figured, "Well, you're in an ambulance, you're not dead, you best go back to sleep now, stay out of any further trouble", and I promptly passed out.

The next time I woke was about an hour later, I'm told. All wired up to the now familiar drip, with a fetching yellow head brace, and a neck one to match. I didn't plan on making any sudden movements, but the medical team weren't going to take any chances, so I was strapped, by my chest, to the stretcher – the stretcher which I felt immediately guilty for occupying.

Some other friends had come into the hospital. They'd been having a nice, quiet night in, only to be interrupted by a panicked phone call from friends telling them what had happened. When I awoke and saw them I laughed a little at the situation, but promptly stopped when the inside of my head suddenly felt like a collapsing building. They told me what they knew about what had happened, and I asked them to get a picture of me with all the braces and drips; it would look great on my band's myspace page. That thought disgusts me a little now, but that was the beginning of Social Media warping how reality is to be judged. On a screen, through the avatar of how you wish to be seen by the world. "Pictures or it didn't happen", was the mentality that was starting to creep into our lives in those years.

My reasoning for that request was that it was the perfect image to show how much we 'meant' it. I may have just came off the worse for wear in a battle of wills with a taxi, but there was no question whatsoever that I wouldn't be doing the gig the following evening. My band meant everything to me. I *meant* it, man.

Punk band with no vocals?

That's right, and?

Ridiculously drawn out, veering on pretentious name?

And proud. We're better than your band.

Hit by a Car before a gig?

Fuck it, let's play.

That's exactly how we were then. Well, that's what I thought.

Once I had spoke with the guys and expressly told them the gig was still on, they went on to get some sleep.

I was kept awake to see the consultant, and I was pretty ashamed to be wasting these people's precious time, if I'm completely honest. Ashamed, yet strangely amused by the whole situation. I also remember thinking, "Why am I in the Royal Hospital on the other side of the city?" I mean, I'd had the courtesy to be hit whilst outside another hospital? They had an A&E, why not bundle me in there?

This feeling of amusement contributed to the conversation I was to have with my Doctor once he found the time to see me.

"You're a very lucky young man, Mr Wright," He dryly, and correctly, opined whilst scanning my clipboard, then turning a disapproving glance to me.

"Yes Doctor, I know, I really am. I'm so sorry to be wasting your time. Another drunken dickhead wheeled in taking other patients time and resources," I replied. It's amazing how quickly getting involved in a collision with a car can sober you up. That, and Catholic Guilt.

"You do realise," he continued, "that if you hadn't been so loose and relaxed from the alcohol in your system, you'd probably be dead?"

What the hell? Was this Doctor advocating booze consumption?

"You do realise," I ignorantly countered, "That if I hadn't been so pissed...I probably wouldn't have blindly ran in front of a speeding car?"

Even I was staggered at my impetuous, however reasonable, retort.

The Doctor, to his gallant credit, smiled at my unintended wit. He briefly resumed scanning my clipboard and said I was to stay overnight for observation, and possibly a few days.

I may have just been involved in a Pedestrian vs Vehicle, idiot's bullfight, but even in my state I knew it best to shut up.

You never tell someone you're going to sneak out, do you?

The next morning I was privy to the delights of a paid-for breakfast, and some chipper exchanges with the endlessly wonderful NHS staff. I was on a lot of painkillers, but there was still a bit of a pain in the centre of my head, successfully vying for my attention. Not enough to cause me to rethink my escape plan, but enough to uncomfortably remind me that when I was out of the hospital, and the painkillers were not, I would have a headache so colossal that the assembled stag and hen parties of the world would've felt better in my presence.

Whilst certainly not on the level of Papillion or Shawshank, my escape plan was thus...

Using the medium of SMS text messaging, I had pre-arranged with the guys to pick me up at the visitors gate at 3pm. This was in the middle of visiting hours so it wasn't uncommon to have people dressed as casually as me coming and going. They weren't to stop, but a mere pick-up. They were to give me a hang-up call (my old brick of a phone had survived being hit by a car) when they had turned onto the Grosvenor road, which, given the volume of traffic at that time on a Saturday afternoon; would give me sufficient time to remove my drip (ouch), the other assembled monitors I was on, and to make my way – hopefully unnoticed – from the fourth floor to the ground via the stairs, to heighten my chances of remaining unseen, because, well, nobody takes the stairs in hospitals.

My phone rang, then abruptly stopped.

With a teeth clenching grimace, and as quickly as I could, I pulled the drip needle from my arm, and slowly raised from my bed, as wooden as I'd ever moved, then proceeded to rip the connecting cords from the chest monitors on my torso. Consciously, I left the round monitor pads adhered, as I wanted to give the guys a laugh. Since, as the Doctor had told me, I was too inebriated at the point of impact to do any real damage to my bones, or even cut the flesh, I had remained clothed minus my shoes and my jacket. I was convinced that I was going to suffer crazy bruising soon enough, but not a single one had yet reared. Movement was still fairly slow and laboured, but would resume normal service soon enough. I put on my shoes, and did up my jacket. I went over to the sink and splashed some cold water on my face. Briefly, I looked in the mirror and thought, "Time to move".

I figured the best way to leave the ward was to be as nonchalant as possible. If I calmly walked by, making no fuss and drawing no attention, no one would notice me doing so. It was a trick I had mastered at many gigs in my teenage years to gain access to the then (by me) hallowed, now (by me) vastly overrated and dull, backstage area. Just walk by the bouncers without a care in the world, avoiding eye-contact and showing no fear. Nine times out of ten, you'll get in. So I did just that.

I opened the door to my room, and as upright as my modestly lumbering frame could manage, casually made my way past the reception desk, to the stairwell beside the Elevators. It was at this point that I started to get nervous of being noticed. All of the staff had switched shifts from when I was admitted in the early hours, but something inside me was convinced the lift door was going to open and my Doctor would walk out, ordering his entourage of burly orderlies to forcibly take me down, and take me back to my room to sedate me with the strongest tranquillisers known to man. It was also at this point I remembered that this wasn't a prison hospital, and I proceeded un-noticed and un-troubled down the four flights of stairs to the main visitor's entrance to where my chariot awaited.

To cut a long story short, I walked out.

We made our way to the gig, as planned. Since news had filtered over to Derry of the previous night's events, I was greeted like a hero by the Fighting With Wire lads and the Nerve Centre staff. I took great delight in being able to poke fun at Craig, FWW's powerhouse drummer, as this gig had been postponed for a fortnight due to 'Doctor's orders'. Craig's wrists had been giving him some grief, and yet lil' ol' Tony had gotten hit by a car and snuck out of hospital to play the show. Craig, being the great guy that he is, took it in good spirit. In Derry terms he, "took his oil".

We had a fantastic gig that night, and started to cast our spell over the Music Lovers of the Maiden City. I was strangely focused, all things considered. Having said that, I would never recommend this particular method of focusing the mind, and I'm sure there's breathing exercises that are vastly more beneficial to your health.

Afterwards we went back to a party, but I chose to go to a quiet room in the house and sleep, as I was going to Glasgow the next day to visit my brother Dario and his soon-to-be wife, Colette. This meant an early rise to get the bus to Belfast, the ferry to Scotland, and then train to Glasgow.

Dear sweet, merciful Jesus, did my head hurt the following day. The last of the painkillers had long left my system, and the natural dopamine high of playing had long since dissipated. It was a long, lonely and painful journey to Glasgow.

At the time it all seemed very heroic and rock n roll. Now it just seems kind of sad, that such a thing were to be in anyway commended.

It is a bitter glamour that drapes itself upon the shoulders of such self-destructive tendencies.

Whilst I'm sure that everybody was just pleased that I was alive, to me I felt like I'd earned some kind of medal. Like a soldier who triumphed in adversity, and saved his fellow troops from missing a noble engagement. When in truth, I wouldn't have deserved even a patch from the Cub Scouts.

But I didn't have time to think about that. A slow, base wind was building at the heels of our band, and through sheer force of want (not to mention a good deal of money being spent), it was quickly becoming a whirlwind, surely to become a tornado, with the potential to be a hurricane.

As it is such with storms, there are often casualties.

6

The ensuing 4 years were both heaven and hell for me. There was no purgatory. No plateau. It was all or nothing, all conquering pleasure or pain. A bipolar existence with the highest of highs and the lowest, most subterranean of lows.

As quickly as we had achieved it in our native Northern Ireland, the band began to establish itself as an important player on the alternative scene throughout Ireland, Britain, and the rest of Europe, as well as making successful forays into both the east (Russia) and the west (America).

We did this largely in the same way we had done it in our home province (except with a few, new helping hands): by working our eager selves to the bone.

In Northern Ireland – tipped off by Cahir – we attracted the interest of a local independent label, Smalltown America; the label started by JetPlane Landing to home their releases, and one that had quickly gathered traction internationally thanks to JetPlane's popularity. And also by putting out some really great records. Andrew Ferris (JetPlane Landing Vocalist and Smalltown America head-honcho) pushed us in the direction we needed to be pushed, and helped us believe that we really could step all of this above and beyond what was thought possible for such an oddly named bunch of experimentalists from Northern Ireland's North Coast. They ironed out our business creases, and would release our self financed debut album, giving us the pedestal we were beginning to believe we earnestly deserved.

Smalltown America had grown interested because of the manner in which we had built ourselves. We jumped up several rungs of the ladder before we had really paid our dues, because of some canny moves on our behalf.

We put out an EP featuring vocals to ensnare some potential fans who were dubious of listening to an instrumental band. It didn't hurt either that some of those guest vocalists were my good friends, and further up the ladder than us. Cahir of FWW, Jonny Black of LaFaro, Neal Hughes of Driving By Night, and Geoff Topley, local multi-instrumentalist and cult hero. Thus exposing us to all of these bands pre-existing fan base.

The initial idea had come to me one night, post work, after endlessly watching *The Last Waltz* by The Band, filmed by Martin Scorcese. *The Last Waltz* had been omnipresent in my parent's house when I was a kid. There were two VHS cassettes that my mum had recorded from TV that we were expressly forbidden from taping over. Live Aid and *The Last Waltz*.

I remarked to the guys one night that it was funny how people thought we were strange for not having a singer, when only a few decades before, it was perfectly natural for a band to play all night and for a series of singers to intermittently join them for a few numbers.

"We should do that". I suggested.

So we did. We called the EP, *Tonight the City Burns*, and put on a gig with all of these other bands opening up for us.

We were cheeky bastards.

Then we came on, played a set, and invited the erstwhile singers to join us one by one, thus placing us at the centre of the circle, the main attraction around which all the others orbited.

The gig itself was a bit of a shambles, but it didn't matter. We had planted the idea that a disjointed scene, full of different genres (different sub genres of rock I should stress; we weren't that unifying), could come together and work as one. And by accidental design, we had placed ourselves slap bang in the middle.

We went on our first UK tour the following day, opening up for the excellent Public Relations Exercise, the band of my oldest and closest friend, Tiernan Welch, who along with his bandmates, had booked most of the shows. It was on this tour that we would meet our future tour mates, the similarly trajectoried, Maybeshewill.

We finally got some mainstream radio play out of it. Our first EP, *This Is Our Machine & Nothing Can Stop It*, had gotten us plenty of attention from radio on our island, which we were deeply thankful for. But there was no way BBC Radio 1 was going to play us.

Until the EPs title track, 'Tonight the City Burns', was recommended to their Alternative Tastemaker, Huw Stevens, by my old friend from PepperBook days, Northern Ireland's very own Rory McConnell. Huw, upon hearing that the song featured Cahir of FWW and JetPlane Landing, was immediately interested and gave us our first national airplay.

Cool.

The next day we were contacted by the editor of the now defunct local music magazine Alternative Ulster, Jonny Tiernan. He told us that he'd received a mail from a very prestigious PR firm in London with the golden dangling carrot of a name, Destiny PR, asking for a contact for the band.

After a few emails back and forth between ourselves and Destiny, we arranged to meet them at their offices when we were in London for our debut show in the city.

It turns out, they had heard us on Huw Stevens show, and liked what they had heard. Even more so when they were to discover we were greener than the island we hailed from I'm sure.

When we eventually found the place after a few hours of our sat-nav playing cruel tricks on us, four naïve young men navigating London on a busy afternoon, we were stunned by the opulence of the place. This was a gated community, leading to the homes of some of London's most loaded &/or in debt. Seriously though, this was a meeting place meant to bedazzle us, and bedazzle it did.

The two gents we were meeting, worked for the company, they weren't much different from us in age, and they were good guys. Their boss would be joining us shortly, but in the meantime we just got to know each other, telling jokes and genuinely bowled over by the residence we were in. I remember being taking aback at the volume of gold and platinum discs on the wall, although my excitement dwindled considerably when, upon closer inspection, they were revealed to be from an array of shiny boy-bands ranging from early Take That, to the one hit wonder ad nauseum of 911.

The boss guy arrived, and again, seemed like a good guy. He had done great things in his field, I guess. He'd produced some huge selling pop singles in the 90s and early 2000s as part of Simon Cowells factory line. He spewed numbers and figures at us, whilst we struggled to keep up, but kept nodding anyway. His two cool and friendly employees started to talk about strategies, and enthused, what I can only assume, was a genuine passion for what we did and stood for. Which was news to us, as we hadn't even really figured that out yet.

None of that mattered though, because we were excited as hell. We'd managed to prick the ears up of some industry pricks (sorry guys, too good a wordplay to not use) in big bad London.

We said our goodbyes, and joined back up with our tour buddies for another gig. We knew we were on the right track, and we were going to have to have a frank discussion about the band going forward. There was no question of us *not* taking it forward with Destiny, it was a matter of *how* we were going to afford to do it. We had to get their services, regardless of the huge sum of money it was going to cost us per month. For the second time in as many months, we were going to jump up a few rungs of the ladder. Take another shortcut. If we could just find the money.

Such actions have only served to teach me that shortcuts are only temporary, eventually you have to take the long path to make up for it.

Of course, we found the money. It came from a few different sources, and I put up the remainder with the last of the money I had been left by my mother.

Like Dan Aykroyd mortgaging his parents' house in *Ghostbusters*. We could now afford to move into the firehouse and start the business of bustin' ghosts, proper.

Obviously, we played a lot of gigs too, and that helped. But bear in mind that on that tour, and subsequent ones to come over the next year or so, we were earning roughly £50-£75 between us each night, which also had to feed us and get us to the next venue.

Things were all looking sunny in our world, and we included a new song with the ballsy title of 'A Little Solidarity Goes A Long Way', on a compilation CD released by Belfast's Oh Yeah Music centre. The title reflected the general feeling of positivity surrounding NI music at the time, and was a further attempt by us at exploiting that good feeling. Not in a bad way, I must stress. Kinda like The Beatles had done in '66 with 'All You Need is Love'. On a much, *much* smaller scale, of course

We even built a small music festival around the sentiment, simply called, "A Little Solidarity", featuring just about every band we had an email address for. Privately, we laughed that we were doing exactly what we had done with, *Tonight The City Burns*, using good sentiment to further leverage our careers. This was not, repeat, not, the intention. Our expensive, private PR team did a great job of using it as leverage, however. And we let them. Hell, we probably suggested it to them as a great piece of spin.

Another few rungs jumped.

During this period, I moved house. I moved in with Jonny, Herb, and Dave of my favourite band LaFaro. The only one we were missing was Al, the drummer. Like families, it was good to see that other bands argued and had issues. Mainly though, we laughed our asses off, dodging mice, in the most dilapidated shared house since The Young Ones had Motörhead over for tea.

We began recording our eponymous debut album with Rocky O'Reilly in Belfast's flowering Start Together studios, and it proved to be a fantastic collaborative effort between Rocky and ourselves. We recorded a great debut, if I do say so myself.

The partnership with Destiny proved incredibly worthwhile too, for the most part. We were getting featured in all the right magazines and websites, and more radio shows were starting to pay attention to this weird little band from the wild Northern Irish coast.

This burst of media coverage brought about the aforementioned attentions of the SmallTown America label and we played them our recently recorded album. Andrew Ferris was brutally honest when he said that he, personally, didn't care for the band's music, but was impressed by the work we had put in, and that our mutual friend, Cahir O'Doherty, had urged him to take a chance on us.

Andrew negotiated us a publishing contract with Sony/ATV, which was to give the band another much needed injection of cash. The irony of ironies being that the publishing contract had been proposed by the very same man who had talked a teenage me into believing I was the future of music, only to suddenly stop talking to me one day. Leaving me wondering for many years, what in the name of God a 15/16 year old could have done to piss off such a man.

I can recall Andrew telling me that it was for this precise reason, he (the guy from Sony) was trying to sign my new band. As some sort of apology.

A bitter pill to swallow no matter how it's viewed.

Still, better late than never, I guess. And at least now we could continue to pay Destiny for a while.

In the midst of all this, I began talking with a music lawyer from Manchester based in London. One of the best in the business, he had negotiated deals for Coldplay and The Verve, amongst others. He would go onto represent us after I had sufficiently courted him.

It was also around this this time that we realised we needed someone else to come on board in a managerial capacity. We were juggling too many balls and needed a proven professional to take us to the next step.

After a gig in Whelan's, Dublin, I, initially, met with one Alan Cullivan, former manager of The Thrills, who immediately impressed me with his enthusiasm and keenness to work with us. The rest of the guys agreed, and we took the discussion across the road for milkshakes at Eddie Rockets. We knew he was the right guy when the first band he mentioned was The Clash.

Thanks to Alan, we got picked up by our agent at The Agency Group, a big-time, powerful booking agency. No more banging our heads against the wall waiting for promoters to get back to us, we had an agent to bang *their* head off the wall instead.

We got matching band tattoos. Andrew Ferris commented at the time that the sentiment was, "Either the coolest, or the shittest thing I've ever seen". It's crazy to think that there are people all over the world who have that very same tattoo now.

Around this time we started to tour in Europe more. We played some incredible big festivals in Europe to crowds of thousands, and Belgium, the Netherlands, and Germany were seeing us more often than crowds back home, a natural sign of a career on the rise. The Republic of Ireland became a more frequent destination than before, largely in thanks to our love-in with the phenomenal and much missed band, Adebisi Shank. It was shameful to think that at that stage we had played more in England than the Southern counties.

We started headlining all across the Republic, and selling out in the majority of venues we played.

Our album came out to much acclaim. Thank God. HotPress Magazine hailed it as one of the greatest Irish Albums of all time. AU Magazine hailed it as *the* greatest Northern Irish album of all time. A smaller pool yes, but still a high plaudit.

We were working ourselves to the bone, not that it seemed like work at all. We were in the most exciting times of our lives.

We supplemented the release of the album with a shorter, punchier record, *The Letters* EP, that was greeted with similar fervour locally. Gone were the swirling post-rock crescendos, in came the grungier, punkier, experimental pop.

It's now deleted, as is the first album, which is a crying shame for music lovers, and my bank manager. Available only in a digital format.

A dream was realised as we played our biggest home-show; a prestigious, Christmas time, headline gig at the Ulster Hall, with a stellar support bill from my housemates LaFaro, Adebisi Shank, and Cashier No. 9. We nearly sold it out too.

I was also crying a *lot* more often, as relations in the band got strained. The night of our Ulster Hall show, whilst everyone else went partying afterwards, I walked around a deserted, freezing, and snow encrusted Belfast. Shivering from the sweaty clothes I had on, and swigging from a six pack of beer, I walked from bridge to bridge, confronting the most awful urges I can ever remember having. Having never been a swimmer, I stared at the River Lagan as a means of escape. Death was on my tail.

I talked to some friends about these attempts and swirling thoughts of self-destruction. Most offered concern. One asked, incredulously, "Why are you trying to ruin this for me?"

I have not confided in that person since.

More and more we forayed into the continent, and then further east into Europe. Poland, Hungary and Czech Republic. We'd started off in Europe, co headlining little venues with our buddies, Maybeshewill, but soon we were coming back to headline our own tours, and then sometimes with American bands.

Johnny was the most made up man alive when we were invited to tour Europe with his all-time favourite band, Clutch. A year later we were back for a series of arena shows opening up for the supergroup that was Them Crooked Vultures, comprising Dave Grohl (Foo Fighters, Nirvana), Josh Homme (Queens of the

Stone Age), and John Paul Jones (Led Zeppelin). What was even more incredible was that those guys were digging *us*.

Around that same time, we toured the United States, thus actually realising a dream and promise that I'd made to myself as a kid, that one day, since I couldn't afford it, music would pay for my ticket to see America.

Amidst all this madness I was diagnosed as being depressed. It was no surprise to me, given the sudden increase in tears, but it was nice to have it made official. We headlined a two week long arts festival called First Fortnight in Dublin, where I told the entire Island of my recent diagnosis on the country's then most popular radio show, Ray D'Arcy on Today FM, in a bid to highlight the issue in a country where suicide rates are terrifyingly high. It was quite the way to, "come out", as it were...

It's one of the moments of my life I'm most proud of. Having mentioned my diagnosis to the festival organisers, they asked if I would be comfortable talking about it on radio. Saying it could be a great help. Not having a therapist or anyone to speak to at the time I thought, "Sure, why not?"

It didn't seem like a big deal to me at the time, but during the show's break for the news, I was read back some of the tweets and texts that were coming in from listeners from all over the island. The outpouring of empathy and honesty was staggering.

Years later, as the festivals wonderfully successful blueprint was beginning to be emulated throughout Europe, I was lucky enough to be in Athens for the debut Greek festival, playing as Ireland's musical representative. I was in attendance with JP and David, who had originally started the festival in Ireland. JP introduced me with some very kind words, highlighting this moment on Irish Radio as being a major turning point in helping to broaden the conversation back home with regards to mental health.

I'd never thought of it that way until that moment, side of stage in Athens.

I smiled broadly, and wept a little, but unlike all those times before years ago, these were happy tears. Happy to have contributed in a small way to a massive issue.

Where were we? Ah yes...we even toured Russia for a few weeks. Russia! And what was even weirder was that the shows were mostly sell outs and they knew our stuff. It was mind blowing.

We switched labels to join Adebisi Shank on the Dublin-based Richter Collective.

Our second album, *Gangs*, came out and the attention and expectation was palpable.

To say that those six years hadn't been a whirlwind would be an out and out lie.

The highest highs were scaled as dreams came to fruition, whilst the lowest lows were plumbed and scoured. Never, in my life, had the words of Charles Dickens ever been so prescient.

"It was the best of times, it was the worst of times".

7

I have always loved the beautiful and historic city of Vienna.

First settled by the Celts some 2,600 years ago.

A city drenched in history; from defining events, to people.

Mozart, Beethoven, Schubert, Strauss, and Brahms could all call it home at one point, and in 1913, Leon Trotsky, Sigmund Freud, Adolf Hitler, and Joseph Stalin all lived within a mile of one another. Admittedly, not all of those names are worth bragging about, but still, in a strictly historical context, it's pretty damn impressive.

The city has repeatedly topped polls such as world's best city, best place to live, smartest city...all manner of prestigious titles have been bestowed upon Vienna.

And yet, it was here in this beautiful and historic place, on a temperate night in early autumn 2011, that the city would remorselessly swallow me whole, nearly killing me through a calamitous combination of misfortune and savagery, and teaching me a lesson that I'll never forget, one that I'm still in the process of learning.

Yet again, I digress. I've warned you I would.

Before and after our second last festival appearance of that summer (Electric Picnic was to wrap things up in Ireland the following day), relations were frosty. To put it mildly. So much so, that when we arrived back to our hotel early that particular evening, I decided to go for a walk and have a few drinks to unwind in a less tense atmosphere.

Around the corner from the hotel, I entered a bar where I was met with two couples; people who had been at the Ottakringer Arena earlier and had seen us play. They were a friendly and welcoming group who invited me to join them, so I did just that. It was a delight. *They* were a delight. We took photos, laughed, and drank. We drank a lot. Not too much, but considering I have never been a big drinker, a lot. We moved onto another bar and continued laughing, dancing, drinking, and all the while my all-consuming troubles faded to an unnoticeable blur in the back of my mind.

I was drunk in the sense that I certainly couldn't drive, there's no doubt of that, but I was in control and had been keeping one eye on the time. It was approaching 11pm, and I knew I should probably get back to the hotel. Our lobby call for the next morning was 8am, so this seemed like a reasonable and responsible enough time to get back to the hotel. Plus, with a bit of luck, everybody would be asleep in our shared room. I said goodbye to my new friends, who pointed me in the right direction of my hotel a few blocks away.

As I walked back, I looked towards the top of the buildings, admiring the mixture of classical, medieval, and baroque architecture. I put my headphones in, and listened to 'Mannish Boy' by Muddy Waters, from one of my favourite albums, *Hard Again*.

When I've had a few drinks, I have a habit of singing along to what I'm listening to, and sometimes at a volume that isn't as appreciated by everybody else as it is by me. Not that I was too worried by doing this on this particular evening, since it was a Saturday night, I was surrounded by bars, and it wasn't even close to midnight yet.

Alas, not everyone was to agree.

Turning a corner, I was on a street with bars either side of the Strasse, and a healthy amount of punters sitting outside, enjoying the pleasant Austrian evening air. When I saw them, I piped my singing down a little, but continued with it, especially when I saw some people laughing and cheering me on. In my beer soaked mind, a mini carnival was taking place. Some customers high fived me as I passed along, spirits were elated. Then, I glanced across the road, where the majority of the customers were just getting on with their evening, mostly unable to hear the half drunken Irishman butchering the blues across the street. Two doormen – both in excess of six foot, and with a build to suit their stature and career – were standing across the Strasse, and they seemed to have mixed feelings about my performance. One was making gestures towards me and the other was laughing. I assumed that they were enjoying the passing spectacle, and that they were up for a laugh also, so I mirrored one of the gestures that the more dour doorman had been making, and I raised my middle finger to him, with a smile on my face, mirroring his less dour accomplice.

This, my friends, was a mistake. As I turned back to my playful audience on my side of the Strasse, the dour man bolted across the street towards me before I had a second to fully realise what was happening.

He shoved me into a group of people who shouted at the two of us in protest as their drinks went everywhere.

Pressed against the exterior wall of this building, he then punched me hard, three times, in the gut. The people surrounding us wrangled him off me, pushing him away, as he returned across the street to his previous station.

A few people helped me up, asking if I was okay, which I generally was, at that point.

But I was furious.

I was furious at an assault that I felt was richly undeserved, but more than anything I was furious and confused at the isolation I was experiencing from certain quarters, and this, regrettably, was where it all came pouring out.

I'd love to tell you it was like a bad film, and that I ran over and fought this man down for an apology, but that isn't what happened.

In spite of the wrongs I may have done in my life, I'm proud to say I have never once thrown a punch in anger. I do not believe in violence. I prefer to talk out a situation. But sometimes, you know, there is no talking, and sometimes you must run. Some may call that cowardly, I call it self-preservation. I call it smart.

I regret that my anger was at boiling point, and I regret that I didn't just walk away from the beating I'd just taken.

They say choose your battles, and I chose mine that evening, for one reason and many others. However, I chose dreadfully and perilously.

I shouted across to my assailant, "POLIZEI!" as I brandished my phone in his direction.

Then, to my horror, I watched as not just one of the doormen, but the pair of them started to make their way toward my, shouting at me in German.

What the hell did I expect was going to happen? They were going to stand and take it?

A few voices beside me shouted, "Laufen! Laufen!" I glanced at them confused, they then translated, "RUN!" I took their advice.

Looking over my shoulder, I could see that this suggestion had also been taken on board by my assailant, and a newer, younger, bigger, would-be assailant. The sight of these two hulking, black clad figures quickly gaining on me, further propelled me down the street.

I took a turn into an alley, which really did seem like a great idea at the time. I ran so damn fast both my shoes fell off.

Still, the two beasts pursued me.

Back onto a larger street, and I was beginning to stumble as my feet weren't used to the impact.

They were right behind me.

I took one stumble too many, and lost my footing outside of a small apartment complex.

Oh no.

As I scurried to get to my feet again, I felt a boot slam into my ribcage with such force that I flew a few feet to my left and slammed into the closed entrance door of the apartment block.

The blow to my ribs had completely winded me, and I was unable to take in a single breath as every time I gasped for life, another boot would slam into my midsection.

I looked up toward these men whom I had angered so greatly, and hoped that if I could make eye contact with even one of them, the connection may be enough to end this brutal kicking that I was being served.

No such luck, receiving a swift stomp to my face.

Then they kicked harder.

I tried to beg them to stop, but my lungs were emptier than the vacuum between the ears of these brutes.

Besides, I could muster no breath to fuel such a plea for mercy.

The blood streaming from my nose, into my mouth, and down my throat, was making any sound other than agonised gurgling near impossible.

Chance, however, decided enough was enough and finally dealt me a favourable hand.

The door in which I lay in front of, had taken quite a pounding as I was flung against it at force, umpteen times.

I was slammed against the old door once more, when it suddenly opened, and with the door I went hurtling inside.

Their final kick to my ribs had also unveiled the means of my escape.

My peril eventually proved to aid my fortune.

With whatever strength I could gather, I slammed the door shut behind me, locking my attackers outside and myself, in.

They didn't even attempt to get in the door, they'd had their fun, like two cats toying with a mouse.

I heard their laughter – interspersed with some German I couldn't understand – fade into the distance as they walked back to their station outside the bar a few streets away.

I had been kicked to a bloodied pulp, and I was in mortified agony.

As I surveyed my sanctuary, I could see that I was in a small foyer, a communal entry/exit for the residents. There were three black doors, one in front of me, facing the entrance, and one to either side. Each were up a small flight of six steps. A security light had initially went on but had now extinguished, leaving the place basking in a low reddish, almost crimson, glow, from the Exit sign.

I was half expecting – and fully hoping – that perhaps a resident had seen what was happening and pressed a buzzer to let me in and to aide my escape, and that they would be there to help me to hospital and contact the police.

This was not the case.

I was bitterly aware of exactly how alone I currently was.

I reached into my pocket to get my phone, thinking that after foolishly wielding it five minutes earlier had helped lead me into this mess, that I must now use it to phone the police, as originally intended.

The front was smashed to bits, but holding together and still usable. I could see Muddy Waters standing behind the obliterated screen. "They got you too, huh, Muddy?" is what I would've thought if I was in a film, which I wasn't.

I dialled the emergency services, which connected me to a German speaking lady, who asked, presumably, what service was required.

I tried to speak but nothing came out.

There was still not enough air in my lungs to verbalise an audible, coherent, and understandable word.

I began to take a deep breath in, and then howled it out in unworldly torture as my ribs dug into my lungs, forcing the gathered air out once more.

This sort of pain teaches the body a harsh lesson that it learns quickly not to repeat.

I took a shallower, slower breath, and although intensely painful, I succeeded in meekly muttering the word "...help..." into my handset.

Noting my language, the lady responded to me in the same tongue.

She asked me a few questions, mostly pertaining to where I was and if I was in immediate danger. It was then I realised that I had no clue where I was and that vaguely replying, "Vienna," probably wasn't going to be beneficial for either of us.

My breaths were short and panicked, as I made noises but spoke no words.

Hearing that I was clearly distressed and in great pain, she started speaking in a calming manner and reassuring me that she was there to help. I could see what looked like some junk mail sitting on top of a mailbox outside one of the apartments, so I said I was going to find out where I was, hoping beyond hope that there was an address on something.

As I attempted to stand up, it became clear that I wasn't capable of that.

My torso straightening mildly felt like I was being pulled apart by horses.

I howled in agony once more, collapsed back onto the floor, the pain engulfing me completely, and I blacked out at the foot of the steps to the apartments.

My mind and body had simply had enough for one night.

8

Some hours later, I regained consciousness, aching like I'd never known before. Dawn was breaking, and the sun was starting to come up over Vienna. I looked again towards the apartment doors at the top of the stairway, contemplating whether or not to try and climb them again to get some help, but in truth, the six steps looked as unconquerable as Mount Olympus on the surface of Mars. That, and I really didn't want to scare anyone from their beds on a Sunday morning. I was at my meekest point, both physically and mentally. This was what the experiences of the recent past had moulded me into. It is not who I always was.

In the distance, I could hear chattering and laughter from outside. People returning home or making their way to another party. I figured they were my best chance of help, so I began my slow, turtle-paced move toward the door that had saved my life hours before. Each movement felt like my internal organs were being held under a flame and rearranged forcibly. Tears were streaming down my face and I wanted to howl, but each minimal vibration of my lungs was enough to stop me dead in my pained tracks.

As I finally got out onto the street, my body demanded that I stay still and recover for a few moments before daring to move any extravagant distances again. I had moved maybe two and a half foot. Slowly, I rolled myself over on the pavement, lifting myself ever so slightly and using my forearms to reduce any further contact to my ribs and lungs. I could see that the people I had heard laughing were several feet ahead and walking away from me where I lay, incumbent.

This was not good.

Knuckling down, I went against everything my body was telling me to do, and took a sopranos lungful of oxygen, and as sure as I had inhaled, I proceeded to exhale with force as my body rejected the volume of air and in doing so turned it into an anguished, pained howl.

My very own, deathly siren.

The good people ahead of me jumped at the god awful wail they'd just heard. They turned and saw my barely moving frame spread over the pavement and mercifully took pity. They started talking to me, and to each other, asking what had happened, was I okay, what they should do.I began softly whimpering three words: "...ambulance...hospital...please..." I could see one was on their phone already and she told me not to worry, an ambulance was coming. The group of young people stayed with me until I was ferried to hospital a few minutes later, trying to calm me as I wept in pain on the street, struggling to catch a breath. I'd like to take this moment to say thank you, kind strangers.

At the hospital I was given oxygen, wheeled in to be x-rayed, cleaned up, then given some painkillers and left in my trolley bed in a long white corridor.

For an A&E in a major European city on a weekend, the place was remarkably quiet. There was literally one other patient, a Polish man who had been bottled in a disgraceful homophobic attack, along with a handful of nurses and one solitary Doctor. The only reason I met the Polish man was that the Doctor had brought him in to translate between the two of us. The Doctor wasn't 100% confident in her English speaking abilities, and I was less than 1% confident in my German. The nice Polish gentleman, who was about to be discharged, had volunteered to translate for us when he overheard the Doctor mentioning this language barrier to the assembled Nurses.

The oxygen and the painkillers were making life a lot easier than it had been for several hours now, but I still explained what had happened in as few words as possible. It's not that I wouldn't have liked to say more, but it was still very painful. The Polish man translated this to the Doctor, she then explained to him what they had gathered from my x-rays for translation. I had two fractured ribs, and severe internal bruising as a result of my assault. Movement would be very difficult and extremely painful for at least a week, and she advised that I should arrange to speak with a professional, as the possibility of PTSD was real.

She then asked if there was anyone they could get in touch with for me. I told them I was a musician, and that the rest of my band was in Hotel Geblergasse in the city. They smiled and I was told it was less than a five minute drive from here. I reached for my phone, and said that I would phone them now. The Doctor and the Polish fellow insisted I lay down and use the oxygen, with the Polish gent saying he would explain and ask them to come and collect me. Being in no position to argue, I agreed and asked him to phone the number I had just pulled up on my decimated screen: my old buddy Johnny.

My new Polish friend walked a little down the corridor and called Johnny. I watched on from my trolley bed and listened to the Doctor explain what had happened to me to the Nurses as they grimaced at the brutality of it all. The Polish man then returned to me with a half smile on his face, looking a little confused.

"Everything ok? You get him?" I asked.

"...Yes, yes I got him..."

"Are they coming?"

"Um, yes. Yes they are. In a few hours," he told me, with a concerned and confused tilt of his head.

"Are you OK?" the Polish man asked me, sensing that I really wasn't.

"Yes, yes I'm fine, thank you so much for your help. I hope you're okay," I replied to this brave man, whose face had been sliced open with glass, who had stayed in the hospital voluntarily a bit longer to help out a stranger, despite just having had his face stitched back together.

As I lay alone in the long white corridor, my only company were empty trolley beds, overhead lights, and firmly closed doors.

I lay trembling in a combination of fear, loneliness, and confusion, as awake and alert as I'd ever been. A million thoughts rushed through my head before I finally settled on one: the last line from Blanche Dubois in Tennessee Williams', A Streetcar named Desire. One of the loneliest lines in all of literature.

"I have always depended on the kindness of Strangers."

The strangers, from the people I drank with, to the people who called my ambulance, to the hospital staff, to this brave man... *they* had all been my heroes that night.

Not all the time but sometimes... sometimes, when it has just dealt you some life threatening kicks, the human race can flip the other way and astound you with their kindness.

Hope; its important.

9

Shortly after 10am, the guys arrived at the hospital so we could go on to the airport. I was in tremendous pain and quite delirious from the drugs I'd been given. Little questioning occurred over what had happened, although in fairness, I think that was because my Polish Knight had informed Johnny of the chain of events on the phone, and they could tell I was pretty out of it, and in pain.

At not one point was I asked whether I wanted to play the festival back in Ireland that evening. Bizarrely, no mention was made of this on the bands official Facebook – ever. Birthdays, illnesses, and shout outs to other band members and bands were made around this time, but never a mention of me being kicked to pieces in a Vienna doorway the night before. At the time, with regards to the festival in question, it wasn't a matter of 'wanting' to play the show, it was a matter of "*of course* I'm playing the show". I was conscious and, mercifully, could still play the guitar. I wasn't going to let the small matter of two fractured ribs, extensive internal bruising, and the inability to stand unaided get in my way.I still meant *it*, whatever *it* is. I still wanted, for better or for worse, to be a member of this band.

ASIWYFA meant the world to me. I'd given it everything I had. Like Mary Shelley's *Frankenstein*, I had given it life.

A wheelchair was arranged for me at the airport, which made the ordeal of checking in equipment and security a breeze. I was pushed past all the queues as I was prioritised entry onto the plane, then moved to the front for extended legroom (not that I need it) and was told that a wheelchair would be waiting for me upon arrival in Dublin for the same service.

I remember thinking that these perks were great, but maybe not quite worth it, but the thought was enough to make me genuinely laugh for the first time in twelve hours. Laughing hurt like hell, so I returned to my morose thoughts like a good boy, worrying about the awful burden I felt I had become.

When we arrived at the festival site, we had roughly an hour to kill before going to the side of stage to get ready to play. The guys went off to get fed, leaving me in our backstage yurt (a kind of oversized teepee).

Our Manager, Alan, was understandably ablaze with queries and concern, along with another one of his acts, Niamh Farrell. I told them what had happened, and he asked, "Why were you roaming about on your own, for God's sake, Tony?" I desperately wanted to tell him exactly why, but was scared of what his response might have been. He shook his head at me, told me that he was glad I was going to be okay, and smiled a comforting smile before disappearing to get some food from the catering tent as well.

Niamh stayed with me. She was concerned about me.

The time came for us to go to the stage and our sound man Andy, very kindly, set up my equipment. He found me a chair to sit on since the guitars weight was too much for my ribs to support, and he set a mic up at a necessary height for me. Not that I was going to be doing much hyping of the crowd.

We played, and the other three went nuts as usual and played as if nothing was out of the ordinary.

To an alarming degree.

They barely came near me.

It was almost as if I wasn't there.

I sat on my chair and played probably the most note perfect show I have ever played, since I wasn't launching myself everywhere for a change.

I may as well have been offstage.

That festival performance, with me seated and ignored, was to be my last full gig with the band I had assembled from my friends, some years ago. I didn't know it for sure there and then, but I certainly had an inkling, and I'm sure that they too, knew it was a possibility that I would soon be gone...

And that could have been it for my 'weird life'. I could have parted ways with the band under difficult circumstances, hung up my guitar, and done the regular thing, putting up roots somewhere, settling down, and trying to make a go of it. But I didn't do that. I couldn't do that. After finding myself being forced to stand on my own, I refused to set down the guitar. I'd spent my teenage years and my twenties with it in my hand and it knows more about me than any living human. I took on a new name – VerseChorusVerse.You see it turns out I'm not the only one to hold my own name, and there's several other 'Tony Wrights' in the business and the public eye.

Some of my favourites include the frontman for 90s BritRock band, Terrorvision, a Labour MP in England, a US Sports Coach, and an album artwork designer of serious repute, who designed the LP covers for the two hallowed Bobs (Dylan and Marley) as well as The Ramones and Marianne Faithfull.

Two of the other prominent Tony Wrights are world beaters, actual record holders! One holds the record for sleep deprivation, and the other for the world's longest phone call. As you can see, I was really up against the wall with the reputations of these gents to contend with. I imagine if we all met at once, it would put the very fabric of the universe at risk, like when a bunch of Doctors cross over in *Doctor Who*.

Hence, VerseChorusVerse. Hopefully the books title makes a little more sense now.

I've released (at the time of writing) a few EPs and two albums. The eponymous debut was produced by the gentleman that is the multi Ivor Novello winning Iain Archer, and the second was a collaboration with my good friend and weird life identifier, Dr. David Lyttle that dented the British Charts and twice topped the Blues Album Charts.

So far, this solo career thing has mostly been a blast, if a little unexpected.

However, to paraphrase the hip hop prophet Mr Chuck D, my wandering has indeed got my ass wondering...

Part Two

10

Travelling by public transport on tour is a dichotomy of delight and burden.

On one hand, you're not confined to a potentially smelly van. You may have a drink if you so wish. You can enjoy the countryside, read, listen to music or podcasts, and sometimes, just sometimes, you can have the most wonderful encounter with a total stranger and enjoy a fun and interesting conversation, which when you're touring solo is a real boon. It can do incredible things for your outlook, nulling the loneliness that is easily felt.

On the other hand, negotiating the length and breadth of a country, or countries, with an absurd amount of luggage can easily become the bane of your very existence. Not to mention how the rest of the commuting hoi polloi views you when boarding a vehicle.

"Christ, look at this idiot in the hat with a guitar. He's bound to hit me in the face with one of his bags *or* his guitar, plus getting by him is going to be a nightmare..."

The last quote is, of course, entirely fictional.

To a degree.

It's what I've extrapolated from many a fellow passenger and the look of contempt in their eyes. I should stress that I've also been helped on occasion with my luggage, and people have also been politely intrigued as to who I am and where they can hear some music. It's just that when I get stressed from trying my best to not injure others, or myself, with the ungainly manner I find myself traveling down railway carriages or coaches, I naturally assume that since I'm pissing myself off, surely I'm pissing everyone off.

Or at least a brave chunk of them.

I travel, almost always, with my guitar, a rather large drag bag that contains a mixture of clothing, toiletries, guitar leads, and Merch to sell on the road (the Merch, not the clothing, toiletries, or guitar leads) along with a shoulder bag that I carry my laptop and a couple of books (in this instance, *Around the World in Eighty Days*, by Jules Verne, and *Innocent When You Dream*, a collection of interviews with Tom Waits).

Everything I have with me is essential to my touring life. The books are the only real luxury items I take with me, and one could argue that they are just as vital as anything else, due to the ease that they can bring my – quite literally – wandering mind. Okay, so the hat may be a luxury item, but it helps with catching up on sleep when travelling in daylight. It can be a nuisance trying to keep it on when both hands are occupied and a sudden gust of wind comes along, which is more often than not.

In my defence, however, I look good in it.

Damn good.

There I go, digressing again...where was I? Ah yes: America. Well, nearly.

On Monday the 2nd of May, 2016, I set sail. Departing the Port of Belfast for Cairnryan, en route to Glasgow, where I would stay for two nights with my brother and his family before flying to JFK in New York, New York.

I was embarking on a networking trip, to liaise with my music publishers in their offices in New York, Nashville, and Los Angeles. I'd be spending 10 nights in each of these legendary musical cities, and hoping to embolden relations with other songwriters and possible creative partnerships in the future.

At least, this is the basis of what I had told the Arts Council of Northern Ireland, who were funding a generous portion of my visit. Whilst what I had told them was entirely true, it was as much a networking trip as it was a quest to try and find the heart and soul – the very purpose – of what it was I planning on doing with the rest of my life. Or at the very least to step a few rungs up the proverbial ladder.

The truth was I really had no clear grasp of where I was going. In a philosophical sense, obviously. Right now I was on my way to Scotland. My ticket told me that much.

Music had always been the vehicle, carrying me forward for upwards of two decades now, but I was beginning to tire of the unknown destinations. Both philosophically and literally.

As I surveyed my peers – both within and outside of the music industry bubble – I was seeing people who were a great deal happier, settled friends with burgeoning families. I was over the moon for all of them, a little envious I admit, but genuinely happy for the stability and love that I saw. Of course, this could all be merely my imagined view of their supposed stability.

A deception of perception in the, "Grass is always greener" mould.

They could very well be envious of the freedom I still possessed and flaunted on the dreaded social media platforms that were now a necessary evil in my field of work; a constant barrage of self-promotion and un-ending manipulative positivity. To a romantic, my life could be seen as a poet musician, a singing guitar player, adventuring across the globe, bound by no constraints that a nine to five-er may be held by. Bringing music to those who wish to listen and escape, through story and song, and to those anchored in their own harbour, having long given up on the dreams that they fostered and aspired to as children. I've had more settled friends tell me such things.

The problem with this, however, is that, to paraphrase possibly the finest example of the romanticised individual I described above, Mr Robert Zimmerman (lil Bobby Dylan, name-fans), the loser now will later on win. That is in no way to imply that anybody who settles with a family and a mortgage is a loser. Quite the opposite. Later in life I rather suspect that my peers who did some actual planning, as opposed to careering through their life with a melody and a wish, will be the winners.

They shall be the ones with a family and security. They shall be the ones who watch their offspring grow into adults and have children of their own, sowing the seeds of immortality, in a sense. Fulfilling the circle of life we all heard about in *The Lion King*. A plot of land and a legacy to blossom in their image, as their parents and grandparents did before them, and, above and beyond all of this, deep, beautiful, nourishing, and unconditional love. Or something along those lines.

Of course, there's always the chance that those flowers won't blossom into such a garden, but let's face it, they have a greater chance than those on different soil. Unfertilised with such seeds.

After all, you reap what you sow.

Don't you?

Or was Lou Reed telling fibs again?

I've been doing this for so long now, and I honestly do feel truly blessed to have been afforded the opportunities I have, to have experienced the things I've experienced. I am a lucky, lucky man, in innumerable ways, and I'm so very thankful, please believe me. I would hate to come across as an ungrateful braggart. But the fact remains that in all the work and miles I have put in over the twenty plus years, I have a deep sense of loneliness that pervades, consumes and, with greater frequency of late, overwhelms me.

I bawled my eyes out yesterday watching the film adaption of *Charlotte's Web*. Some pig.

I guess I should probably have written a song about it, you might say?

Well, I have. Many of them in fact.

Songs with big blatant names like, 'No-one as Lonely', and the giant neon billboard of a song, surrounded by fireworks and a 20ft finger pointing down from the heavens, 'If I Just Knew Your Name'. The first line of which, "Won't somebody fall in love with me", is, I'm reliably told by my good friends on Kepler-1, the only song lyric visible from space.

The longing contained there within is enough to power a journey and colonise the aforementioned exoplanet, with an extensive, self-sufficient line in aquaponic agriculture for the population to survive a million millennia.

I digress, again.

But yeah, I'm a lonely soul and have been for a while now, after what happened all those years ago – life has been, well, *solo*.

The very cliché of a skint, love starved, wandering singer-songwriter.

Nomad, vagabond, call me what you will.

I hope, in some way, that the trip to America, may signpost me to a more secure future. Crazy as it sounds, I hope that the meetings with my publishers may open up some gilded opportunity that may help me on this twisted highway. That I might go up to perform at some open mic night in any one of these three titan cities, and Frankie Sharp from Sharp Records may leap from his platinum throne and pronounce that my songs are exactly the thing he has been looking for, to soundtrack a confused and frightened generations journey from the unknown – terra firma unexplored – into ultimate enlightenment and infinite contentment.

Not too much to ask, is it?

Oh yeah...America...

11

I landed at JFK at approximately at 1845 EST on May 4th. The flight had been mercifully routine.

By the time I had collected my luggage and figured out how to get to where I was staying in the East Village, it was getting closer to 2100. After a little help from a kindly security man at Jamaica St Station, I was on board the Subway & going all the way to Broadway-Lafayette. The journey took about 45 minutes, and as mentioned before, you're never the most popular guy on public transport when you have a guitar in an unwieldy, but vital case, a huge 4 wheeled drag-bag, along with a shoulder bag containing a laptop. Negotiating the turnstiles with all of this is tremendous fun for sadists.

As I emerged from underground to the slightly chilly New York night, I felt the thrill that millions before me had felt.

Ma! I'd made it – Broadway, Ma!

I tucked myself into the nearest corner away from the throngs of hip young things crossing the street to get my phone out and check I was heading in the correct direction. Something I would do several times after a few blocks to reassure myself; this was the furthest I'd ever been from home without any travelling companions. I persevered towards my destination, the residence of musician, bar owner, and all round classic New Yorker, Jesse Malin. A total gentleman too, I must add.

I'd first encountered Jesse in 2003 when I was living in Liverpool, although he hadn't encountered me. Jesse was opening for Ryan Adams at the Royal Theatre on his "Love is Hell / Rock n Roll" tour. This gig was memorable for several reasons, the main one being that this was the gig when Mr Adams, blindly lost in music, took a few steps too far forward and fell a considerable drop into the unused Orchestra pit some feet below, breaking his wrist in several places and having to abandon the gig and the remaining dates of the tour. I too, was lost in the music that evening and hadn't noticed what had exactly happened; I was convinced he was going to come back onto the stage, miraculously recovered, in some kind of homage to James Brown. That didn't happen.

I then encountered Jesse for the second time in 2015 when I opened for him on his acoustic tour of Ireland in Belfast, Dublin, Galway, and Cork, as well as joining him onstage each night to relieve him of guitar duties on his song, 'Bar life'. Other than that, I stayed out of his way mostly on the tour, giving him and his touring compatriot, Derek, space.

At the end of the last date, I thanked him for having me on the tour and asked if he'd be able to help me out should I ever make it over to the States. He was monumentally positive about the request in his beautiful New York drawl. "Sure! Come to New York! You can stay at my place! I'll introduce you to a bunch of people! It'll be great!"

So that was what I had planned to do.I arrived at Jesse's place a little after 2200. The twenty minute walk from Broadway-Lafayette to East 2nd Street seemed like a few hours with everything I was hauling in an unfamiliar environment. Not aided by my periodical stops to check maps on my phone in order to make sure I was going the right way.

I buzzed his door and he let me in, shouting down from the second floor in that great accent, "Second Floor!" I negotiated my way up the narrow stairway, trying not to damage the paint work of the building. Ultimately, a fruitless endeavour.

Jesse welcomed me into his apartment, which was achingly cool and organised.

Along with all the classic records and movies, neatly compartmentalised in shelves, he had more notebooks than anyone I've ever met. Now, I've got a lot of notebooks, any writer of any discipline does, but there were hundreds, and pretty much all the same make. I was quietly impressed. Jesse gave me a quick tour of his place, showed me my room for the oncoming while, then he told me that my name was on the door for one of his clubs just up the block from his place and that a great band, Hollis Brown, was about to start their second date in a month long residency, and that I should go down to get a beer, relax, and enjoy. Despite how tired I had been just thirty seconds before, it sounded to me like the greatest idea in the world. I was in New York City and already my name was on the door at one of the coolest little underground venues in the Village, Berlin.

Look Ma! I made it!

Jesse said he was going to do some writing (those notebooks don't fill themselves), and would join me down there in a little while. So I made my way down and introduced myself to the doorman, Patrick. He stamped my wrist and I continued further down into the bowels of the building, where in the corner a band in the fashion of The Band, Warren Zevon, and The E Street Band were playing their own songs to a packed little venue contained by a suitably enthused, entertained, and hip audience.

I ordered a beer and began my confused, islander, relationship with tipping. I drank in the night and thought to myself, "Well...*this* is pretty cool".

The next morning I rose early. By all rights, I should have had a hangover, but for some reason it didn't rise with me. It must've been the excitement. I didn't have any engagements for a few days, so I decided to just go and walk the city. I must've walked 10 miles that day. I took in a lot.

I walked to nearby Little Italy, and had breakfast in a little establishment on the corner called Azzura Gusta, which was playing a radio station that only dealt in Frank Sinatra songs.

It was bliss.

New York has a way of making you feel like you're starring in the coolest scenes of your ever un-folding life-long movie.

I walked around a while, found myself in Greenwich Village, then walked a little more and found the Fire Station that had been used in the original Ghostbusters movies, which was disappointingly obscured by scaffolding. I must admit to feeling a genuine thrill when, later, a bus drove by with the Ghostbusters logo and infamous tagline of, "Who you gonna call?" emblazoned upon it, heralding the new movie. Seeing it here in NYC made me feel like a kid, however momentarily. Another cool, if little surreal, sign I would see on the Subway was, "No HoverBoards". "How would Marty escape Biff?" I thought, before remembering that *Back to the Future* was, alas, fiction.

A friend had recommended I go and see the High-Line, whatever that was. So I checked my maps, and decided I would walk along the Hudson River to get there.

When I got to the High-Line. I discovered it was an old, well, high railway line; connecting Gansevoort St (surely one of the street names that had survived from the days of the early Dutch settlers when the fledgling settlement was named New Amsterdam) between 9th and 10th Avenue to West 34th Street between 11th and 12th Avenue. Twenty-one blocks in length. The railway had been removed some years after the line itself had been closed, and weeds had taken it over. Now, in place of both the rail and the weeds, were beautifully realised gardens, wooden walkways, and rest spots where photo opportunities await you on every conquered block of the bustling New York traffic, below my fellow wayfarers and I.

As I reached the end of the High Line, I wanted to go to the Official Liverpool Football Club Supporters bar, 11th Bar, to watch the European Semi-Final between Liverpool and Villareal. The only problem being that the bar was 3 miles away on East 11th street, only a few blocks from where I'd set off from early that morning. Still, that should only take me a little over an hour. So off I set, if my calculations were correct I should get there with time to kill before the kick-off. My calculations were indeed correct, and I had time to burn. Which I could probably set alight with my now on fire feet. No matter, there was a match to be watched, and it seemed I had arrived just in time as, shortly before kick-off, the doors were closed due to the bar being at capacity.

The atmosphere in the place was formidable, and held the most famous red shirts I'd ever seen outside of the UK congregated in the one place. Some were ex-pats from England, but the overwhelming majority were Americans, and they knew ALL the songs. They were singing from the get-go, and in a strange hybrid Scouse/US accent. It was hard not to be impressed and taken in with the passion on display. I've always tended to be quite a reserved viewer of football, but I was completely swept away with it. Liverpool comfortably won 3-0 and we all celebrated like newly liberated loons, and very contented ones at that. It was apparent, should all continue to plan for me, I would be watching Liverpool play in a European cup final somewhere in Nashville, Tennessee, in a few week's time.

After the game, I checked my phone to discover that Jesse had been in touch and invited me to see a New York band called Caveman, who were opening for someone at Terminal 5. Naturally, I said yes, and he told me that we'd be on the door, which opened at 7.00pm.

I really should have checked where Terminal 5 was. It was nearly 4 miles away at West 56th Street, and closer to the point I'd set off from the High Line some hours ago. As I looked at the maps I figured, "*it's cool* (New York was beginning to permeate me), *I can walk this.*" So I walked. I walked into the hordes of traffic, both human and vehicular, headfirst against the tide, like I always seemed to do, for as long as I can remember.

Somewhere on New York's oldest street, before I reached Times Square, I finally admitted to myself that my boots were not making this epic stroll any easier. I began to keep my eyes open for a pharmacy to buy some cushioned in-soles.

Very Rock n Roll, I know.

I picked up some of the gelled comfort variety for $13, and proceeded to make my way north, very slowly. Not only was I about to get to the neon and giant screened, Ballardian advertising nightmare that is Times Square, but the heels of my feet were in great distress, and thus I needed to get my recently purchased in-soles inside my boots, and quick.

I was in a race against time, in my head.

With the benefit of hindsight I'm sure I could have just sat on a Street corner or window ledge, and inserted them there. Everybody is going from A to B, and the surrounding skyline spectacles draw the eyes up, not to some red headed schmuck taking his boots off. But nope, I had to find somewhere I could do this comfortably, and out of eye-shot. Amazingly, I found an empty McDonalds toilet, went in, locked the door to the cubicle and then proceeded to remove my now hypothetically smouldering boots to slip the gelled life preservers in and give overdue mercy to my poor suffering feet. Only, in my haste, I didn't lock the door. Within a moment of taking my boots off, an elderly gentleman, in dire need of what the cubicle is intended for, burst in. He was already starting to undo his belt, when much to his surprise and forgivable chagrin, he found an equally startled, afore mentioned red headed schmuck staring back at him. I apologised and quickly gathered my boots, in-soles and bag and cleared out to the toilet to try and finally introduce in-sole to boot.

There is nothing comfortable about trying to do this whilst men are pissing just across the room and wondering what in God's name you are trying to achieve in a room mainly intended for the expulsion of bodily waste.

In McDonalds.

On Times Square.

In New York.

Whilst in my Hugh Grant-like state of delightful befuddlement, I hadn't quite put the soles in correctly, but my time was running scarce. I didn't want to be late or have Jesse waiting outside the place for me. I still had a few blocks to go, and definitely wasn't going to make it for 7.00pm. I sent Jesse a text as I stumbled on, with my feet in a state of neuroses, half eased and half distressed, saying I'd be five minutes late. As I arrived at T5, I received word back from Jesse. "No rush".

He'd only told me doors were at 7.00pm, I'd falsely deduced that we would be meeting there at that time. Of course there was no way a guy as cool as Jesse was going to be there as soon as doors opened; he'd be there in time to see the band, but he wasn't going to be queuing up to get in, he was going to walk straight in, get his ticket, and stand casually at the side just in the nick of time for the band to start. I realised my folly and asked one of the security guys if there was a bar nearby, which there was of course. Right around the corner, a little NY dive bar called the Green Door. As I went in they were playing Frightened Rabbit over the stereo. After a couple of songs by the same band, it slowly dawned on me that it was Frightened Rabbit who were playing in T5 at a sold out show.

The last time I saw them play was at 2000 Trees Festival in Cheltenham, England in 2014. I had played the modestly sized acoustic stage to a respectably gathered crowd at the start of a scorching summer's day, and they had headlined the festival that same night. The last time I'd seen them before that was in Paris in 2010, where they had played the Flech d'Or venue, a night before ASIWYFA had played it, and we had helped them out with some equipment. They were genuinely nice guys and thoroughly deserved all their success as they worked their asses off and had great songs, but I couldn't help but ponder at what point our lives had grown so disparate.

Nature definitely played a part, of that much I felt certain.

You see, the day after our gig in Paris back in '10, we had slept in the van on the outskirts of a Parisian council estate. That morning we were due to fly to Glasgow, before flying back to Europe to continue a month long jaunt. We were scheduled to play a show in Glasgow's legendary King Tuts venue that was going to be broadcast live to several hundred thousand people on one of the UK's most popular radio stations, BBC Radio 1. There's little doubt in my mind that this level of exposure would have introduced us to more new listeners and potential fans than every show we had played up until that point combined.

Nature, fate, destiny, circumstance, whatever your preferred term, had other ideas.

A volcanic explosion on the far south of one of Iceland's Ice caps, Eyjafjallajokull, put paid to that possibility whilst we slept, blissfully unaware. We were as devastated as the ice cap itself when we woke to the news, knowing the opportunity we had lost to force majeure. The ash cloud from the volcano had grounded all European flights for the foreseeable future.

As the Spanish would say, que sera sera.

Thankfully I didn't dwell too long on it, although it would pop into my mind from time to time in the coming weeks. I privately laughed it off over my beer in the Green Door, awaiting Jesses text.

After the opening act, Caveman, had finished, Jesse turned to me and asked if I wanted to share a cab back to his place, but I opted to stay and see at least a little bit of the headliners, whose path we once shared. Not only this, but by a strange coincidence, a lady I knew from Baltimore (whom I'd met with her family in Portstewart, NI, but that's a whole other story) was also in attendance. Fran is a cancer survivor. A phenomenally strong minded person, she in part credits her survival to the music of her favourite band, Frightened Rabbit, and the honesty within their music, acting as a beacon of hope and empathy, and a direct reason as to why she came through that most frightful of diseases, that terrible thief, cancer. She had been following the band since their early US tours, and as a result had gotten to know them. Throughout her diagnosis, right up to her remission, they have always repaid her faith in them in kind. Fran was attending four shows in total and was getting the full VIP treatment for her unflinching support. I met her briefly beside the VIP section and gave her a hug. We caught up, talked about how cool it was to see each other in NY, and then said our goodbyes so she could take up her place in the wrist-banded area again, in readiness of seeing her favourite band for the umpteenth time. The band that, along with the love and support of her family and medical team obviously, had helped cure her from cancer, such was her belief in them.

Music.

Wow.

I suspect this belief and loyalty that they have the ability to inspire, may be the reason our paths as musicians had grown so divergent, and I would be lying if I said it didn't make me take a look long, hard and deeply within myself, as both an artist and a human being.

I watched Frightened Rabbit thrill the audience in the sold out T5 for about 15 minutes, but I was feeling anxious. I've never been great at watching gigs, as I've always felt the urge to be on the stage playing too. I don't know whether it's a need to be the focus of attention, a cockiness that leads me to believe I could do a better job, or a need to connect with other musicians and communicate with music, but I'm sure that a large part of it is the want to entertain.

What better feeling than to make others happy?

So after a quarter of an hour I decided to leave and start the long walk back to Jesse's place. Stopping off for a few beers along the way, of course.

I knew that if I got to Broadway, I could just walk south for about 45 minutes and I wouldn't be too far from Jesses place. So I reached for my headphones and started my long walk south, sound-tracked by Billy Joel ("New York State of Mind", what else?), dazzled along the way by New York by night, quite literally. The glare of Times Square and the endless stream of yellow cabs and movie advertisements is a blitz for the senses. Sometimes it's welcome, and sometimes it can be a little too much. On my way to the gig, in my supposed race against the clock, it was quite overbearing, but now on my relaxed stroll back, paired with Mr Joel's gentle and familiar croon, it was everything you wish it to be.

You make temporary travelling companions on every street in New York.

Some you will overtake, only to meet them again at the next set of traffic lights. You quickly learn that there really is no point in getting ahead of yourself. Move with the city, breathe like the city, let it set your pace, synchronise your rhythms.

At this point I'd been in America just a little over a day and I felt like I was settling and becoming at ease with the world's most famous city.

So far, so good.

I passed by Rockefeller square and News Corps building, opposite Radio City, and marvelled at the size of the place and how an empire could be built out of the manipulation of information to suit one's agenda. As I pondered further on it I came to realize that historically that has been the basis for all empires – and eventually their downfalls too.

A taxi cab passed me by, advertising sunglasses with a Barack Obama lookalike modelling them, and I tried in vain to imagine a similar image back home, with either an Enda Kenny, Arlene Foster, or David Cameron doppelgänger being used, and failed to see how it would boost sales for any company.

I got back to Jesse's apartment around midnight, where I met Davy, his very cool and beautiful girlfriend, and briefly told of my extended sojourn around their fair city and said my goodnights. I crawled into my bunk in the spare room, switched on the fan, and passed out to dreams of people forgotten, and times that never were.

12

I didn't rise until after midday the following morning. Which, given the distance I had covered on foot, and the change in timezone, was entirely forgivable. As I woke, I could hear Jesse on the phone, and it sounded like he was giving an interview, so I lay in my bunk until he was done. Eventually, I emerged from my room and he apologised for the noise, thinking I had gone out already. I laughed off the apology and told him not to worry about it for a second.

Now, before I had arrived, Jesse had mailed me saying that he had some other friends staying for a few days over the weekend, and if I could make other arrangements for those few days, I would be fine to return on the Tuesday. He told me that today was fine again, but tomorrow I'd have to ship out for a few nights. He also told me not to worry, as he was trying to get me on a bill in New Jersey, as an opening act.

For The Zombies, legendary 60s pop icons from England.

My gaster was flabbered, but of course I did not let it show. He explained that they were playing a house show at a little place in Ringwood, New Jersey, and he was trying to get me to open through his friend Drew who put on the house gigs, and this was their special 200th show. "Live at Drew's" was the gig and Jesse himself had done it at least 14 times, with a highly attentive, respectful audience.

Not bad for my second morning in the Empire State.

I had a quick wash and cleared my way out of Jesse's place to give him his space, and enjoy the Big Apple that little bit further. It was a rainy afternoon in Manhattan, so I wore my hat. A brown hat I had bought in Granada, Spain, for the quite different purpose of shielding me from the sun.

Off I went in my daily search for breakfast. Around the corner I discovered that I was staying quite close to the Mercury Lounge, the venue where I had played my first ever NY gig with ASIWYFA some six years previous, and a wave of nostalgia swept over me like nausea. I shook it off and saw the famous Katz Delicatessen ahead of me on the corner of East Houston and Ludlow, but the queue outside put me off and I continued my trek for breakfast, well... brunch, at this early mid-afternoon hour.

In New York there's an option of eatery every few buildings. Faced with this plethora of choices, I continued walking for a long time, until I finally gave up and opted for a two slices of pizza and drink $5 deal. Reasoning with myself that it was now after 2pm and a perfectly acceptable time to eat Pizza, regardless of it being the first thing I'd have that day. My inner child was over the moon with this result. As I contentedly guzzled down my pizza slice, feeling ever more like a New Yorker with each mouthful, I figured that going to the cinema (or Movie Theatre – to go native with the lingo) would be a good way to spend this rainy afternoon in the city. I'd seen a movie theatre on East Houston St the previous night, and I walked around to see what was playing.

Awaiting me at the Box Office of the LandMark SunShine Cinema was an effortlessly cool Villager. After I enquired as to what was showing, she asked me the question I would get asked more often than any other along the way in the US: "Are you from Ireland?" It was always a pleasant thing to be asked, and it made me feel that little bit more welcomed in a land so vast and so far from home. Given America's fondness for Ireland and vice versa, it is mostly safe to assume that this question is asked with a curious warmth, as opposed to a disdainful mistrust.

I confirmed her friendly suspicion and she told me that she was going there for the first time in a few months, to the west. "Galway?" I asked with a smile. "Right!" she replied with surprise in her tone, eyes and smile. I assured her she would have a fantastic time and told her of a few bars that she must check out, and then purchased a ticket to a truly American movie about two titans of American history, for better or for worse, *Elvis and Nixon*.

By the time I emerged from the Cinema, the sun had given up trying to break its way through the clouds, but was letting its presence be known in the form of a warm, but dull, evening.

I walked.

I walked and I walked.

Buoyed in every step by both my gel in-soles, and the thrill of being in New York on a Friday night, I really wanted to hear some blues. I searched "New York's best blues bar" on my phone, and top of the list of suggestions, quite unanimously it would seem, was Terra Blues in Greenwich Village. So I walked back towards the village and sought it out. As I approached from around the corner I started to hear an ensemble of musical sounds, which grew as I was drawn closer. Stopping outside at the bottom of the steps to the entrance to the google proclaimed 'Best Blues Bar', I rolled a cigarette and took in the sights and sounds around me. Beside me, there was a glass case with pictures and listings of the performers coming up that night and beyond. A doorman shouted down to me that there was no smoking in the immediate area outside the bar, where I was smoking. I made my apologies and stepped half a foot to the left.

I was fine there.

There was a $15 dollar cover charge on the door, which was more than reasonable, but I was very wary of how little cash I had to do me on my trip, so I made up an excuse about finding an ATM, and left.

I do regret this now. I'm a musician and know the financial hardships that go with this choice of life, so why wouldn't I pay a measly $15 to see some masters of their craft? Not cool, Tony. Not cool. The bar next door to Terra Blues, was free entry and there was a covers band interpreting some material by the recently departed Prince. I'd earned a beer, I thought, to raise a glass and tip my hat to the Purple Maestro.

The night was advancing and I remembered passing the Mercury Lounge earlier in the afternoon, where I had popped my American gig cherry all those years ago. Perhaps fuelled by a few drinks, I remembered it fondly this time, not with nauseous nostalgia like before, but what a great gig it had been, and how we felt like we'd conquered America after our bottom of the bill, opening performance. How we all got so drunk on the Jameson we were paid with that I had fallen asleep at the nearby Bowery Electric, which, ironically, was/is one of Jesse's establishments.

After that particular gig, we'd returned to the Mercury Lounge to collect our gear in some of the worst rain I have ever seen, only to be greeted with a Mercury Lounge that was shut for the next few hours, whilst MTV set up for a secret, invite only gig with the buzz band of that year, MGMT.

Around the corner there was a dive bar advertising 4 bottles of beer for $10. With prices like that, we knew this was the spot for us.

We took up residency at the bar – as there was no-one else there – and made our acquaintance with the welcoming Puerto-Rican bartender. The jukebox in the corner was jam packed with punk rock classics from the Ramones and New York Dolls onwards. I can't overstate the joy we collectively felt when we saw songs by Stiff Little Fingers and The Undertones amongst the assembled classics. Naturally we put them on as we drank further to celebrate our successful first gig in the city so nice they named it twice.

As the beers flowed and sobriety went into hiding, I proposed that we should try and get on the bill for the secret MTV gig around the corner. I mean, why not? Our equipment was already in there, and we could use every ounce of our bountiful Irish Charm to ensure our rightful place on stage at the Mercury.

Since I was the one most enamoured with this inevitability, I was charged with doing the talking, as was the norm back then. Filled with the most Dutch of courage (after all New York was once a Dutch settlement), we filed around the corner in the biblical rainstorm, ready to take our rightful place at the table of our fortuitous destiny.

Ignoring the "Closed To The Public" sign that adorned the front, we simply opened the door and made our way in. Interrupting a live interview with MGMT on MTV as we went. The singer and I made eye contact and we both giggled like kids at our unfortunate intrusion. Someone took us to one side and asked us, justifiably enough, "What the fuck are you doing in here? This place is closed to the public, didn't you see the sign?" "We're not The Public", I bullishly countered with bullshit. "We played here last night, and we're here to get our equipment from the live room" The kind gentleman gave us a reprieve but told us to hurry up, as the band would be sound-checking soon. "No sweat, we'll be outta here in a few minutes".

As we entered the live room, the sound engineer was checking frequencies, looking agitated and clearly quite busy. I thought this an excellent time to interrupt her and ask her if the TM (Tour Manager) was around. She didn't even look at me, but answered promptly, "You're looking right at her," as she continued teasing feedback out of the PA. This was my moment. My opportunity to blurt out our identity and lay out our intentions, surely only to be greeted with a positive response. This was America after all, where acorns turns to oaks and dreams come true.

"Cool! It's just, you see, we're from Ireland, and we played here last night, we completely killed it, and we were just here to pick up our equipment, when we heard about this show happening tonight, and we thought you may need an opening act for tonight, and, you know, seeing as how our stuff is already here we..."

"Yeah, I'm pretty much 100% sure that's not going to happen," she interrupted, without looking away from the stage once. "Sure! No problem!" I replied, thumbs aloft in a Paul McCartney-esque fashion, as we hurriedly picked up our stuff and exited the venue, pissing ourselves with laughter at the gall of it all. Hey, at least we gave it a shot.

These were really fond memories at a genuinely thrilling time in each of our lives.

Old enough to know and do what we wanted, and too young to give a damn about the consequences.

I thought I should retrace my steps a little bit and see if the dive bar that held such special memories was still there.

Would the Jukebox still be packed with gems of yesteryear?

Would the entertaining bar maid from Puerto-Rico still be serving up drinks and laughs?

I got to Mercury Lounge, and turned the corner onto Essex Street, and I walked up and down it a few times in case somehow I had missed it. But no, it eventually dawned on me that the un-named dive bar was consigned to history, like those relationships. Those great memories were just that – great memories.

Foolishly, I decided to have a beer for old times sake and for absent friends. The place wasn't even busy but the bar tender, kept ignoring me in favour of just chatting with the girls at the bar. I started to feel old and I started to feel alone. Eventually, I got served and I took a seat in the corner of the room, as far from the rest of the clientele as possible in such a small place. As I supped my over-priced beer, I tried to shake the nostalgia that was in danger of overwhelming me. It was at this point that I noticed the song that was playing over the speakers. It equally eased and distressed me.

'Swim Until You Can't See Land', by Frightened Rabbit.

Summoning up those divergent paths once more.

13

The following morning, I gathered a few items to begin my trip out of state to see
The Zombies play an intimate house show in Ringwood, New Jersey.

Alas, I hadn't got the support slot Jesse had angled for, but I was more than
happy to go and see such a legendary group play up close and personal. To make
amends – even though he didn't need to – he told me I would playing on the
the upcoming Wednesday, at Berlin, if I wanted to. I accepted and thanked him
profusely, then grabbed my stuff and went on my way.

Whilst walking to the station, a small but significant thing happened.

In the UK and Ireland I am often accosted in the street with references to
my red hair. Most people who find the need to comment on it are harmless
enough, with a reference to Simply Red's Mick Hucknall, since we both have the
same colour of curly hair. They revel in their comic genius, clearly confident that
in my 35 years on this planet I will have never heard this comparison before.
Bizarrely, it's usually bald men who have reached their quipping peak, and
sometimes they'll grab me to take a picture, without my consent. Invasive, yes,
and sometimes a little frightening, but hardly the end of the world. Some take
it a little further, spitting and physically assaulting me for no other reason than
umbrage with my hair colour.

Anyway, I was crossing the street, when a stunning African American lady
smiled at me as we passed each other, and made my entire month with four
simple words: "I really love your hair." "Why thank you, and I yours...", I replied
in reference to her beautifully and immaculately half braided and half natural
hair whilst she ran her fingers through mine, making sure my accent was noted
in the hope of giving her a further kick.

I know hers had certainly given me one.

A kick, I mean.

Shame on you.

Continuing my stroll up Avenue A, I walked past a mural of the late, great
Joe Strummer outside a bar called Niagara, another one of Jesse's bars, and I
reflected on the inspiration this man had given me throughout the years. Just
7 months previous I had made a pilgrimage to the beautiful city of Granada
in southern Spain, where Joe had spent a lot of time in the aftermath of The

Clash splitting, trying to find himself, and at the same time ingratiating himself with the locals to such an extent that they posthumously renamed a little square in his honour, "Placeta Joe Strummer". I was there at the time to help make a short independent film, highlighting the struggles of the people of Spain since the big financial crash of 2008. In the film I was searching for the spirit of Joe, and how I had found it in the people there who were fighting for their rights. A phenomenal and truly sobering experience, and a whole other story. *"Know Your Rights"*.

Jesse – being a total hero – had arranged for me to be picked up at the station in Ringwood by his good friend Tom Baker. Not the Fourth Doctor Who alas, but still a damn good guy. We got a quick bite to eat, dropped my belongings off at my home for the next two nights, the Comfort Suites just outside of Mahwah, and made our way to Drew's for the gig.

Drew's place was like a storybook. It was beside a beautiful lake, and surrounded by magnificent trees, as well as a great deal of neighbours who weren't as keen on the legendary house shows as the committed attendees, there for Live at Drews 200th night.

Opening that night was a David Bowie cover band, the sensational Michael T and The Vanities, who played a delicious set with rockier songs from Bowie's 70s and 80s catalogue.

In between sets, I stepped outside for a smoke and everybody was keen to introduce themselves to the stranger. I got the impression very quickly that the audience was very faithful, and that everybody knew each other quite well from gigs over the years.

Bob McAdam, a retired pharmacist who was spending his retirement the right way, going to as many gigs in the tristate area as possible.

Alirio Guerrero, a Professor at Columbia University, who was enthused to tell me about his friend, Alejandro Escovedo, and even more enthused when I told him I was already a big fan.

Laura Werner, an absolute diamond of a person who would later bring me a bottle of award winning wine in New York that was hugely appreciated.

Michael Waters, another professor, and also a poet. He was there with his wife, and their young son, who stood outside during Michael T and the Vanities set, playing some excellent air guitar.

Everybody was incredibly friendly, very cool, and so passionate about live music. It was heartening, and good for the soul. I drank whatever was offered my way, and listened intently as conversations drifted from music to Bernie Sanders, Hillary Clinton, and Donald Trump. I kept my mouth shut. Having grown up in Northern Ireland during the nadir of our troubled history, I'd learnt it best not to discuss politics when in the company of relative strangers. But for the record, I felt the Bern.

The Zombies, well two of them, Rod Argent and Colin Blunstone, played to a full house, who hung on their every note. I listened to the bulk of the set from outdoors where, given the absence of drums, the sound was perfect. From the outside looking in, I gazed through the window at the audience marvelling at all the smiles and the eyes alight from the music being performed in front of them. It's a sight I never really get to see when I'm playing myself. Perhaps I don't elicit the same emotion, you may be thinking? How rude. No, it is due to the lights in my eye, and very rarely making direct eye contact with anyone, okay? Honestly...

After the gig, the fourth doctor, Mr Baker drove me back to my hotel, and promised me he'd see me at my gig during the week at Berlin, Jesse's place. I thanked him, entered the hotel, and approached the gentleman on reception.

"Excuse me, I was wondering if I could buy a beer?" I asked with a slight, but definite, slur.

"I'm afraid not sir, but if you look at the back of your key card there will be directions to a bar you can get discount at...it's an Irish Bar actually," he unknowingly patronised me. "It's only a five or ten minute drive, depending on traffic."

"Are you seriously recommending I drive to a bar for a few beers?" I enquired, culture shock inflecting my query in a theatrical manner.

"Oh of course not sir, uh, there's...uh, there's a burger joint a few places up to the left of here that serves beer, but you'll have to jump over a few hedges and fences to get to it. You are on the freeway, after all..."

"Very well! Then that is just as I shall do. Thank you! To the left, yes?"

"Yes sir, to the left, just after the drive through bank."

"A drive through bank? Brilliant..." I tailed off with a smile, exiting the hotel and making my way past another motel, the drive through Bank of America that I found so amusing, and then arriving at Boom Burger.

There was at least two dozen televisions showing just as many different sports, with a handful of couples scattered amongst the establishment. I had a few beers, and watched everything from basketball to golf to rodeo, before deciding I should hit the hay for the evening.

The hotel was my base until Monday, and Boom Burger was the most exciting thing for miles. It became apparent that a hotel day loomed for me, before the first of my meetings, and I wanted to be fresh and sound of mind. Not to mention I'd need all the energy I could muster for the ensuing few weeks.

14

Back in NYC and the military were everywhere.

I'd seen on the morning news that they were having drills to test their personnel on how to react in the event of a chemical attack on the subway. For this drill, they would be using coloured gas for maximum realism. Having never been a fan of seeing the army on the streets – and also having watched one too many conspiracy theory documentaries in my time – I opted to stay above ground as much as possible.

Thankfully, my hotel in midtown Manhattan wasn't too far from my publisher's office on Times Square, where I was scheduled for a meeting with one of the heads of their NY creative section, Ms Sarah-Jane Smith. So staying on foot wasn't a problem.

Three hours needed killing, so I figured I should stop somewhere for a coffee and really get my head in the right space for this meeting. After all, the chief reason for me being in America was to try and foster these ties as much as possible, and to try and take my career to the next step.

I needed to be on my A game, I needed to be confident, and know what I wanted to get out of our relationship as publisher and client. I couldn't come across as smalltime, despite that being exactly what I was.

Walking up 8th Avenue, I kept my eyes peeled for a coffee house that wasn't too crowded, and that wouldn't necessarily object to me sitting there for a couple of hours nursing one cup of coffee. I passed a bar that for some reason stood out to me.

The Houndstooth Pub. It rang a bell, somewhere, in my head.

It all became clear to me when I went inside. Surveying the walls, I saw a large Irish flag, and beneath that hung a platinum disc belonging to my fellow countrymen, Snow Patrol. The disc was for their fourth album, *Eyes Open*, which had been a monstrous success. On the adjacent wall there was a signed poster from Snow Patrol's good friend and associate, Ed Sheeran, from his sell-out run of shows in the nearby Madison Square Garden the previous year.

Mr Sheeran is a talent, and there's no questioning that, whilst not my particular cup of tea, he's a phenomenon. I can only laugh when I think of how poor my timing was to branch out as a solo musician. As I, a weird looking redhead, started out on my own, armed with only my guitar and voice, who steps out of the shadows to become arguably the most successful musician on the circuit? Another weird looking redhead, armed only with his guitar and his voice, lucky ol' Ed. Yes, I can only laugh, as it makes the tears look like happy ones.

I took a seat at the bar of The Houndstooth, and sent an email to Nathan Connolly, guitarist with Snow Patrol, a shareholder in the bar, telling him where I was. The bar was populated with a mix of business types and tourists; unsurprising given its proximity to Times Square. It was quite different to the bars I'd previously been to, and the ones I would end up in on the remainder of my trip. The bartender approached with a menu, and I declined, asking only for a coffee, to which he smiled and duly brought one over.

Nathan got back almost immediately saying how he hoped I enjoyed it, and to tell everyone he said "Hi". When the bartender (who was the manager, as it turned out) came back with my coffee, I introduced myself as a friend of Nathan's, presented the email and said "Hi", as instructed. The nice gentleman would then return every twenty minutes to refill my coffee, whilst I scribbled in my notepad, readying myself for what could be a very important meeting.

Buoyed with caffeine and confidence (mainly caffeine), I made the short trip to the a building on Times Square, where my publishers had their offices on the 11th floor.

Ninety minutes later, I left the meeting, fairly pleased that it had all went very well. Sarah-Jane had been excellent to talk with, making me feel very much part of my publisher's operations, and that we could move things onto the next step by introducing me to other writers and different members of the creative and sync teams. I couldn't have been happier with how it had went.

I returned to The Houndstooth bar, took the same seat that I'd held before, ordered some French Fried Onion soup, and talked with the new bartender when she wasn't busy.

The urge to play some music was fast becoming a fervent need, so I searched for Open Mic Nights on my phone, which told me that one of the longest running and coolest Open Mics in the city was taking place at a bar called the Sidewalk Cafe at 94 Avenue A. Which, of course, was the other side of Manhattan, and about five minutes from Jesse's door, where I would not be staying that night.

I went to settle my bill, and the very cool Polish bartender told me to forget about it. Nathan had been in touch, and my drinks and meal were all complimentary. Wonderful news and supremely kind of Nathan, but if I had only known this in advance, I would have had something a little more substantial than soup. I guess that's why they don't tell you these things until afterwards... Still, mustn't grumble. Graciously fed, and even more graciously watered, it was time to move on.

The Sidewalk Cafe is something of a legend on the Open Mic circuit in the city, known for being the epicentre of the 'Anti-folk' scene. Regina Spektor, Lana Del Ray, Lach, and The Moldy Peaches are amongst just some of the notable performers who have performed there at the beginning of their careers, so it seemed a fine place for me to yell incoherent melodies down a microphone in New York for the first time.

It is a dark and dingy place.

I immediately felt at home.

The main bar is pressed along the left hand side, and the open mic takes place in the larger back room, where I was escorted through to upon asking the waitress where I was supposed to go for sign up. She showed me in, told me sit anywhere I liked, and then took a drinks order from me. The place was still relatively empty but she assured me it would get busy soon enough, which it proceeded to do in no time.

The way it works, is that the lady who runs the evening, Somer Bingham, would ask all attendees to form a queue, and then a lottery would take place as to when you would get your chance to perform.

Joining me at my table were a nice Belgian couple, Francois and Scarlett, a handsome Italian man, Sergio, and a hippie girl called Lindsay. We chatted amiably and talked about how we'd come to the city, and how none of us had been at the Sidewalk before. The time then came to queue, so we formed an orderly line, and collected our numbers. I had randomly selected number twenty seven, which is somebody's lucky number, I'm sure, but not to the members of the club named after it.

There was roughly seventy performers – along with thirty or forty punters – and Somer told us that we'd all get a chance to perform if we stayed, and that chances were, not everyone would stay, so our numbers were bound to change. Somer kicked things off, as she did every week, and she was excellent. The very essence of Village cool.

Sergio was first up from our table with number five. He took to the stage and sat behind the upright piano before introducing himself. It was only then that I noticed he had a smaller left arm and hand, which (and this is conjecture on my behalf, as I thought it rude to ask) may have been from the condition known as Phocomelia. This did not in any way, shape, or form hamper his piano playing.

He played with all the flair and confidence of Jerry Lee Lewis, and had a rock and roll voice the Killer himself would have been proud of. He was the first performer of the night to get everyone really pumped up, and he finished to great applause. He briefly re-joined us at our table, finished his drink, and went on his way, as seemed to be the way of a lot of performers.

Turn up, play, get your fix of applause, move on.

Some of the following contenders included an albino stand up, an over dramatic show tunes mangler, who performed twenty second requests (probably my favourite of the night), and a poet who refused applause or recognition of any sort, storming out the fire exit at the rear of the stage when someone dared to whoop in approval.

Number sixteen rolled around and it was Francois' turn to get up, whilst his girlfriend Scarlett filmed from her seat. Francois was quite nervous and dedicated his song to the lady he had written the song about, his girlfriend and the love of his life, Scarlett. Half of the audience groaned, and the other half let their hearts flutter in appreciation of their love. I am not ashamed to say I was in the latter group.

Alas, Francois' nerves seemed to be getting the better of him as he fluffed chord changes and drifted out of key. But this mattered not, for as soon as he was done, he got a huge roar of appreciation and encouragement from us all, as it became apparent that the only person he cared about enjoying his performance was his other half.

They never took their eyes off each other the entire time.

Everyone unified in regard for their love for one another being so much stronger than his musical ability. The very fact he'd braved a New York audience, just to show his feelings for his girlfriend was truly a beautiful thing.

I stepped outside and rolled a cigarette, wary that I was drinking too fast, and that if I didn't slow down, I was in danger of doing a realistic, but poor Shane Magowan impression when my number finally came up. Outside, Lindsay and her friend from our table, joined me and lamented that they may not be able to stay.

"Why not?" I asked.

"Well, I got number forty, and it's only at seventeen now. It's been going for nearly two hours...we don't really wanna hang around that long," Lindsay replied, reasonably enough.

I tried to talk them round.

"Aw c'mon, you've lasted this long, you're nearly half way there. I'd really like to hear you..."

"Really? Aw that's sweet, but you got it right, we're *nearly* halfway there, it's gonna be at least another two hours," replying once more with reason, albeit pessimistic reason. Then she asked, "What number did you get anyway?"

"Twenty-seven, but I promise I'll stay to hear you if you're afraid of everyone leaving." Right on cue, Francois and Scarlett exited the building and said goodbye to us, mirroring what most people seemed to be doing once they had played.

"Hmmm, we'll think about it. See ya inside," Lindsay finished, smiling, returning indoors with her friend, whilst I remained for another few minutes and finished my smoke.

Back inside, the numbers had thinned out, but there was still a healthy enough crowd there. A few more people had joined us and the room was still relatively full. More performers got up for their moment in the spotlight, and as chance would suggest, some soared and some crashed.

Then a curious thing happened. As I was reaching for my guitar, Somer called for the next performer.

"Number twenty-seven, Lindsay Mellows!"

Huh?

The Peace and Love loving, nightmare hippy girl had taken it upon herself to switch numbers with me whilst I was still smoking. I would have been more pissed off if I hadn't kind of admired the outright chump she'd made of me. I laughed and tried to make eye contact with her friend in order to convey my initial feeling of, "what the actual fuck?" She didn't bite and clapped enthusiastically for her friend who was taking my place on the stage.

To be completely fair – unlike her number swapping trick – Lindsay was sensational.

She set up a loop station, and relied only on her voice to set up a beat and a bass loop before topping it all off with an impressive and catchy vocal line. She was far and away the most impressive performer of the night up until that point. I guess if I was going to be played for a fool I might as well be played by the second most talented person left in the room. Ahem.

Lindsay left the stage to great applause. She quickly gathered her loop station, then rushed down to give her friend a passionate kiss. They were closer than I first thought. Then they turned and smiled at me, Lindsay mouthed, "Thank you", apparently sincerely, and they disappeared into the New York night.

Nightmare Hippy Girl, by the way, is an excellent song by Beck.

Oh well, I thought, *I guess that makes me number forty. Only thirteen more to go...*

By the time forty rolled around, it was after midnight. I'd been there for nearly five hours, and somehow wasn't too drunk. The numbers had diminished significantly, with only twenty at most still in attendance.

"Number forty, Tony! Tony? Is Tony still here?" Somer enquired over the PA, and I raised my hand in acknowledgement, taking to the stage.

"Alright party people, give it up for...Tony!"

There was a sparse round of applause from the remaining few that faded as soon as it had started, and I waved back in thanks as I plugged my guitar in. Regardless of the thinned audience, I was excited and more nervous than I had been for a long time in front of an audience.

"Hi...I'm Tony..."

"Tony, you don't sound like you're from round these parts, any of these parts for that matter... You Irish, Tony? Where ya from, Tony?" Somer asked me from her spot by the mixing desk, answering herself before she asked me a question.

"Irish, yeah, that's me," I said, tugging on a red curl on my head, as if reaching for tangible proof.

"Okaaaaay, Irish Tony, you're very welcome here, now sing us a song will ya?"

"Sure..."

I took a deep breath, and readied myself for my first solo New York outing. I thanked everyone for staying around this long and then introduced my song, 'Have Some Soul'.

It was over in a heartbeat. The near four minute song seemed to last the blink of an eye. Which it kind of did because once I started it, I closed my eyes and didn't open them again until I hit the final harmonic.

The twenty or so remaining stood and applauded.

It was the first time it had happened that night, and the first time it had happened to me. I was stunned. I took a step back and bowed, like I'd always seen The Beatles do in their early performances. This thinly assembled rabble of notoriously hard to please New York anti-folk musicians and artisans showed me their appreciation, and I felt like I'd just reached the summit of Mount Olympus on Mars, again.

Look Ma! I made it! Top of the Red World!

"Well, holy shit Tony!" Somer commented, "Wanna play another?"

"Yeeeaaaah!" came the reply, but not from me. From the audience.

Negating one of the oldest and truest rules of showbiz, "Always leave 'em wanting more", I played one more (a song called, 'Shakedown Sally'), and got an equally enthusiastic response.

I thanked them from the bottom of my heart, got off the stage, and took my hard wooden bench seat where I had been sitting for nearly five hours, and I would've waited another five to play again if I could. I was shaking from the adrenaline surge like I hadn't done in such a long time.

That's not to say I haven't enjoyed playing in the past, but when I stepped off stage in the Sidewalk Cafe, Avenue A, I felt like I'd aced some sort of endurance test that had been going on for years, decades even, and every molecule in my body was fizzing with excitement.

I'd finally sang in New York City.

15

The next day held a new adventure. As everyday should.

Today would introduce me to some new faces and places, just as the past five had, but would be topped off with seeing a familiar old face, from my past, present, and future.

I would be traveling upstate to meet an old friend from home: Paul Clegg, his wife Meghan, and their little boy, Crosby. Before any of that however, I would be taking my first ever trip to the centre of the Hipster Universe, Williamsburg in Brooklyn, to meet with a stranger, Liza Sun.Paul had suggested we meet and maybe try to do some writing together, so we had agreed to get lunch and get something arranged.

I had met Liza once before, for a few seconds in Dublin when ASIWYFA had opened for her band, Gogol Bordello (at this point, I should probably add, my friend Paul is part of Gogol's management team, hence the connection), with whom she had parted ways from only a few months previous, completely at her own behest, and with no malice from anyone involved. Which is always nice to hear.

After I checked out of the East Manhattan Hotel, forgetting the sheer terror and unreserved suspicions I had held the previous day concerning the NY underground, I descended into the Subway to catch the L train to Brooklyn.

Standing and idly thumbing through Reddit on my phone, I was approached by two friendly, smiling, elderly gentlemen.

"Excuse me sir, you know how to get to uptown from here, yes?, one of them asked me in a Spanish accent. Confident that I was now practically a New Yorker after less than a week here, I replied, "I think that may be the other side, but yes, I'm fairly sure you can get there from this station".

"Oh...are you not New Yorker?" he enquired upon noticing my accent. I was about to respond, when he suddenly exclaimed, "Oh! Look! A little mousey!" as he pointed toward a huge rat scurrying along the line below us. "We're from Rio," he continued, with their smiles never wavering. "We too have little mousey in the subway!"

I liked these gentlemen.

I walked them over to the large transport map and showed them what they needed to know, then we shook hands and wished each other the best on our respective trips.

Having successfully passed on transit advice, I felt sure my green card would be issued imminently, and my candidacy for Mayor of New York would be met with great celebration in the Five Boroughs. Next stop on the campaign trail, Brooklyn.

Getting off of the subway train at Bedford Ave Station, it was immediately apparent I had just arrived in the Elysian Fields of Hipsterdom. I mean, I was aware Brooklyn was now cool in a different way to before, but nothing really prepares you for it until you get there and see it for yourself.

People of all nationalities swarmed on and off the train, just like in Manhattan, or London, or Berlin, and it is glorious. But all of these folk, in comparison with myself, were so young, and I'm only thirty five. Not only that, they were so...so... so... *hip*.

Tapered trousers, or shorts with roll ups and long tees to match (or not), beards, severe undercuts, with long hair to one side and none to the other, mullets and moustaches, beards, glasses ranging from Buddy Holly-style frames, to the styles popularised by Harry Potter and his father Gandhi, beards, an abundance of sleeve and leg tattoos ranging from the harshest of conflicting colours to the finest of black outlines, beards, moth eaten wooly sweaters with garish designs, and more deck shoes and winkle-pickers than every 1980s Oxfam outlet combined.

And then there were the hats...ascot-caps, Balmoral-bonnets, beanies, boaters, bowlers, buckets, chullos, deerstalkers, fedoras, flat-caps, gatsbys, panamas, porkpies, rastacaps, sun-hats, top-hats, trilbys, and truckers.

One strong gust of wind could have serious implications in this neighbourhood.

And beards.

So many damn beards.

The hipster is a much maligned, multi-faceted tribe of youth. Mostly – but not exclusively – this malevolence comes from older people, and, ironically, older hipsters.

Hipsters love irony.

They are mocked in much the same way that goths, or punks, or hippies, or beatniks were before them. These are simply young people reacting to the generation that preceded them. So the majority of the people so upset at the sight of them have no one to blame but themselves, since the hipster's world is merely a contrary reaction to the former one that their elders created and inhabited.

If someone's age, gender, race, sexuality, creed, choice of how they live, or dress upsets you so much, you really should find a new hobby and spend your time on something else, as yours is fast running out.

There are much more productive ways to spend ones time than judging others. Unless you're perhaps a Judge.

Remember, you were young once too, and take comfort in the fact that they may well too look back at pictures of themselves and possibly cringe. As you probably do at your early twenties and teenage years.

Those last few sentences are aimed as much at myself, as they are anyone else.

Liza and myself had arranged to meet at an establishment called Cafe Mogador on Wythe Avenue, two blocks north west of Bedford Street station. I arrived a little early, and emailed her to let her know that I had made it, but there was no rush. Whilst waiting, I received word from Paul – who I was staying with that night – that I should get in touch with his friends Paolo and Emily, who were also joining us that night.

Bang on time, Liza arrived. I had told her to look out for the most Irish looking man she could imagine, adding that I had a guitar too, in case there was a sudden flux of us. She immediately recognised me, and I her, although I had a distinct advantage being a fan of her old band.

All smiles, we exchanged hellos and pleasantries, ordered two coffees, and told each other about ourselves. Liza was very cool, full of wonderful stories, and just as intent on listening to others as she was telling her own. A very striking looking woman, that drew the eye towards her. She was of half Chinese and half Scottish descent, and had held onto her mild Glasgow accent beautifully; it was a delight to be called, "Hen", so far away from a city that I hold very dear to my heart.

After our coffees, she took me on a brief stroll around the neighbourhood that ended up in a nearby bar, where we enthusiastically discussed music, life, and the difficulties of readjusting to being in one place for an extended period of time, as Liza was now doing after ten years of relentless globetrotting with Gogol Bordello. We couldn't find a solution unfortunately, but we did agree that it was demandingly difficult to do so.

It was approaching time for me to leave, and she told me to pass on my love and regards to Paul and his family, as well as Paolo and Emily (it turned out that Paolo was – and remains – Gogol's tour manager) and that we would meet again in a few days to try and do some writing together.

Astoria Blvd station is East of LaGuardia Airport, where Paolo and Emily were staying. I disembarked the train and took a picture of the Station sign that bore its name. You see, the Fish and Chip shop that my parents owned – and we lived above – was called the Astoria. I'd grown up there, it was where I had learned how to play guitar and mope. It seemed like a nice picture to send my Dad to let him know I was safe and sound.

Paolo and Emily picked me up, and we travelled north to Nyack, getting to know each other along the way. Paolo, as I mentioned before, is Gogol Bordello's TM, and they had arrived in the city a few days previously, where the band had begun rehearsals for their upcoming jaunt around the colonies. Emily, Paolo's girlfriend, worked as a driver for a festival booker, driving the headline acts from hotels, to sites, to restaurants. She had the most incredible stories, which unfortunately I can't share, for fear of some of them possibly going to prison.

As we departed the city, the surroundings became greener and the traffic eventually thinned out, allowing us to arrive just before seven o'clock.

Paul, Meghan, and little Crosby were waiting outside to greet us as we arrived. We were all hugs and laughs, and Crosby commanded all of our attentions the way only a happy toddler can.

Their house was a beautiful, large, detached two storey property, in a quiet leafy neighbourhood. The perfect place to raise a family, which is precisely why they had moved there I imagine.

We moved inside, Paul fed Crosby some supper, and then Meghan put him to bed. We ordered in some Mongolian food, and sat down to feast.

As is the norm when gathering with both old friends for the umpteenth time, and new friends for the first, stories naturally turned to how everyone knew one another.

Myself and Paul have known each other for just shy of twenty years.

A phenomenally smart individual, he graduated from Queen's University Belfast with a degree in History and Politics – I think. He'd been the singer in a band called Consume, from Ballymena, when we first met.

Consume were very much in the mould of Rage Against The Machine, and had toured Europe with successful US bands of a similar genre, such as Biohazard and Downset. Paul was doing this whilst my band PepperBook was struggling to get a gig in Belfast.

They worked their asses off and gathered a good following outside of Northern Ireland, yet were given little to no credit in their home, despite European tours and positive recognition from magazines like Kerrang! and Metal Hammer.

When Consume started to wind down, Paul began trying his hand at tour managing professionally, since he'd been doing it for nearly half a decade with his own group. Working with mainly US rock acts to begin with, as his reputation deservedly grew and grew, he was soon working with bigger and more mainstream acts. He was never afraid to put himself out there, and I've never seen him show a flicker of fear, despite some of the truly terrifying positions he's found and put himself – and occasionally myself – in. He's always had an ace up his sleeve to get himself out of these situations, and if he didn't, he didn't once let it show. Such was the fearlessness and confidence in his own ability.

One such small example of these perilous instances occurred in 1999, when PepperBook and Paul joined forces for a few gigs, with the ultimate goal to just have a good time and laugh as much as possible.

This should have been obvious from our preposterous name, "Big Jim and the Twins".

Our set consisted of a bunch of PepperBook songs that Paul inserted new rapping verses to, as well as medleys of classic rock songs that Paul would, again, rap over, with always hilarious, when decipherable, lyrics.

All of this was done with tongues very much in cheek.

To add to our sheer ridiculousness, we wore excessively baggy clothing. Paul's mother had at one stage owned a shoe shop, so he took some large, fake plastic gold letters he had found in his garage, and turned it into a necklace that read, "HOES".

If anyone took us seriously, they really ought to have taken a deep, hard, long look at themselves. Unlike ourselves however, a lot of people did take us seriously.

One Saturday in November of '99, we were playing two gigs in Belfast. A matinee in Katy Daly's, followed by a support slot later that evening in the Duke of York.

For the first gig, we were part of the bill for Belfast's long running Distortion Project, a popular hard rock and metal showcase. We were supporting Sons of Massey, an excellent band consisting of, amongst others, the amazing Kilrea songwriter Robyn G Shiels, and Michael McKeegan of NI rock royalty, Therapy?

It was fairly evident soon into our set that a lot of the regulars at the showcase did not appreciate us or get the joke. Soon we had sections of the audience hurling the immortal phrase *"Death to the false Metal"* our way at the end of every song.

I'd be lying if I said it wasn't fairly intimidating, but since I wasn't the frontman of this band, I wasn't the recipient of the majority of ire being shown to us. Paul, with his equally high energy and pitched rapping style, was getting the glut of the disdain, but he didn't bat an eyelid in the face of any derision.

Just before we played our last song, Paul finally took it upon himself to address the scorn being levelled toward us.

"Wow, so you guys don't really dig us, do ya?" he asked the angered punters, whilst pacing the stage, smiling to himself, and then to us, as we did our concerted best not to show any sign of fear, or look at the audience.

"*Fuck you guys!*", "*You suck!*", "*Get the fuck off the stage, assholes!*", and the now familiar "*Death to the false Metal!*" being chanted at us in ever increasing numbers.

One guy was taking particular exception to our efforts, and was standing on his table launching both insults and cigarette butts our way.

Paul decided it was time for some action, and he spoke directly to this indignant fellow.

"You think you could do better, huh? You wanna get up here and show me? C'mon, big boy, get up here and show me how it's done! I've got a six pack of beer here for ya if you prove that you can do better...", and he wasn't lying. To our collective astonishment, Paul produced six bottles of beer from a bag at the side of the stage, right beside a pint glass of blackcurrant juice that had sat untouched, along with a bottle of water. A huge roar of approval came from the furious crowd as the embittered metal lover accepted the challenge levelled his way, urging him to show us up.

The gentleman in question jumped onto the stage area to take the microphone. He was a six foot plus hulk of a man, clad entirely in black, with more tattoos than the populace of a Brooklyn subway station combined. As he gripped the mic, he let rip with a long and deep, sustained metal growl that would have shook a sleuth of bears into hiding, and the audience loved every lingering, rumbling second of it, cheering him all the way.

Revelling in his clear victory, he then launched into what I can only presume was a popular metal song, a cappella. Or perhaps he was riffing. Either way, the audience went wild, further cheering him on as he smugly passed the mic back to Paul, awaiting his winnings.

"Well dude, you really showed me..." The audience were still applauding for having witnessed the peddlers of false metal be put in our place, but Paul then continued, "...But if you really wanna prove what a tough guy you are, I bet you another six beer you can't down this pint of blackcurrant in one. Whaddaya say? Double or quits, big man?" He reached down and produced another six beer, then held forth the pint of juice, goading his challenger on with a grin.

Buoyed by his schooling of Paul, and the adulation from his peers, he didn't bat an eyelid as he snatched the glass and sank every last drop, opening his throat to ensure it disappeared in double quick time. Once more, the audience pealed in raucous approval at his one-upmanship of our seemingly beleaguered frontman.

We didn't know where to look.

Despite the un-dwindling abuse coming our way, Paul didn't flinch.

He made good on his word and handed over the twelve bottles, to a huge cheer, before announcing that this was our last song to huge hybrid bellow of delight and disgust.

Delight, that we were finishing, and disgust that they had to sit through one more song.

It was easily the biggest reaction we had gotten that afternoon.

We finished the set to a handful of claps from the sympathetic few at the back of the bar, but for the most part, nobody even noticed.

I unplugged my guitar and switched off my amp, glad that the ordeal was over.

"Well, I guess that guy really *did* show you," I said to Paul, vocalising what the four of us in PepperBook were thinking. I was pissed off at the crowd but, and I regret this now, I directed it toward my friend.

"You think so, huh?" Paul retorted immediately. "Come with me," he said, before walking offstage and motioning for me to follow. Paul pushed through the crowds whilst I tailed behind him, making our way towards the guy's toilets.

As we approached the door, the misted window which took up half of the door had been sprayed by some lumpy, fetid purple fluid. Kicking it open, we were welcomed by a putrid miasma, a stench far worse than your average bar toilet on a Saturday afternoon. A streak of foul purple led from the floor, and onto the sink on the right hand side. Some of it had splashed upwards onto the mirror, and then onto the urinals beside, where it dripped to form repugnant puddles of vomit and urine, leading ultimately to the cubicle, to which the door was closed.

It sounded as if some kind of self-imposed exorcism was taking place within.

The unmistakable sound of a man's stomach rejecting all that it contains.

You see, the blackcurrant juice was undiluted; no gut could hold down that sugary poison. Especially not one filled with an afternoon's worth of beer.

Paul looked at me with a grin that opined "who showed who?" He didn't need to say it, and I certainly didn't doubt it.

Just beside the urinals, two six packs sat, undisturbed.

"I don't think that guy is gonna need these," he conjectured, probably correctly.

Picking up the beers, he turned to me and said, "Dude, let's get out of here, it fuckin' stinks," definitely correctly.

Later that same night, we (Big Jim & The Twins), were in the Duke of York, where PepperBook had played our first Belfast gig three years previously, when I was fifteen, opening for John Robb's band, Goldblade, and Dischord Records' achingly cool, The Makeup.

At this point, we were all pretty drunk. Ever the young professionals, we'd made sure to drink every last drop of our first rider for that day, and we were making a decent dent into our second. We had been laughing ourselves to distraction at what had went down in Katy Dalys just a few hours before, not thinking for a second that some of those disgruntled punters from earlier may come along to the gig that night as well. After all, Belfast nightlife for those into rock music was pretty limited, considering the size of the city.

We were opening for a band called Zerotonin, who were kind enough to let us use their amps and drum hardware. Zerotonin enjoyed a pretty decent following in the city, and the Duke of York isn't the biggest of bars, particularly when the gig is confined to the narrow back bar. If forty people showed up, the place would be rammed. Which it was.

The gig started off without a hitch and a pleasant atmosphere; a lot more people seemed to get that we were out to offer a bit of fun, and that this band was in no way to be taken seriously. Paul wore a huge golden, "HOES", chain around his neck for crying out loud.

It was Saturday night in the city and people were feeling good.

Towards the end of our set, from the back of the room, we started to hear a few voices of discontent, and those voices were chanting a phrase with which we had all become so well acquainted with earlier that afternoon.

"Death to the false Metal!"

We ignored them and kept playing, going nuts as usual, and trying our best to entertain those who were enjoying it and who were getting the joke. Slowly but surely though, the kvetsching throng had battled their way to the front, and were once again clearly very unhappy that we were daring to have fun whilst playing heavy music.

"Death to the false Metal!"

Our penultimate song had been played, and half the audience cheered us whilst the other half booed us to high heaven. Paul had clearly had enough of this.

He launched into a justified tirade, aimed directly at the minority that had infiltrated the front and found it acceptable to show their disdain for us, but weren't too happy when a mirror was held up to them and their shortcomings were pointed out to them.

I won't go into specific detail, but Paul being a smart guy, and quick witted, fired off a diatribe of hurtful truths at those who deserved it and cut them down one by one with his superior reason, aided by – most importantly of all – a microphone.

As correct as everything Paul said was, coupled with how hilarious it was to watch the faces of those whom his truths were aimed at drop, I would not advise anyone on a stage to do this. For comedians this course of action is fine, at a rock gig however? Not so much.

For one, you may incite a riot, and secondly, you may be limited in your escape options if the possibility previously mentioned should happen to manifest.

To further both these points, as you may have guessed by now, I speak from experience.

The audience started to sway a little, back and forth and from side to side, like something was about to erupt. A pressure cooker, if you'll forgive my obvious metaphor. We started our last song, warily. I looked towards my bandmates, Aidy, Graeme, and Johnny, whilst Paul was laying his verse with more venom than I'd ever heard. Not that I could make it out due to the rising noise from the audience, but it seemed he was freestyling, and those freestyles were about the people he'd just been cutting down moments before. It was safe to assume this from the finger pointing and flipping that was taking place. It was tense.

Somehow, we got to the end of the song when, our friend and van driver, Big Paul (not to be confused with Mr Clegg), had forced his way to the front. He pushed a few people back so he could open the fire escape which was just in front of the stage, and firmly told us, "Get the fuck out and get in the fucking van... now." Big Paul – as his name would suggest – is not a gentleman that people tend to disagree with. We gathered our distortion pedals and ran to the end of the back lane, with our guitars strapped on and cables dragging behind us, to where the van was sitting, waiting for us, with the sliding door unlocked.

We piled in the back laughing, buzzing from it all. Paul sat, cross legged, cool as ice, against the opposite side of the van. Big Paul, jumped in up front, in the driver's seat.

"What the fuck do you think you were doing, Cleggy?" Big Paul yelled from the front in his Huddersfield accent. "Those fuckers wanna kill you," staring at Paul over his shoulder in disbelief.

"So? I don't care..." came the laconic response, and he really didn't.

It was at the point that some people started pounding the van, trying to get in. Our laughter soon stopped.

Retaining the same demeanour, Paul didn't flinch for a second.

"Cleggy," Big Paul continued yelling, "I'll go out and fight for those four," pointing at the PepperBook contingent of Aidy, Graeme, Johnny and I, "but not for you. what the fuck were you thinking stirring them up like that?"

The van was really rocking back and forth now, and for all we knew we were about to be torn limb from limb by the gathering mob.

"Death to the false Metal!" could be heard being shouted from all corners outside the relative safety of the vehicle.

"Dude, I really couldn't give a fuck, they deserved it," Paul said, and I believed him. We all did.

Big Paul started the engine and leaned out window telling people to back off, loudly, and colourfully. When Big Paul spoke, and especially when he spoke loudly, people tended to listen.

It was like having a Yorkshire Stone Cold Steve Austin berate you.

So they backed off, and we drove away.

Their chants faded out within seconds and for what seemed like an age, we all sat in relative silence in the van.

Finally, Paul broke the silence with the most welcomed words we'd heard all of that day. "Yo, who wants a beer? I've got like twelve bottles here from earlier..."

Stories such as this were bandied back and forth across the table from each of us. Eventually I moved onto telling a story about the first European Tour I had been on, whilst I was at college in Liverpool, which Paul had TM-ed. Without going in to too much detail (and believe me, as I touched upon at the beginning; there are enough horror stories from that tour and various repercussions, to spawn a saga), there was a show in Milan, towards the beginning of the millennium, where I nearly got cut up into little pieces and served as anti-pasta by a bunch of bikers. My crime? Putting the band's backdrops over their coat of arms at the back of the stage. As it turns out, this was the first time Paul (& I) had met Paolo and, never forgetting what a great job the young show rep had did, Paul offered him his current job with Gogol years later when he moved onto the management team. I had a distinct memory of Paul complimenting the show rep repeatedly once we left the venue. Funny how life throws people back together. A job well done – fittingly rewarded.

We finished our food and stories then called it a night. Paolo and Emily drove back to their Hotel at LaGuardia Airport, Meghan said her goodnights and went to bed, whilst Paul and I sat up a little longer catching up and talking nonsense; as old friends do.

After a great night in excellent company, and a good eight hours sleep, I awoke ebullient, knowing that I had a gig that evening.

Meghan and Crosby had already left by the time I made it downstairs after a wash, so Paul finished up a few phone calls and emails, then took me into the pretty little town of Nyack for a breakfast of eggs, bacon, home-fries, and coffee, as had become the norm for me in the past six days.

After we ate Paul took me on a little tour of the area, which was clearly quite affluent and brimming with entertainers and creative folk who had done well. We passed by houses belonging to Bill Murray, Rosie O'Donnell, and Mark Kostabi (Kostabi is an artist, his best known work probably being the covers of Guns n' Roses albums, *Use Your Illusion I & II*). The much celebrated artist Edward Hopper (responsible for the American classic, Nighthawks) came from this little gem of a town.

We left Nyack and crossed the bridge over the Hudson River to the east bank, on our way to Tarrytown, where the train station was. We stopped by a little village made famous by America's first international best-selling author, Washington Irving. The village of Sleepy Hollow, where the aforementioned is buried, along with Elizabeth Arden, and Andrew Carnegie. In separate plots, obviously. I, along with several busloads of school children, took pictures of the bridge that is said to have inspired the now legendary tale, and a particularly arresting metalwork sculpture nearby of the famed headless horseman chasing poor old Ichabod Crane.

Paul dropped me off at the train station in Tarrytown, I thanked him for everything, and we said our goodbyes. He told me to sit on the right-hand side of the train if possible – riverside – as it is a beguiling train journey along the banks of the Hudson River.

He wasn't lying.

It was a beautiful day, and looking out the window on the right, I could have been racing along the side of the Danube or the Tiber, such was the beauty of the wide river reflecting the trees and endless sky. But the adjacent left hand side was unmistakably New York.

Both were equally beautiful, but in quite different ways.

16

I arrived into Grand Central Station a little after 1pm, so I still had a lot of time to kill.

Killing time in a city like New York should be a fairly easy thing to do, right? Even when you're on a limited budget, yeah? Well, it can be if you're not lugging around a guitar and a case full of clothes, which both unfortunately and fortunately, I was.

After getting the subway towards the village (still no sign of the Chemical Gas Attack drill yet), I alighted then briefly stopped in a bakery for a coffee, croissant, and a gallon of water. I got in touch with some friends from back in Northern Ireland, Rory and Grainne, who happened to have arrived in New York the previous day, and arranged to meet them at my gig that night. I told them they'd be on the guestlist, which felt pretty good, I must admit.

Continuing on my quest of time wasting, I was struck by how the village was awash with beautiful young things, the majority of which were vaguely bemused by the sight of me, clad in black, wearing a denim jacket, and carrying all that I was, in these blistering hot temperatures. I'm not sure whether people were getting out of my way due to politeness, or because they were terrified at the sight of this exhausted red headed and faced, sweat factory in denim, attempting passage through the narrow streets, seeking shade wherever it was cast.

I'd successfully seen off a few hours, but knew that I needed to get off of the streets and take some refuge from the unforgiving sun. At this point I was on the same street as Berlin and it made sense for me to linger around here for a little while until I could ditch my stuff in the connecting bar above at street level, 2A. There was a bar just across the street called the Double Down Saloon that looked particularly grimy, with no danger of sunlight breaching the said griminess. Plus, it was happy hour, and I could nurse a beer for an hour or so. No problem. Of that much, I was sure.

Only it wasn't as easy as that, really. You see, after I ordered my beer and took a seat at table where I could easily store my guitar and bag without getting in anyone's way, I then noticed, and I really don't know how it had escaped my attention when I entered the bar and ordered, every television in the establishment was showing grainy, 1980s VHS quality, hardcore pornography.

The volume wasn't blasting, but it was audible as soon as you noticed it, eyes and ears coming into synch when presented with the visuals.

I watched momentarily – not quite believing my eyes at first – then shook my head like an old man, with an expression of "Well I never..." and a bemused grin, before reaching for my book to kill a little more time. I buried my head in the book, but the combination of cheesy eighties porn soundtrack, all wailing guitars and saxophone solos – possibly played by Bill Clinton himself – along with generic moaning, is a fairly distracting one that doesn't really allow the mind to settle into the required state to fully immerse oneself in another's prose.

Go on, try it.

Anyway, casting aside the fear of reprisal from my all-consuming catholic guilt, I allowed my eyes to be drawn to the nearest screen. Most of it was laughable, but some it was pretty dark stuff, so I drank my beer a lot quicker than I had first intended and went on my way. I wasn't so incensed as to waste a beer. That would be the real sin.

Walking north up Avenue A, I arrived at Niagara which had just opened. I stuck my head in and quickly looked at the screens, fearing I may find out that it was National Porn Day, and that I'd just have to get used to blushing that much in public. Thankfully, they were showing *The Warriors*, so I sat at the bar and ordered a beer. Aware that I hadn't eaten anything since breakfast and I was now on my second drink, I asked the barmaid (Danielle was her name, a great lady) if there was any bar food available.

"We got Popcorn, want some?"

Naturally, I said yes, and passed the next few hours watching *The Warriors*, washing popcorn down with a beer, and getting to know Danielle a little better. Soon it would be showtime.

That night I was first on a bill of three. Headlining was the up and coming New York band, Hollis Brown, whose main support was – along with his band – a gentleman with the impeccably cool given name of Don DiLego. I knew both of them from seeing their names down as support to Jesse around Europe, but I'd never met or spoken with any of them prior to this evening.

As I arrived in Berlin, Hollis Brown were in the middle of soundcheck, so I briefly introduced myself to the sound engineer and the band between songs.

Meaning, in effect, I stood in between the stage and sound desk and yelled, "Hi! I'm Tony! VerseChorusVerse! Nice to meet ya!" Real smooth. I then dropped my guitar and bag, and retreated upstairs to the quieter confines of 2A, to try and placate my ferocious nerves.

Bob McAdam, the cool retired pharmacist I'd met in Mahwah a few days earlier was there, and we chatted whilst I drank water. The barman was a friendly, smiling man by the name of Tom Clarke. Everybody knew Tom, and everybody loved Tom. With good reason, too. He's a fantastic person who makes you feel at home instantly, as well as being a great songwriter, as I would later find out. Tom and Bob were so full of conversation that I felt my nervousness ease for a few sweet minutes.

When I heard the low rumblings of music below us cease, I returned downstairs to properly introduce myself, say my thanks for being added to the bill at the eleventh hour, and to get a quick soundcheck.

The stage was rammed with the main act's equipment, and I asked whether I could borrow a guitar lead. That was a fun conversation.

"Hey, may I possibly borrow a guitar lead please? Mine are upstairs in Jesse's place and he's not around yet..."

"Borrow a...what?"

"A lead?"

"I'm sorry, a... what? Borrow a 'what' now?"

" A guitar *lead?* A lead?"

"Oh a *cable!* A guitar cable! Of course man, no problem, why didn't you just say?"

On reflection, Cable is a much better choice of word. After all, I'm not taking the guitar out for a walk. Well... I suppose I am...kinda. You know what I mean... Ah, sweet, sweet semantics.

After my brief but productive soundcheck, I asked whether I had time for a quick smoke. A cigarette before singing probably isn't the best idea, but it helps settle my nerves a little. Which were now about 85% of who I was. The sound engineer said he thought that should be cool but I'd be on pretty much straight after that. He was half right. I got to smoke half of it before I was told that I had to go on there and then. It was just after 7pm and I had a strict 25 minute set time.

I walked back downstairs into the basement venue of Berlin. I made my way toward the stage. It wasn't a long or difficult journey, it was a small place with very few people in, as the doors had only been open twenty minutes. But it initially seemed like I was walking into an operating theatre for surgery, and they were all out of anaesthetic.

A tiny terror can make vast waves.

To dispel these now all-consuming nerves, I breathed slowly and deeply with each step, as discretely as was possible.

My eyes fixed on the microphone stand, as everything went into slow motion.

This suited me fine, as it slowed my heart rate down, which was required unless I wanted to drop dead in front of the fifteen or twenty people that were scattered amongst the room. I mounted the stage, picked up my guitar and proceeded to play.

As soon as I played my first chord I felt my confidence rush back through my body with a sudden jolt.

The guitar sounded so damn good.

Unlike two nights ago at the Sidewalk open mic night, I kept my eyes open the whole time, staring at the spaces between people, giving the illusion to each person that I was staring down the person next to them.

I roared out my lyrics, hitting every note with precision both vocally and on my guitar.

A visible reaction from the small crowd started to become more apparent, little by little, bit by bit. Some took a few steps forward, some started swaying in time to the music, some of the bar staff stopped in their tracks and started nodding in appreciation, feet started tapping and heads started nodding. All sure signs that I was doing good.

Every doubt and worry about my ability chased away with each descending strum of the guitar and harmonious howl into the aether.

A few more punters arrived, and were soon caught up in the moment. I stared at the spaces between them too, drawing them into the musical spell.

It was bizarre to feel at home, so far away from my own land, as though life had suddenly leapt into light speed.

The twenty five minutes disappeared far quicker than I could ever truly have expected, as time sped up, catching up with itself from the slow motion dysphoria prior to getting onstage, before finally returning to a normal pace for the final cheer from the crowd, mercifully giving me the momentary chance to cherish it.

I retreated back up the stairs and exited Berlin to the warm evening air to roll a cigarette and enjoy the exhilaration that comes after a successful gig. Sarah-Jane – from my publishers – had made it to the gig, shaking my hand as she raced by me. "You were great! Lets talk soon! Got another gig to go to, bye!" Several other punters followed me up, congratulating and thanking me. Amongst them was some of Hollis Brown's management team and, with them, an Englishman by the name of Steve. They had recognised me from house show in New Jersey a few nights previously, and I them, explaining to me that they looked after The Zombies as well. Steve was the drummer. He went on to ask me if we'd met before, which I didn't think we had but it was entirely possible. He then asked if

I'd been in a band before, to which I replied "Yes", but he'd probably never heard of us, going on to say the bands unwieldy moniker, And So I Watch You From Afar. Much to my surprise, he had, and he started to get excited at the mention of our name.

It turned out that our eponymous debut album was on the jukebox at his local pub back in London, and he and his drinking buddies were big fans. Even going so far as to ask for a picture with me to send to his friends back in England. I was taken aback, but gratefully obliged, amused by the absurdity that the drummer from such a legendary band would want my picture. Surely it should be the other way around? It made the post-gig buzz all the sweeter.

Whilst I was outside, Jesse arrived, apologising that he'd missed the gig and asking me how it went. Everybody replied for me, telling him how great they thought I'd been. I was genuinely humbled by their kind words. Jesse smiled and congratulated me; I was so ecstatic that I hadn't let him down, considering the chance he'd given me.

I spent the next couple of hours between the now packed gig, downstairs in Berlin, and the upstairs bar talking to Tom Clarke, accepting a plethora drinks being bought for me by the folks who had been in attendance for my slot.

A lady called Jayne approached me. Jayne was the Entertainments Manager for 2A, and asked if I wanted to play another gig upstairs in the loft area of the bar where a covers band was playing. Naturally, I accepted and was told that at some point, when the band took a break, I was welcome to get onstage and play. Regretfully, the band didn't take a break and I spent my time running between the three floors to see if it was time to play yet. On one of my trips back into the bowels of the building, I discovered that Rory and Grainne had finally arrived. I was totally cool with them having missed my set, since they'd seen me plenty of times, and I can assure you that they didn't seem bothered either.

It was just so damn nice to see them.

We retreated upstairs to 2A where we could talk easier, and proceeded to drink way too much as the night ran away from us.

After a few hours, they ordered an Uber back to their hotel at the other end of Manhattan. Before they left they asked me what I was doing.

"Well, I'm here for another few days, then Nashville, then Los Angeles".

They looked at each other, having a whole conversation with each other through only a look, in the way that only a couple so in love and so in tune with each other can. They looked back at me, with a potent mix of curiosity and concern, then Rory said, "We know that, but what are you doing? What's your main plan?"

At this point Jesse politely interrupted, introduced himself to my companions, then asked to speak with me for a few seconds. He again thanked me for playing and went on to tell me he would be out of the city for the next few days, not returning until after I had left, and that his buddy, Randy Schrager, would be staying the next two nights. I thanked him, hugged him, and really expressed my thanks at the vast generosity and kindness that he had afforded me. He told me not to worry about it and left me with the kind words of, "You better still come and see us when you're a big star", as he dropped his apartment keys into my hand with a big smile.

Although I'm sure he says it to all the aspiring songwriters that pass through his life, whether he meant it or not, it made me feel like a million bucks. He said his goodbyes to the three of us, and then departed.

I turned back to Rory and Grainne, where they then reminded me of the question.

"I dunno really, that's kind of what this trip is about, trying to formulate the next step. I..."

"You should move here," interrupted Grainne. They both had sympathetic and worried looks on their faces, recognising a lost soul when they saw one.

"I...uh...well...maybe..." I meekly countered.

"Look at the opportunity you're going to come across here," Rory offered. Grainne then continued, "Everybody here already knows you, it's like you've always been here."

A silence came over us.

They knew what I was thinking. I knew it, and they thought it too.

What did I really have to go back to? As much as I love home, and being near my family, it really didn't feel like I was making any great leaps forward in my life back there. My progress as a human being was stagnating, possibly even regressing. I felt the shadow of my former life in the band looming over me like a malevolent spirit, like everything I achieved had been ripped from me in the awful manner in which that chapter of my life had so violently finished. Only it hadn't finished, not completely. I was living in the midst of a terrible hangover from it. Here I was, five years separated from it, and still suffering the aftershocks.

They'd asked a question that I've asked myself a thousand times, only to brush it off and feverishly find another distraction every damn time.

"Just think about it, you've got friends here too, and you've got a talent that's languishing at home," said Grainne, breaking the silence. Rory's phone beeped; their Uber had arrived. All of a sudden we were all smiles again, and they both gave me a hug that I really needed.

I sat on at the table for another ten minutes or so, finishing my drink and trying to pull some sense of who I was and what I was doing, into a semblance of a coherent strategy. Not the easiest task at the best of times, and certainly not with a head and gut full of alcohol.

I rolled a cigarette and headed outside to smoke it.

Standing just beside the door, on the street, the tall doorman politely informed me that I couldn't smoke in that particular spot, since the smoke would bellow in through the door. I apologised and moved toward the lip of the pavement.

After a puff or two a guy approached me and asked me if I had a couple of dollars to spare, and in all honesty I didn't have any on me. I'd been fortunate enough to not need any that night, as people had kept setting drink after drink in front of me. I told him I had no cash, and said sorry. He went to walk on, used to the usual refusal, but I asked him if he wanted a smoke and to talk.

He stopped and looked me up and down. "What do you mean?" he justifiably asked me.

"I mean, I'm sorry I haven't got any money, but if you wanna smoke, I can roll you one, and if you wanna talk for a few minutes, I'd be delighted to talk with you, that's all...I'm Tony," I said, offering my hand forward to shake his. I was still running from the question Grainne and Rory had just reminded me of.

After a little trepidation, again justifiably, he extended his. "Yeah...ok...Nice to meet you Tony, I'm Larry."

Larry was a young black guy. He had shoulder length dreadlocks and a handsome, oval shaped face, with a movie star smile. Not that he graced me with it too often, to begin with. He was definitely at least ten years younger than me, and once he got started, he really liked to talk, and he had plenty to say. Larry went on to tell me his concerns about our generation, about America in general, and especially about the media and its influence on the two former topics. Larry was a smart guy – that was evident – and he was putting himself through community college studying philosophy and politics. We talked for nearly an hour, and I rolled us both a couple of smokes each in that time before he went back to his shelter to make sure he got enough sleep to be fresh for college the next day. We agreed on a lot of things and I learnt a lot from Larry. He was easily one of the most interesting people I'd ever met. I think about Larry from time to time, and while the thought of him makes me happy, the thought of his situation makes me sad. Mostly though, he makes me happy.

Afterwards I walked back into 2A to say goodbye to Tom Clarke and grab my guitar. Upon leaving the doorman stopped me.

"Hey, I was watching you talking to that dude who asked you for money.

That's about the coolest thing I've seen anybody do whilst I've been on here working, you're alright, man".

"Oh hey, thanks. It was nothing, Larry's the man!" I shook his hand, and walked towards Jesse's apartment, cursing myself that I didn't ask the doorman his name.

It was easily my most New York of days.

The conversation with Rory and Grainne rang in my ears. *What was I doing?* I almost felt an urge to escape, like an unwanted shadow was catching up with me, even here, all this distance away from home.

The unfortunate thing about shadows being, of course, that you can't outrun or escape them.

They can only be accepted. If you exist, you have a shadow. It's an unbreakable law. In truth, you should be happy you have a shadow. Peter Pan met Wendy when he was trying to get his back.

17

The next few days blurred into one. I was feeling a little overwhelmed, partly due to the questions posed by Rory and Grainne the night before, but I suspect mainly due to the vast amounts of booze I had put away in the past week. It's only now I see the parity in the cause and consequence of this. An existential hangover, if I may.

Initially this manifested itself in a desire to sit around Jesse's flat, and idly thumb through books for a few hours, but the trouble with books is that they have a sometimes irreversible tendency to tickle your brain into thinking. If you're lucky. Awful business.

No, what I needed was some dumbing down. Television was what I needed. Chewing gum for the eyes. Although I think I may have already butchered enough grey matter by then, as I sat struggling for twenty minutes trying to figure out how to get some volume from the damn thing, before eventually giving up and going on a long walk.

Not forgetting the one duty I had, I put the spare set of keys in an envelope and scrawled 'RANDY' on it in large letters, then stopped into 2A downstairs to drop it off.

I roamed the city, listlessly, splitting my time between bars and coffee shops. Staring out of windows when sitting, and at then at my feet when walking.

Eavesdropping all the while.

I wondered how much those dedicated teams of people going through the trash bins for plastic and aluminium made in a week.

I listened to monied twentysomethings talk about how awful their lives were because their boyfriend didn't do this or their girlfriend didn't do that, and how they hated their parents for cancelling a credit card, and how were they ever supposed to survive with just two?

Then I looked back out at the old lady going through the trash.

I saw the weight she was carrying in two oversized, opposing bags tied on either end of a stick for balance, perched on her shoulder, and I immediately felt bad for having ever complained about lugging my guitar and bags anywhere.

It was an incredibly sobering experience to watch this happening outside whilst listening to the bile of privilege being spewed inside, and knowing that I shared more in common with the idle complainers that I shared the establishment with, both literally and figuratively.

These colours always seem more domineering when you're looking for them.

It's hard to pick out the sunshine from behind the clouds but you *must* remember, it *is* there.

Easier said than done, I know.

I must've walked ten miles around Manhattan that evening, although with none of the euphoria of my first day in New York only a week before.

A seemingly unescapable loneliness had caught up with me once more, in the world's most densely populated city. Oh, the clichéd, poetic irony. My thoughts were fogged with angst and the confusion was layered, compounded with self-disgust at not being able to appreciate how lucky I was to be in the situation I was.

By the time I arrived back at Jesse's apartment, the elusive Randy had arrived and gone to bed already. The next afternoon he was away before I awoke. The weather reflected my outlook as it poured down in thick sheets of rain from a dull, grey sky.

I took myself and my guitar back across the water to Willamsburg on the L train to meet again with Liza at her apartment, as arranged, to try and do some songwriting. Sometimes this blinkered, miserable outlook can help spark a song into existence, but that was not to be the case today. I blamed my inability to appear enthused on a crushing hangover, but in my head it was because of a heavy sadness that was bearing down on me. Truth be told, it was one feeding the other. Liza was cool about this, and instead we traded travel stories and instances where we had gotten way out of our depth. She had a fantastic story about a terrifying border guard on the Trans-Mongolian express, and one about nearly being arrested on a flight to Rio due to an inadvertent mix of a sleeping pill and champagne, and I found my mood lifting somewhat. Before we knew it, evening had crept up on us, and we said our goodbyes as I left her to her night's plans. A beautiful person, and someone I hope I meet again.

I caught the L back into Manhattan and walked down Avenue A.

It was Friday night in NYC, and the great and the good were starting to make their way out into the night. The heavy downpour earlier in the day had made the air a little clearer and lighter, both physically and metaphorically. Instead of seeing the darkness I had actively sought out the night before, this time the couples holding hands, and the groups of friends stood out to me. I was sad inside, but I was happy that these people appeared to be in good spirits, and I wondered what the night held for them.

2A was starting to fill up, but there was one last seat at the bar. Well, there was two, but one of them had a drink with a napkin on top sitting in front of it. I sat down at the empty seat and was greeted by the ever affable Mr Tom Clarke. He bought me a beer and a Jameson, and we drank to our health. A classic and contradictory salutation.

The owner of the seat beside me returned from wherever it was he had been. We briefly engaged, glancing at each other and doing that weird half smile thing, where you make your lips disappear whilst raising your eyebrows and a nod that translates universally as, "Hello fellow human, I acknowledge you, but we need not verbalise this acknowledgement".

After I finished my beer, I asked Tom for another. It was when I spoke that the guy in the seat beside me turned and asked, "Tony?"

"...Yeah...?" I sheepishly replied.

"Haha! Hey Tony, I'm Randy!" he exclaimed, as he spun on his seat to greet me.

A greeting that would give a stiff upper lipped Englishman a fright, but I'm Irish, so I was fine.

Jesse had told Randy there was an Irishman staying at the apartment too, so as soon I ordered that beer, my accent had been a dead giveaway.

Randy was a cool guy; a fellow musician, he played drums professionally. As we talked it turned out that we had kind of met before at a festival in Latvias capital of Riga. A few years back he'd been drummer with Scissor Sisters, and my old band had played just before them. I remember it so well because I'd taught Jake Shears – their singer – a few Latvian pleasantries before they went onstage. Well, I'd helped him brush up on the pronunciation. Funny how life throws people back together. Randy was also drummer for Jesse's live band, and was in the process of trying to find a new apartment in the city. We talked and we drank, and we drank and we talked, exchanging stories of the road like two old soldiers from different infantries.

Eventually, we went down into Berlin, where a friend of his was having a birthday party. It had only opened, and people were starting to filter in, but the birthday girl was already there with a bunch of friends. They all worked in film and television, and to some extent – barring introductions – that was pretty much all they talked about. Randy was able to muscle in on the conversation because he had worked with a few of them before on music video shoots, so he had a point of reference. No matter how I tried to join in, I felt very much the outsider, and I was cool with that. It wasn't my party after all.

After standing at the bar for a quarter of an hour or so, I saw that Randy looked pretty in with everybody, so I executed a textbook, "Irish Goodbye", and departed without a word, retreating to 2A.

Upstairs I bumped into the entertainment manger, Jayne. She was just about to do a tour of the other bars nearby that were under the same ownership, or "The Empire", as she referred to it. She kindly asked me if I wanted to join her, and I accepted, first stop being Niagara a couple of blocks north. Next stop was an almost 'speakeasy'-like bar; just around the corner from Niagara, right beside the Joe Strummer mural. It was interestingly called, 'Lovers of Today', a tiny little hideaway that was packed with hip young things, eager to neck as many cocktails as they could before the bank caught up with them. It's a nice place that has an actual hidden bar behind it that I'd been in once before with Paul and my old band. It's a hideaway for touring bands and actors that may be passing through New York, a very exclusive place. Well, except for that one night that I was in it.

We then cut across Tompkins Square Park for the final bar on our circuit (they have another bar, Bowery Electric, but we didn't make it there that night), and probably the most popular, if that particular night was anything to go by, Dream Baby. Even though Jayne was Entertainment Manager, we still had to wait a few minutes to get in because the place was so packed. The doorman told us, "One in, one out," without looking at us, or the other twenty people hoping to get in, admirably not betraying health and safety laws with steely determination.

Ordinarily, I'd rather be in the emptiest bar around so I can get a drink easier. This may be a contributing factor to the loneliness I complain about, so I was happy enough on this occasion to wait, and to check the place out at the very least.

When we eventually got the go ahead to actually enter the bar, I felt like a sardine with a death wish. We squeezed past the sweaty mass of people and, eventually, got to the bar. The barmaid was nothing short of astonishing, as Jayne had told me she would be. In the face of this heaving bulk of thirsty beauties, she was a smiling, cocktail making machine, never missing an order, an ingredient, or an ice-cube, making her way through the waiting throng with ease.

Her tip jar was deservedly as busy as the bar.

As impressive as all this was, I had to get out. I could barely breathe, and it wasn't my scene at all, at least not right now.

Jayne ordered a cab to go home as her duties were done for the night, we said goodbye and I thanked her for showing me around The Empire.

Waltzing back towards Avenue A, I stopped by into the Sidewalk Cafe on the off chance that I may bump into some of the people I'd met at the Open Mic at the start of the week. No such luck. Fortune favoured me in the form of a different friendly face however, when I bumped into Randy as I was walking out.

By this stage we were both pretty drunk, and we walked around for a while before settling...somewhere. Yes, at this stage I have very little recollection of where we stopped. All I can tell you is that it was owned by a guy that used to be in a punk rock band, and it wasn't Jesse. Sorry, I have no more detail for you than that.

My memory picks up a little when we left around 3am and made our way back towards the apartment. Randy produced a little pipe and some weed he'd picked up from a random earlier that night. He packed it and offered it to me.

It's never a good idea to smoke weed when you've had as much to drink as I had that day, but when you've had that much, the wise little voice that generally offers you that valuable information has already given up and gone to bed, because he's the smart one.

"Sure!" I yelled, as I huffed down a lungful, then passed it back to Randy, whose hands it should never have left. He took a hit from it and then went for the apartment door.

"You coming, man?" he asked me as he was unlocking the door.

At this point I was reaching into my pockets, hunting for my headphones.

"Nah man. I'm gonna go walkabout and enjoy this weed, man!" knowing that the next night I'd be in bed relatively early to get up for my flight on the Sunday.

"No sweat man, see you in the morning, be safe," he said before entering the building and I waved him on.

(Usage of the personable term, 'man', increases 75% when a little marijuana has been introduced to one's system, this is scientific fact. There's no proof or evidence of this figure, but it is – I assure you – irrefutable fact.)

Somehow, with one eye open and one closed, a shoulder against the wall to stop the damn horizon dancing, I managed to roll a cigarette to accompany me on this stroll. I plugged in my headphones, put the Beastie Boys on shuffle, and began my own shuffle around the streets.

After a little while, I realised I'd been singing along. I also realised I'd become *that guy*. I was the guy that people were crossing the road to avoid, as I bumped off walls and trash cans, singing along at a level that can only be described as "Public Nuisance". If this had been the forties, I would have been soaked by a bucket of water from a disgruntled New Yorker. I'd listened to about six tracks without a clue where I was going, roughly twenty five minutes of walking in any direction, going wherever my clueless feet took me, and I didn't care. Not one bit. Vienna entered my head, so I piped down on the vocals, straightened myself up, and got my bearings. I walked back to the apartment with a smile as wide as the Hudson.

18

My final day in New York was a relaxed affair. I rose around midday, and Randy had already left. He had left me a note saying goodbye, and a little bit of the weed we had picked up in a sealable bag. I gathered my dirty laundry, then looked at Jesse's washer and drier for about twenty minutes without a clue how to operate it. I was like a dog at the steering wheel of a stationary car. Accepting defeat, I took my stuff to a laundromat just around the corner from the apartment. Whilst I was waiting for them to dry, I received an email from a very nice guy called Nik, at the New York Irish Arts Centre, with whom I'd briefly been in contact with. Nik invited me to a performance that evening. I replied that I'd love to attend, and thanked him for thinking of me.

I pottered around for a few hours, stopping into cafes and bars that I'd enjoyed people watching in, talking with both customers and staff alike. Then I took one last long walk, this time to the Irish Arts Centre on West 51st Street.

Upon arrival, I collected my ticket from the Box Office, still vaguely unaware of what I was going to witness. All Nik had told in the email me was that it was a "Masterclass" performance. I neglected to follow up on what was actually being performed, preferring to have a surprise that evening.

I was one of the last to arrive, and my seat was at the back of the smallish auditorium, which held roughly 150 people. Giving in to my peaking curiosity, I glanced down at the program I had been given to finally unveil some of the mystery.

Masters in Collaboration X: Colin Dunne Meets Nic Gariess.

So I was about to witness *two* masters in their field, up close and personal.

Upon further perusal of the program, Colin and Nic were revealed to be dancers – step dancers to be precise. Colin had been part of the world famous Riverdance show, as well as Artist in Residence with the University of Limerick, while Nic was something of a rising star, re-imagining movement as a musical activity. It was clear from the bios of each of the men that they were mavericks in their field, and fantastically talented. This was even clearer when they took the stage and started talking about their craft in detail, and about the people that had influenced their lives and work so profoundly. I have always found it moving and inspiring to listen to anyone talk about their chosen outlet with such fervour and passion, and that was something these two gents did eloquently.

The only trouble being that once the performance started – given my seat was at the rear of the theatre, coupled with the modest incline of the arranged seats – I could only see them from their waist up; I couldn't see their feet.

Now, I have never been, and probably never will be, an encyclopaedic authority on any form of dancing, but I am fairly confident that a view of the dancer's feet in this particular discipline is a big part of the appeal.

This was akin to going to watch a master magician perform mind boggling and eyeball defying sleight of hand card tricks, but only being able to see them from the elbow up.

I was determined not to let this small, albeit fundamental, discrepancy blight the evening.

So instead, I closed my eyes, and tilted my head toward the ceiling, listening and marvelling in the rhythm of the two masters tap skills.

Everybody else just sat slightly more upright.

Upon returning to the East Village, I roamed the streets one last time. I took in the neighbourhood that had become my home for the past few days, and tried hard not to get too romantic about it. Which is difficult in a city like this.

Every time you stop – even if it is only for a second – the city can take the shape of so many different art forms, all at once.

The sounds of the city, with its kaleidoscope of audio through its many languages, accents, music, traffic, roadworks, and life is different from anywhere else.

Everywhere you look, a drama is unfolding.

From the most trivial of exchanges, to an encounter heated and flamed by love or by rage, often both.

In almost every direction, you can pick out a potential album cover.

Every intersection, if suddenly frozen, is a renaissance style event, with so much activity and wholly divergent episodes, momentarily entwined in glorious, chaotic, and contradictory existence. This isn't only true of New York of course, but it's a city that has captured our collective imaginations so brilliantly in recent history, that every perception we have and every observation we make here is amplified magnificently.

New York has taken the mantle of the world's most vibrant theatre, a city of constant comedy, tragedy and romance.

If all the world's a stage, New York has become the Globe.

Standing on a street corner that evening, minding my own business and simply smiling at the civilised pandemonium taking place all around me, I briefly made eye contact with a guy making his way up the street. He was slightly bearded with long greying hair, in ripped jeans and an INXS tee. He was ten or fifteen years older than me and he was muttering to himself about something. Our eyes briefly met as I surveyed around me, but I quickly looked away, not wanting him to feel self-conscious since he was talking to himself, or, kill me. As he got closer, I glanced back at him as he continued walking, and stopped muttering whilst proceeding to look me up and down, a face as stern as an angry teacher. He then said, "My band was better than your band in 1987..."

...and continued on his journey, resuming the conversation he was having with himself only moments before. It brought the widest smile to my face, which I masked by putting my hand over my mouth, stifling any laughter from being heard. I will always wish that I came back with, "But I wasn't in a band in 1987..."

Goodnight, New York, New York.

Part Three

19

Tennessee is considerably warmer than New York.

An obvious and well known fact yes, but never made more apparent to me than when my Uber driver dropped me a mile from my accommodation in the blazing midday sunshine, on the surprisingly long street known as McGavock Pike, East Nashville.

Annoyingly, I only deduced this after he had driven off and taken his $5 tip/ schmuck tax.

Luckily, I was dressed entirely in black, wearing heavy boots, without any sunscreen on my near translucent skin, and only had a large case, a guitar, and a shoulder-bag containing my laptop to carry.

An ample amount of pick-up trucks drove by me, neglecting to do the very thing that the name of their vehicle suggests. I lumbered onwards, losing body-weight through sweat and patience, wondering where this fabled southern hospitality I had heard so much about was. In fairness to the passing drivers I must've looked quite a sight.

Another dreamer with a guitar, not used to the ways of Music City just yet, and probably the only one they'd ever seen with such a blindingly white, reflective body surface.

To compound this, I was the only human that was both dumb and unfortunate enough to be walking in this crippling heat, never mind being laden with luggage, clad head to toe in black.

I pressed on – with little other choice – marching towards my ultimate destination and my home for the next ten days. I'd gotten myself a room through the AirBnB site for the first time, and had little idea of what to expect.

The house was just off the street with a long driveway, the building itself obscured by a multitude of trees and other assorted greenery. I climbed the few steps to the porch and knocked on the screen door, hoping this was the right place, and after a minute or two the door opened to reveal my hostess, Anita.

Anita welcomed me into her home. She and her daughter, Isabella, were just about to depart to go thrift store shopping. We exchanged pleasantries and she gave me my key. From the start it was obvious that these were exceptionally good people. They made me feel at home immediately and introduced me to the family pet, a lovable and mild mannered muscle of a dog called Ralphie.

They wished me luck and told me to get in touch if I needed anything, and then they were gone, leaving Ralphie and I to get on with it. Whatever "it" would turn out to be.

My bedroom was a generous size, and contained the coolest looking four poster bed I'd ever seen. It looked like the gateway to another dimension, which I suppose sleep is, if – as Jung would suggest – dreams are anything to go by.

Each post was topped by a painted wooden flame, like a perpetually burning Olympic torch adorning every corner. The headboard continued with the flame theme, except in the centre where a large shipping style clock sat. The numbers ran 0-5-4-3-2-1-0-1-2-3-4-5 clockwise, furthering the mystery of the nocturnal vessel upon which one would set sail to the land of dreams, hopefully avoiding the perilous waters of nightmares.

The clock itself was surrounded by more globe-like colours, of blue and green with unrecognisable landmasses and oceans akin to a map of a similar but ultimately alien planet.

The headboard reinforced this otherworldly motif; it contained eight panels that looked like a star-map of some kind with imaginary constellations linked up by dotted lines.

It really was a most remarkable bed, hence my remarking on it.

But enough about this bed, for right now.

I'll get back to it, and the very strange impact it had on this portion of the trip. Nothing sexual though, alas.

My time in Nashville was very different to the blitzkrieg of the senses that New York had been.

I was fortunate enough that opportunity had seemed to bombard me at every corner in the Big Apple. Now here I was, just another songwriter, miles from home and with very few leads, in a city where everyone is fighting for their shot at the Big Time in the music game.

Chances are, every bartender, waiter, or waitress you may encounter in Nashville could very well be harbouring some of the greatest songs you've never heard, or a voice that could bring light to the darkest of hearts.

Whereas a city such as NY has every means to overwhelm one with its sheer vastness and supposed impersonal touch to it, I found it to be quite the opposite. Nashville, whilst being an amazing place and full of incredible people, seemed to intimidate me a lot more than New York ever did. As a result of this, I spent a great deal of my time on the street I was staying on, McGavock Pike.

Instead of constantly venturing into the unknown that I had so embraced in Manhattan, I chose to remain in this beautiful little village, hidden in plain sight, in the heart of East Nashville. This is also down to how welcome I was made to feel there.

On my first day, I got a cab into downtown Nashville to go and check out some of the sights and sounds. The cab driver tried valiantly to understand my accent but it was too much, which is odd as my accent isn't too harsh. Even in my native Northern Ireland, when I first moved to Belfast a decade ago, most locals assumed I was a Scot, and when I've had a few drinks I do tend to drift into Ewan MacGregor territory, trying to disguise any creeping slur. So in order to further attempt communication with my driver, I unwisely drifted into an American accent, but since I'd just been in New York I went into some bastard hybrid of Joe Pesci and Lady Gaga. Incomprehensible to even myself, I gave up and went into an exaggerated Northern Irish vernacular – a mid-Ulster drawl – which to my astonishment he seemed to understand, and thus we chatted for the remainder of the drive. It became my go-to tactic when the good people of Tennessee were having difficulty deciphering my well intentioned gibbering.

My first port of call was a blues bar called Bourbon Street on the legendary Printers Alley. They had two different acts playing 4 to 5 hour sets every afternoon and evening, never the same combination of bands. The act I caught was a three piece blues outfit, whose name I'm afraid I neglected to get, a fact I lament even more because they were so damn good. Piano, vocals, drums, bass, and enough grooves to shake a mountain to the ground. I listened to them for about three hours, putting a few dollars in their jar every couple of songs.

As I noticed the time had not so much ran away from me, but hopped in a record breaking land speed vehicle and disappeared into the past for good, I figured I should go and check out the main music strip that I'd heard so much about. Legendary bars like Tootsies, the Bluebird, and Roberts. Record stores like the ones you would see in movies as a kid, street performers so good that they made me want to sell my guitar, live music pumping out of almost every building, ranging from the tightest country acts you've ever heard to the most god awful karaoke singers mangling your guilty pleasures of yesteryear; exactly the way karaoke should be done. Guys in the most ridiculous oversized Stetsons, girls in the most equally ridiculous (and distracting) denim shorts, Cowboy boots for sale every other store. It really has to be seen to be believed.

I was impressed by it all, but not particularly enamoured, and I couldn't quite place my finger on why. The strange feeling started taking over the navigation part of my brain, and before I knew it, I was back in Bourbon Street, listening to, and feeling, those sweet, sweet blues. They never seemed to be too far away at this stage.

I got a cab back to McGavock Pike, the Village Pub to be precise. I was aware of almost every eye being drawn toward me as I made my way from the establishment's front porch to the bar, a stark contrast to the gleeful anonymity I had enjoyed in New York. It really was like in the movies when a stranger enters the town saloon and the music suddenly stops, except the music didn't stop, but every eye was on me. I put it down to this not being a part of town or bar that strangers often stray into since it isn't in the heart of the city where the action is.

"How ya doin sir," the barman said, with no inflection as if to imply a question; it was merely a way of leading on to what he really wanted. "I'm gonna need some identification".

His delivery reminded me of Dan Aykroyd's portrayal of Joe Friday in the eighties movie remake of *Dragnet*. Firm, in an efficient public service manner. My hand was already in pocket, reaching for my wallet. "Sure, of course, no problem," I said, before handing over my driver's license.

Being asked for ones ID in the states is nothing new of course; it's not that they think you may be underage, but to make sure you're an actual person, living on the grid as it were. Old Father Time himself (whoever he may be...lets picture the much loved Sir David Attenborough for this scenario) may have been trying to order a drink and they would still ask for some proof of identity, regardless of the fact that he's clearly over 21 and he's Sir David Attenborough.

The barman instantly became friendlier. Satisfied that I wasn't an escaped convict, he passed me a drinks menu and skipped directly to the beers.

As I sat on my lonesome, wearing as welcoming and friendly a smile as I could muster, my fellow imbibers became that bit friendlier as they grew used to me taking up space.

The barman, Michael, was exceptionally good. He knew everybody that came in and had a straight faced, dead pan wise crack for every last customer as they came and went. Which made the whole scenario that little bit more like a western as the time passed and my glass emptied.

Leaving the bar, Michael encouraged me to come back whilst I was in the area and stressed I was very welcome. He had a different way of showing it of course, but I was suitably impressed at his skills as a bartender, having been one myself for some years. Except Michael was a lot better than I ever was.

I was sure that Michael never played, "The Prick Game".

A game invented by myself and a gent called Pete, when I worked in Katy Dalys back in Belfast many years ago.

The overall aim of "The Prick Game" was to see how many times you could get away with calling the customer – you guessed it – 'Prick,' without them commenting on it. The glory of the game being that no-one ever commented on it, as the delivery was always so nonchalant and fast (a loud, busy bar helps too, obviously), and most customers don't really listen to the bartender, when they really should. Not only is it basic manners, but they may be seeing how many times he can insult you unnoticed. Then the ones that did notice would wear a confused look on their faces, unsure if they've just been called 'Prick' an unspecified amount of times. A typical game would go something like this.

"Alright prick, what can I get you, prick?"

"Uh...Three stout and a coke."

"Ok, prick, three stout prick and a...a coke was it? Prick?"

"...Yeah, a coke."

"Alright prick, no bother prick, coming right up prick."

"..."

"Okay prick, there ya go prick, Three stout and a coke, prick...that'll be £11.40, prick, please, prick."

A bemused silence would invariably follow, coupled with glances as they hand over the money, telling themselves their ears must be deceiving them.

"Cheers, prick, and there's your change prick, £3.60 prick. Thanks prick."

And there you have it; you've unleashed a barrage a pricks (now, now...), getting away with calling a poor innocent customer Prick no less than fifteen times.

You're now a Prick Master.

A Prick's Prick.

A terrible thing to do – I think we can all agree and you should feel suitably ashamed of yourself – and something that Michael, the Nashville bartender would never have indulged in.

That is, unless he was *really* good at it and I never noticed.

I returned to my adopted Nashville home, where Anita was sitting in the back kitchen. I noticed a framed photograph of Frank Zappa performing on the kitchen wall, I expressed how cool I thought it was, and she told me her husband, Mark, had taken it. She invited me to sit, then she explained that Mark would be back the next day. We talked about music and politics and we were both equally delighted to find out we both love The Clash, so it was safe to assume our politics wouldn't be too far apart. Which they weren't, so we discussed the current players in that particular theatre. Bernie, Hillary and Donald.

They sound like a trio of kids who are explorers on the Disney Channel.

Anita, who was from out of state, had owned a restaurant in Nashville before retiring, and Mark was a retired professor. They had two kids, their daughter

Isabella whom I had met, and their son Wilder, who had just moved to New York. Ralphie, the dog, was rescued by them and showed them all the love he could to them in return, which was a lot, and the family reciprocated in kind. They are a beautiful bunch.

As I mentioned before, Nashville was a very different experience from New York, and though outward adventures weren't as forthcoming as they had been in NY, inward adventures and turmoil were in no short supply. But the home and company of Anita and Mark provided great refuge, warmth, and love. I returned there every night to sit with them on their porch, exchange stories, and enjoy many, many laughs. There wasn't much in life that they hadn't seen or experienced, and their enduring love for one another was nothing short of inspirational.

20

My subconscious started to push itself to the forefront in these ten days.

Dreams came thicker and faster than at any point in my life I can ever remember. They became more and more realistic, no matter how absurd or other worldly they were, to a startling degree. As a result they were much easier to remember the next day, and thus became deeply affecting, as my isolation led me to ponder them.

Some of the dreams even took on the shape of Hollywood action movies, guest starring actors such as Natalie Portman, Kenneth Brannagh, Jennifer Lawrence, Idris Elba, and Daniel Bruhr. Sometimes even leading to appearances on America's many late night chat shows, from Conan to Kimmel, sharing a couch with Simon Pegg and Zoe Saldana.

The country was clearly soaking in through every nook and cranny available in my mind.

Or was I simply losing it?

The lines between dreams and day to day events became blurred, which was worrisome as surely that detachment from reality could be construed as the onset of madness?

As I woke each morning, it took a while for me to readjust to this conscious realm. Had I been alone too long? Not on this trip, but in general? Or was it this strange new bed? Was it some kind of dream amplification device? Had I stumbled upon a dream intensifier facility in the quiet Nashville street? Why had the reality dial been turned all the way to eleven in this dream weaving four poster sleeping vessel? All colours were brighter and all interactions truer, all voices louder and all textures firmer.

This intensification of my subconscious had both its drawbacks and advantages.

On my second day – both feet firmly planted in waking reality – I stayed relatively close to the house. Spending my time playing guitar, sending emails, and strolling the local area. In a Dollar General Store, I bought a commemorative Life Magazine on Walt Disney, thinking it would be a nice gift for my Aunt. I ventured toward the Deli I had spotted beside the Village Pub the day before, where I ate a sandwich that redefined sandwiches to my palate. I nursed a root beer with this sandwich for a long time, reading the news via an App on my phone, and barring the odd glance around me, I was largely oblivious to the people going about their everyday business.

An hour or so passed, easily.

The Deli thinned out as the lunchtime crowds left and went about their days. Songs played on the large jukebox just adjacent to me, whilst I read about the impending vote in the UK about whether or not to leave the EU. Nothing out of the ordinary really.

Then, something happened.

The deli was practically empty, and a few notes rang out from the jukebox that I hadn't heard, or thought of, in a very long time.

The piece of music in question was by a Texas band called, Explosions in the Sky, and the tune was 'First Breath after a Coma'.

In less than the time it takes to register the thought of a single blink I was taken on a physics-warping return journey. I was transported from a Deli table in Tennessee to a late night party in my halls of residence in Liverpool thirteen years previous, where a friend had first played me this song, changing my life forever. Then I was jerked from there to standing in the old Liverpool Barfly a few months later, eyes shut tight as the band played it in front of me as I fought back tears at the sheer power of this music I'd never experienced the intensity of live before. Then several billionths of a millisecond later, I was in my old bedroom in Portstewart, playing the song to the guys from a then unformed ASIWYFA, delighting in blowing their minds as mine had been only months before in Liverpool. And then in an even quicker instant, my entire life from that point onward blasted through my mind like a shockwave.

The good times, the bad times, the beating in Vienna, the emptiness, the battles within myself, the loss of friends, and our backs all turning on one another at the same time, the misunderstandings from all corners, the miles I have walked with a guitar in hand, going from stage to stage, country to country, person to person, song to song, table to table...and with that I was back at my table in the Deli.

I landed with a jolt, gripping the table as my eyes widened and my pupils dilated, exhilarated through fear.

Where the hell had I just been?

How had I forgotten that song, that band?

Maybe I died in that Viennese doorway?

Was the sandwich *that* good?

My immediate life around me pulled back into sharp focus, and I was no less scared than I had been in less than the blink of an eye before. My eyes darted around me, looking to see if anybody had witnessed me being taken from my seat and thrown thirteen years into the past, across oceans and through time, an involuntary passenger in my own already played out timeline.

The Deli was already pretty empty, except for the staff behind the counter, but at that precise moment it felt like I'd just crash landed in the world's emptiest place. I started to pace my breathing to calm myself down, and then I just listened to the rest of the song. It both soothed and burned, but I knew I had to listen, and that I should probably have done so before this.

Once the piece of music finished, I gathered myself and my things, then stepped outside into the fresh, late afternoon air. It was a moderate temperature for that time of year in Tennessee, it felt very much like a good day at home. I breathed steadily and deep, eyes closed, and soon my heart rate returned to normal.

This short, sharp shock of my past would reverberate into my dreams that night, and many nights after. Everything got very strange in my subconscious.

Uphill confrontations with ghosts from my past, quite literal ones as I marched and climbed an infinite mountain; coming face to face with absent friends and unsettled arguments.

Giant boulders avalanched past us, knocking us further back from time to time. Sometimes together, sometimes alone.

Occasionally we pulled each other out of the way of danger and other times we pushed one another in front of them.

Huge ruptures in the rock face would fracture the surface we clung to, and as someone from my past either fell into the holes or climbed on without me, soon I would face another.

We were under attack from all directions as huge winged beasts would swoop down upon us, we both depended on the tumbling rocks to take them out but we never once thought to work together against the beasts and make our journey to the dizzying summit that little bit easier, and likelier.

One of the winged terrors clasped me in its talons and whisked me from the mountain face.

Its claws dug into my shoulders and blood streamed down my arms, dripping from my fingertips like red rain as we flew far from the crumbling mountain below. I could only watch on as the mountain turned to flatland and disappeared altogether as I was taken farther into the heavens, flying higher and higher until soon we were above the weather.

We burst through the gathering storm clouds and into the vastness where blue meets black, straddling the atmosphere and almost touching space, I realised I was no longer in the claws of the beast and was floating alone and aimlessly.

The more I reached toward the stars above me, the little more I dropped toward the clouds that I was miles above.

I watched as the clouds below me parted to reveal an endless ocean, and with one final grab towards the moon, I flipped into a dive; accepting my fate and began the plummet at thousands of feet per second towards the sea below. Waving at the birds perched on lower clouds who were pointing and waving back. Looking back at the waters surface, which I was about to breach at a speed well beyond terminal velocity, I smiled and closed my eyes, awaiting what lay ahead.

As I braced for impact, I instead found myself in an long, narrow corridor.

The floor and the ceiling were perfectly black and the walls a deep, unsettling crimson.

Thick, oak doors on either side stretched on for as far as my eyes could see.

I could hear music coming from behind some of them, and behind others I could hear voices from my past.

Frustratingly, each of the doors were marked, "PULL", but had no handle with which to do so. I pressed my ear against them and the music was a mishmash of songs I had written, or had loved. The voices I could hear were all voices I recognised.

Some were as familiar as family and old friends, and others were indecipherable, although I could hear my name being sporadically mentioned.

I walked on and eventually I could see all the doors were open, but as I approached them it became apparent that there was nothing in them, and that they led nowhere.

When I say nothing, I mean nothing.

A vacuum is the nearest I can even begin to describe the sheer nothingness they contained.

There is no way of accurately describing the terror of that unknown.

Like a black hole, the darkness promised to swallow anything or anyone that dared set foot within its emptiness.

After what seemed like hours, I started to walk firmly in the centre of the corridor – being careful not to get too close to these rooms – but sometimes my curiosity and boredom would tease me back towards them, before my creeping inertia would warn me back.

Just ahead of me, I could see that there was a door, slightly ajar, and I could hear sounds of a city.

I approached and tried to push it open but it was useless, the door was stuck fast. I pushed my face towards the door to peak through the crack to see what was within.

It took a second for my eyes to adjust to the twilight, and when they did my heart began racing in horror. Two large men, all dressed in black, were taking grim delight in kicking and pummelling a sorry, collapsed figure who was incapable of fighting back as they booted him time and time again in the doorway that he lay. From outside the door I yelled and pulled and pounded on the door, screaming at the assailants to leave him – me – alone.

I called for help, but there was nobody nearby either in the past or in my current corridor.

The door then slammed shut, blasting me back with a force of air that surely saved my fingers and nose that had been in the doorway from being sliced off as I had tried to find a way in to try and aid my past self.

I continued vainly beating and pointlessly scratching at the door as tears of rage and fear rolled down my face, shouting for help and getting more and more frustrated at my seemingly unending isolation. When, as if to add insult to injury, one by one the lights in the long Black and Crimson Corridor began to switch off.

My voice got quieter with each extinguishing light, silencing my angry and scared pleas as the darkness approached.

"OH GREAT! WHAT THE ACTUAL FU..."

A cimmerian nothingness enveloped me.

I could still think and breathe. Bizarrely, I could still hear too as I could hear myself breathing, but as an actual physical being, I was bereft of presence.

As my brain sent the signal for my hands to search for the rest of me, I became aware that there was nothing to feel, and I was without the hands to do so.

Was I just a central nervous system?

A set of lungs and pair of ears adrift in a total void?

I bet that would be quite a sight, not that anyone could see it.

A short beam of brilliant white light, either tiny or in the far distance suddenly became apparent. The distance being hard to tell when you're just a curious and distressed spine with airbags floating in an endless vacuum.

Then another – seemingly across from the original one – followed suit.

It was the doors.

One by one they were opening, a little quicker as each blinding light led to another, until soon they were all open in infinity in both directions and with the light filling the now translucent, glass corridor; I realised I was whole again.

I patted myself down for good measure, and I turned to walk up the corridor, but this wasn't possible.

Instead I floated, with total ease.

The corridor was warm, as you would expect a glass surrounding to be, but a cool breeze blew toward my face and ruffled through my hair, cooling and easing me no matter what direction I turned.

Beautiful Orchestral music bellowed from the doors in perfect harmony, from one a string section and from another the horns, and so on and so on.

It was divine.

After floating in near indescribable bliss for sometime, I eventually came to the end of this great glass corridor and was face to face with an Elevator door, but with no button to summon it.

I surveyed around it and the only discerning feature it had was a large sign above it that simply read **When,** *whilst below the sign and the top of the door was an old fashioned dial – that generally would have the floor numbers on it – and an arrow pointing to the one the lift was currently at. It didn't have any numbers on it though. Instead there were three words, two the same and one different. One on the left, one in the centre – where the arrow was currently pointed – and one on the right.*

Then, Now *and* **Then.**

In that order.

Eventually I came to the assumption that the first **Then** *meant the past, and the second; the future. But surely I had just been in my past? But then again, that was a different corridor, in every sense. Both aesthetically, in how it had made me feel and also, most obviously, quite literally.*

With this realisation, I decided to put it to the test and turned to one of the infinite open doors behind me. I closed my eyes and took a leap of faith into the blinding whiteness, only to find myself exactly where I had been in glass corridor facing the Elevator. Each and every time I stepped through one of these doors, no matter how far I had gotten from the Lift, without fail I would land in exactly the same spot, facing the closed doors.

Until I let my building frustration get the better of me.

I found my annoyance growing and I kicked the seemingly un-openable door. The hitherto un-penetrable Elevator doors then opened and an unseen force pushed me inside.

As I turned to see the doors then close, I looked above at the identical Dial on the inside.

It vibrated slightly as the lift began to judder into life. From the sounds of it, this was the first time it had been used in a while.

My eyes scanned the interior. It was quite basic, with a beige carpet, wooden paneling and a handrail encircling three quarters of it. As the mobile room continued juddering with increasing vigour, I gripped the handrails and readjusted my gaze to the Dial above the door. To my initial curiosity, it started slowly moving left toward to the first **Then.** *My curiosity shifted to panic as the speed built to a frightening degree. Soon the only thing that was keeping me from slamming against the roof was the handrail I was now gripping for all I was worth. The Elevator then slowed, slightly, and as the Dial finally settled on the initial* **Then,** *we came to an abrupt halt and I* *connected with the nondescript beige carpet. The doors opened, with a ping, before the lift then spat me out onto the regrettably familiar black floor.*

I was back in the Black and Crimson Corridor.

I picked myself up and turned to rush back into the comparable sanctuary of the Elevator, but it was gone and I was faced with this seemingly never ending, cursed Black and Crimson Corridor once again. I screamed out in anger and frustration, and with that the lights behind me extinguished in sequential consequence; each one heralded by a deafening boom, louder and more menacing as the darkness approached.

I covered my ears as it grew painful to listen but stared down the advancing nothing.

Until it stopped, inches from where I was placed.

Slowly, I allowed a semi victorious grin to etch itself onto my face, silently mouthing, "Yes!", as I raised my fists from my ears to the air.

This slight celebration was short-lived as the still visible oak doors around me started to creak.

The wood moaned as it contorted; as if something was pushing out from the other side.

It became swollen, and pushed back and forth, in a most un-natural way for anything made from oak. The deafening booms returned and it sounded like the footsteps of a thousand advancing armies, growing louder and closer.

I ran for a while, pointlessly.

It became clear that no matter how far or fast I ran, it was the Black and Crimson Corridor that was moving and not I.

So I stopped and did the only thing I felt I could, I bravely assumed the foetal position. Then screamed for help. Momentarily, this seemed like a great idea as all at once, the sound of the advancing armies and the distorting, creaking doors ceased, and I was met with a punishing silence.

I could hear every internal movement my body was making.

From the blood coursing through me and the pounding of my heart as it pumped it through me to the formation of antibodies and the hairs that line my lungs to-ing and fro-ing with every breath. Summoning some petrified defiance, I screamed once more, mercifully ending the internal soundtrack but unfortunately, to counterbalance this brief respite, every door blasted open into smithereens all around and over me.

I got to my feet and dusted myself down.

From each doorway, now exposed, a different voice was calling my name. All the voices I could recognise, but not one could I place.

Tentatively, I stepped towards one of the door frames, my name getting quieter as I approached. There was a glass pane where the oak had once been, and behind this first one was my pudgy, twelve year old self in my school uniform, wandering the school grounds at lunch time, and wondering why my friends had suddenly stopped talking to me. I was wearing headphones and I could hear what my former self was listening to, it was Lithium by Nirvana. This view of my past was certainly less violent than my previous encounter through the crack in the door, but no less harrowing as I was consumed with same confused sadness my twelve year old self had been.

I turned from that door and with morbid intrigue I looked through another to see myself, earlier that same year rehearsing a play in a summer theatre group, laughing and carefree. The play was Peer Gynt and I was playing the part of Dr. Begriffenfeldt, director of the Cairo Asylum.

The irony was not lost on me, but I was mostly taken with how happy I seemed.

As I allowed a smile to take over my face, the light illuminating this vision of my past went out and I was thrust by the unknown forces towards another door at the other side of the hall.

This time I could see myself as a fourteen year old, receiving another beating, this time for the crime of having long hair and standing up for a friends girlfriend, six other teenagers pummelling me in my hometown, whilst the people I was with fled.

I looked away, grimacing and brimming with anger.

I was pushed from door to door being exposed to a litany of emotion provoking memories in vivid colour, often in juxtaposition to the last. At one I was sixteen, playing a gig to a rapt packed house and feeling the rush that comes with it, in the next I was twenty two and being dumped by my girlfriend, wondering where our love had gone, in the next I was a child in Italy with my family stuffing my face with pizza and wearing a grin that beamed contentment, then I was a scared ten years old on Friday the 13th of November 1991 and looking out of my skylight window in Coleraine, watching the town burn after a bomb had levelled the centre. I saw myself in Belgium, at the Pukkelpop music festival with ASIWYFA and the communal thrill and wonder we shared as we walked onstage to be greeted by four thousand people at our first gig there; conversely I then saw myself in bed in Belfast after my last gig with the band, bruised, battered and broken and no one visiting or even calling or texting as I lay with two fractured ribs. Crying in pain, physically and emotionally. Wondering once more, where had our love gone?

I could feel my abdomen aching profusely as if my ribs were suddenly broken again. Then came the real sucker-punches.

I was planted in front of a door where I was sitting on the edge of my mothers bed, eight years old, wielding a guitar for the first time as she sat with me placing my fingers in the correct position for an A chord. I was wincing as the nylon strings pressed against my soft fingertips, but press them I did. She played, "Leaving on a JetPlane", by John Denver as I tried to keep to keep up with simple chord changes of A, D and E, all the time she was singing and smiling, each as sweetly as the other as she encouraged me. The melody eased me and the pain from my ribs had vanished, contentment washed over me. Unfortunately, it seemed that once an emotion took grip, that was when the unknown forces would decide that I'd had enough of that *particular scene and I was whisked away to another memory.*

I was nineteen years old and I was sitting at my Mothers bedside in hospital, holding her hand as she slipped away from us.

The memory froze.

My heart tightened and I couldn't breathe.

I couldn't see for the tears flooding my eyes.

I howled, and I howled.

Every muscle in my body tensed and yet I was weak as a kitten.

The long, Black and Crimson Corridor extinguished to nothing and I was lit only from the light emitting from the memory, which was fading too.

I stood with my head bowed and shoulders slumped, accepting and awaiting the impending darkness.

The lightless emptiness descended once more, and I was less than impressed with whatever or whoever was orchestrating this Dickensian trauma. It occurred to me that I best not express any malice toward it – whatever it was – as each time that happened I was pulled into the horror of my own psyche, reliving a cavalcade of intense memories, mostly at my peril.

So, straightening up, I blanked my mind, and steadied my breathing.

It took some time, whether it was seconds, minutes, hours, days or weeks I cannot be sure, but eventually, I calmed.

Then, out of the black, like a reset button had been pressed, I found myself back in the elevator, facing the door and looking up toward the Dial.

Some music was being piped in, and whilst I say music, I mean it in the loosest sense.

Some Muzak was being piped in.

An awful panpipe rendition of Lithium. I nearly smirked.

The Elevator then began to slowly move, and with it the Dial did too.

As the Elevator moved from down to up, and the Dial from left to right, I noticed the Muzak change too. It shifted from butchering Nirvana, to a Muzak rendition of a song by my first band, PepperBook, a medley was forming.

*Around midway between **Then** and **Now**, it shifted seamlessly into a Zombie Safari Park song, my second band.*

*About three quarters of the way to **Now**, a horrendous panpipe interpretation of the ASIWYFA track, "Set Guitars to Kill", blended with the last monstrosity, and by this time I was unable to control myself and I was laughing like I hadn't done in a long time.*

*The laughter grew to near uncontrollable levels when the VerseChorusVerse song, One Fine Day, came along about an inch from **Now** on the Dial. I was expecting the lift to stop at **Now**, but truthfully I was beyond caring whether it did as I was too amused at the renditions I was hearing, plus I had learned that it was best not to* *expect anything in this strange, strange place.*

*The Dial began to pass the **N**. A song from my first album played – "No More Years", then onto the **O**, and a track from my most recent album played – "Have Some Soul". As it passed onto the **W** a panpipe version of a song from my unreleased album played – "Category".*

*It moved on from the **W**, and the music faded. Then the Dial moved towards completing its trajectory; onto the second, **Then**. I felt a sense of intrigue and wonder come over me, but not a drop of worry. The passage was mainly smooth from here on in, with intermittent rattles and judders as I was ferried onwards and upwards, seemingly into the future.*

A wave of excitement built in me from my tip of my toes to the ends of hair.

Could it really be?

Were all those repeat viewings of Back to the Future, Bill and Teds Excellent Adventure and Doctor Who about to pay off?

Was I about to step into the future?

A philosophical, paradoxical and rhetorical question then ousted all others from my thoughts.

Surely every step, yet to be taken, is a step into the future?

The Elevator ping-ed.

I had arrived.

The doors began to part and as they did a blinding white light began to fill the lift and I had to shield my eyes with my hand, peering out through my fingers.

A warm breeze was blowing in my direction and the heat felt welcoming.

My sinuses felt clear and my senses invigorated. My eyes adjusted and I could see outside of the Elevator there was an infinite horizon in a glorious field, where the sun was breaking on a brand new day.

Birds were singing, trees and flowers were in bloom.

The world unfolded in an endless vision of opportunity, possibility and purpose; urging and encouraging exploration and education as my eyes, ears and nose tickled my thoughts back into action. I braced myself and took a step out into the soft grass that lay as far as I could see.

I was barefoot and as my first foot touched the tender terrain, the sensation was tingling and ignited my sense of touch in delight. I lifted my other foot from the Elevator to share in the prickling delight, but as it settled onto the ground, time sped up.

The sun rose in the distant horizon, peaked and then began its descent all in the space of a few seconds.

It then repeated this process.

I watched as the summer turned to autumn and witnessed the green leaves brown and begin to fall. I saw autumn turn to winter and heard the birdsong cease; the winter led to spring and the trees started to blossom once again.

All this in just over five minutes.

At first it was magnificent to watch, but soon I realised that although I appeared to be moving at my own speed, my body was taking its cues from the quickening passing of the days, and I was ageing at an alarming pace.

Soon I was an old man.

I had stood still for too long and life had accelerated by me. I took one last look at this utopia that was laid out in front of me and thought of the things I didn't do and the places I wished I had went.

I closed my eyes, my heart stopped and my future was now my past.

21

I opened my eyes. I was back in my crazy four poster bed/dream vessel in Nashville, Tennessee.

I wish I could tell you that I leapt from my bed and ran outside, down the street wishing everyone a 'Merry Christmas' like Jimmy Stewart in *Its A Wonderful Life*, but that would have been as crazy as the dream I'd just had. The truth being that I was fairly shaken by it all, understandably I'm sure you'll agree. I lay there for a little while, pondering all that I had seen and felt in this most vivid of fantastically, nightmarish dreams. My notebook was on my bedside table and I picked it up to scribble everything I could remember from it before it dissipated, the way dreams do, then mustered my will to raise my bleary head out of bed and shower.

I was due to meet up with a fellow called Chris, whom I had only talked with via a few brief emails. To the best of my knowledge, Chris worked for the office of the Mayor. Nashville is a twinned city with Belfast, and Chris worked for the department that dealt with relations between the two cities. The meeting had been suggested by some friends at home who had worked with him in that capacity. We weren't due to meet until around four o'clock, so I figured I could, and should, get in a little sightseeing first. Anything to try and shake the David Lynch movie that had unfolded in my head the night before.

It was 11am when I left my McGavock Pike residence. I took the bus into the city, trying to save a little money. Firstly, I checked out the Country Music Hall of Fame, which was nearly $40 a ticket, and not being the world's biggest country music enthusiast I declined to take the full tour. It's not that I don't enjoy some country music, but I'm not into it enough to spend that amount of money seeing items of clothing worn by people I have little to no knowledge of. Not on my budget anyway.

I passed by the Ryman Auditorium, home to some legendary gigs and hopefully so for many years to come. Again, I wandered up and down the main strip where music was still pumping out of every doorway and window, and again, I failed to be moved or invigorated by any of it.

I don't blame any of this ennui on the great city of Nashville; I could have been strolling the Hanging Gardens of Babylon and I think I would still have felt as listless. The total feeling of apathy that I was bathing in before had only been intensified by the harrowing events that had taken place in my subconscious the previous night.

There was only one thing for it, a damn good sandwich.

Beside the Johnny Cash Museum lies Luigi's, an American-Italian restaurant that offered good food and a temporary respite from the heat. I placed an order for a Meatball Sandwich, and soon I was taking refuge from both the sun and my blues, for the meantime anyway.

Chris emailed and said he was going to an In-store Gig at Grimeys Record Store in the east of the city, and that we should meet there a little earlier than planned. My friends who had set up the meeting spoke nothing but positively about Chris, as well as his enthusiasm for music and life, and I was in dire need of a little of both.

After killing some more time in Luigi's, I ordered an Uber and made my way to Grimeys. Getting into the back seat of the car, I attempted to initiate that most predictable topic of conversations.

"Man, it sure it is hot."

I was met with a confused look in the rear-view mirror as my eyes met with the driver.

"Where the hell you from, man?" asked the driver. I sensed that it was my accent again.

"Ireland, sorry if you can't understand me, we... talk... a little...... fast," I said, slowing my speech to a Shatner-like pace.

"Nah man, I understand you fine. Ireland, huh? What's the weather like back there in Ireland?" came his inquisitive response.

"The weather?" I was delighted that my boring conversation had taken hold. "Well weather like we're having today would be probably a freak occurrence. Everybody would take the day off work and disposable barbecue sales would go through the roof...the roof we'd all be hiding under so we don't get burnt..." I was hoping he got my, admittedly poor, joke.

"Really?" he replied, without a hint of amusement. Couldn't blame him.

"Yep, really..." I confirmed, with a big dumb grin on my face, trying to reinforce that I was trying to joke too.

"And when did you get into town?" he continued, not permitting a smidgen of light-heartedness into the exchange.

"Two days ago. I was in New York before..." before he interrupted.

"Man, you gotta take your red ass back to Ireland."

"...I'm sorry? Excuse me?" I asked, shocked.

"We've had shitty-ass weather here for two days now and I ain't cool wit' it! You gotta take your pasty red ass and this shitty weather back to Dublin with you! Or wherever it is in Ireland it is you came from! I moved here from Chicago to get away from all that cold weather shit, and here you are bringing it back to my new backyard!"

I couldn't quite believe what I was hearing, and I was about to tell him to pull over, when he suddenly burst out laughing, probably at the indignant silence I was spewing.

"Maaaaan, I'm just messing with you man! Welcome to Nashville!" he said between guttural roars of laughter.

"Oh...right...yeah...cool..." and then I started laughing too. It was impossible not to, his laugh was severely infectious, and we laughed all the way to Grimey's. Admittedly the laugh began to grow awkward as we dragged it out a bit, but then the driver would slap the steering wheel and start roaring again. In hindsight, I think he was totally testing me. *Well played, sir.*

As I got out of the car, still laughing, albeit more a giggle at this point, I reached into my pocket and pulled out a few dollars to give this master of both physical and verbal delivery a tip through the driver's window.

"Thanks man," he said, looking me in the eyes with a huge friendly smile. Then his face turned and he deadpanned, "Seriously though, take your red ass back to Ireland man, I'm done with this bullshit," grabbing the money from my hand and speeding off. I heard him laughing as he went, and I'm still not sure whether he was serious or not, but it was totally worth it, if nothing else for the masterclass in acting I'd just received.

Since I was a little early, I mailed Chris to tell him I'd arrived and would wait outside, telling him he'd recognise me with my usual self-description: "The most clichéd looking Irishman you can imagine". He replied near instantaneously saying he'd be there in a few minutes, and that he knew me from VerseChorusVerse and ASIWYFA, so he'd recognise me. True to his word he was there in minutes. We shook hands and made our way in to the gig that was about to start.

Grimey's is a very cool independent record store. The place was filling up nicely with a broad mix of age groups, all fervently awaiting the band that was about to come on. I still had no idea who that was. Chris told me it was an indie rock band from Virginia, Car Seat Headrest, who had just signed to Matador records. I joked with Chris that their band name was so bad, I could've been a member. Again, my attempt at humour falling flat. I imagined that this is how Bill Murray would feel if he wasn't a megastar. Or funny.

The band came on and didn't disappoint. They were magnificent, and richly deserve their growing reputation. It was a perfect mix of lo-fi angst, interesting song structures, smart lyrics, and the right side of shambolic that makes for inspirational garage bands. For forty minutes they reminded me of the joys of being in a band.

After the show, we went to the little coffee house beside the record shop and got talking. My friends hadn't been wrong, Chris was an exceptionally nice guy who knew a great deal about the current and past Irish music scene, listing bands, singers, and songs that he loved.

He asked about my trip so far, why I had left the band, and what my plans were. So I told him about staying with Jesse Malin, the open mic slot, the gig, and how I had went over so well, photo requests from The Zombies, then I gave him the abridged account of my exit from the band, and how I was still trying to build the future.

I couldn't exactly tell him – as I discovered the night before – I was going to stand in a field and age decades in seconds.

I asked him about his trips to Ireland, the Belfast-Nashville connection, and his job, and to my surprise he told me that he didn't work for the Mayor any more. He told me that he now worked for this big music management company, who handled many international acts. Big acts. Interesting.

Now, part of this whole self-employed musician/artist deal is that you have to hustle nearly constantly. If you sniff an opportunity, you have to take it, otherwise you'll end up forever in the slow lane. Sometimes, people get plucked from the slow lane through either sheer talent, good fortune, or good looks. Sometimes all three. Mostly though, it's two of the three, and I'm no oil painting (and apparently becoming quite the cynic, too). I asked Chris more about this management company, and he graciously answered all my questions, with an unerring enthusiasm. I then, half jokingly, asked whether or not they had room for me on their roster. Chris was very diplomatic in his response. He threw me an olive branch when he mentioned that his boss – a gentleman named Jim – was very tight with Jesse, as they both knew each other through working closely with Bruce Springsteen over the years (I did my level best to remain cool, usually a pointless endeavour). He recommended that I ask Jesse to get in touch with Jim to sing my praises, and that he would do the same.

A praise lavishing pincer movement.

He said this was really all he could offer to do, since he was new to the company and, no offence to me (none was taken), I didn't have the biggest profile. Grateful for his honesty, I thanked him, expressing that this was more than enough, and any help tended my way whatsoever would be hugely appreciated. I told him that I would get in touch with Jesse in a couple of weeks, asking him to do as Chris had suggested, but that I didn't want to ask him immediately given the huge favour he had already just afforded me.

He offered me a lift back to McGavock Pike, and apologised that he wouldn't be around more when I was in town, but he was heading out of state to help his girlfriend move back from college. I gratefully accepted the lift and headed back with him, listening to new music in his car along the way, passing through Five Points, and taking his advice of the cool places to check out.

Later that evening, wary of being alone and thinking about the dream too much, I swung by the Village Pub just to be around people. Michael, bartender extraordinaire, welcomed me back as I sat down where all people entering bars when on their lonesome sit, at the bar. He offered me the beer menu, and I asked for whatever it was I had drank the last time. Michael, being such a professional, remembered what it was, poured me one and set me up a tab. He then introduced me to some of the locals and other recent drifters that had breezed into the area. Among them was a cool German man, Igho, based in New Jersey for the past nine years. We talked about European football for a while after I had expressed my admiration for several German teams, but principally for Liverpool FCs son of the Black Forest, Jurgen Klopp. Igho was a font of knowledge who possessed a dry German wit, and we shared several beers together before he went on his way.

As I went out into the pleasantly warm night air to have a smoke, a little wobbly at this point, I got a phone call from my good friend and associate, Paul Clegg. He was checking in on me and seeing how my travels had been since we last spoke. He then went on ask when I was going to Los Angeles. I answered, and wondered aloud to him why he was asking, was he due to be in California around that time?

"Nah dude, not me, but Gogol Bordello are starting their US tour in California around then, you wanna open up for them in Berkeley and Napa? They'll be pretty big shows, you'll play to about 2000 in Berkeley and about 1000 in Napa, then they're playing a festival in Napa Valley the next day, you should just hang with them. We can fly you from LA to San Francisco and then back after the festival, we'll book you into our hotels too. Whadayasay?"

Naturally, I flatly refused and told him to never contact me again with such frivolous and nonsensical requests. Thankfully, my brain caught a hold of my tongue before it was able to verbalise said refusal, rearranged some of the letters, dropped others and then spat out the following in gracious acceptance: "Sounds good, I'm in, thank you!"

Paul told me he'd email details through in the next few days, and when to announce via the various devilries of social media and – being a busy family man – promptly hung up before I had a chance to ask him anymore details and thank him again.

I reflected that, all in all, it had been a pretty good day. The harrowing dream was still knocking on my frontal lobe, so I decided I should settle my bill and go for a walk, listen to some music and clear my head a little.

An excellent song to listen to when you're tipsy, in America, and feeling a little lost emotionally, is David Bowie's 'I'm Afraid of Americans'. It provides the perfect amount of empathy from the lyrics and never lets up on the paranoia. Perhaps it's a terrible song to listen to then actually...

Regardless of the paranoid lyrics, it jams. It's a great song, and, in my experience, best listened too after several ales, in a city you're not familiar with and staggering down a busy main road, in this case, Gallatin Pike. The strip is lined with McDonalds, Dollar Generals, Pawn shops, Wendy's, Popeyes Louisiana Chicken, Discount Liquor Stores, Car Washes, and mechanics, their multi-coloured signs all bearing down, as pick-up trucks and lorries the size of cruise ships rocket by. Also being the only pedestrian for miles in either direction, in a populated area, is an interesting feeling. Or perhaps that was the alcohol.

Stumbling on down Gallatin, my senses equal parts inebriated and titillated, I noticed a one storey dive bar hidden between the many neon signed drive thrus, Mikey's. It was barely lit at all, had just a few cars outside, and the sign was as basic as it could come. The "I" slightly sloping to the left, but hanging on in there against the odds. What a metaphor, I remember thinking. It could hardly be described as inviting, but to me it looked beautiful.

Why not? I thought. And I entered.

The place was actually pretty busy and loud, but loud from talking as there was no music playing. There was a pool table and a jukebox to the rear, before an entry way into a room with a few dart boards. The bar itself was about twenty foot in length, and there wasn't a seat to be had at it, but the many tables scattered around the long thin room didn't have a soul sitting at them. As much as I would've preferred to sit at the bar and maybe strike up a conversation with some interesting stranger, that wasn't going to happen. I reasoned that it would've been a 50/50 chance that the person may have been interesting, they could have been boring as hell.

I ordered a beer and a Jameson, paid the man, and placed my drinks at a table near the jukebox, briefly considering to try my hand at pool, before quickly dismissing the notion. I can barely play when stone cold sober, never mind when I'm three sheets to the wind in Tennessee. The prospect of getting laughed out of the bar didn't appeal to me.

Instead, I took my four quarters, and pumped them into the jukebox.

I immediately saw the song I really wanted to hear, the song I *really* wanted as my soundtrack to sitting in Mikey's Dive Bar. But then I'd have to put on two more songs, and knowing how indecisive I can be, that could take some time.

My logic was as follows, first song had to be a song I liked, but not one that I wanted to *really* listen to, more a soundtrack to choosing the other tunes.

The second song was the song that I actually wanted to hear, and the one that I felt really projected who I was to this room full of strangers, and the third song...well, the third song was kind of a mix between the two.

After a quick scan of the music on offer, my first song leapt out at me, 'Magic' by The Cars. Perfect, and at a length of just under four minutes, should give me ample time to input my second selection and find a third.

A few feet started tapping and I even heard someone shout their approval at the music choice as it piped out through the speakers.

Hurriedly, I keyed in the digits for my favoured second song, and then began my hunt for whatever the third track would be.

I perused and perused.

I should also mention at this time that when I was younger I would spend hours and hours in the local video rental place looking for a film to rent, which in modern terms is like scrolling through Netflix for hours to finally watch a film that would take up a fraction of the time to actually view.

Time was running out and, at the final chorus of the first song, I opted for a stone cold classic by Aretha Franklin, 'You Make Me Feel (Like a Natural Woman)', and sat at my table.

My second choice, you may have been wondering, was my favourite single of all time, and one close to home too, 'Baby Please Don't Go' by Them.

The opening riff cut through the overall murmur that had been permeating the room, the bartender even turned it up. I noticed people drumming along with their fingers at the bar, some people were singing along and I sat, satisfied at my selection.

The underlying panic from the vivid, fantastical, nightmarish dream that had never been too far away throughout the afternoon and evening was finally conquered with a combination of alcohol, good news and, ultimately, Them and Van Morrison drowning out the demons with the greatest sounding two and a half minutes ever committed to tape.

It was the best I had felt since I'd played in New York the week before. As the song finished I awaited Queen Aretha to come on and soothe my soul further. Only, she didn't.

In my haste to retake my seat before the start of Them, I had fumbled the tracks selection number.

Oh no...

Instead, on came the EuroPop nightmare that was 'The Macarena'.

My god...what had I done...

Apologies if that song is now in your head, sincerely, but imagine, just for a moment the mood in the bar as that song invaded the ears of the gathered socialisers of Mikey's dive bar in East Nashville. I certainly got a few strange looks as I sat and pretended as if nothing out of the ordinary was going on.

Who was this sickly pale stranger with a penchant for mid-nineties novelty dance tracks?

Why had he come to infect our brains with this trash?

The only way it could have got conceivably worse was if I jumped on the pool table and started performing the dance. Or maybe, just maybe, that would have made it better.

I neglected to find out as I finished my drinks and made for the exit, failing to suppress my giggles any longer..

"I think they liked it," I thought to myself, zig-zagging down the pavement. It was clearly bed time.

A few other notable things happened in Nashville in the next week. I watched Liverpool lose the Europa League final to Sevilla, deservedly, I'm afraid I must admit. But hey, it had been a good ride. The better team won. I talked with a nice guy who chose to support Sevilla just to make it interesting. He was an artist called Rick Lobdell, who would take me around Nashville later in the week, bringing me to, among other places, his art studio (where I met a nine foot rabbit, truly) and Jack Whites Third Man Records, where I would cut a two minute acetate record in his recording booth for $20. A nice gift for my brother.

I met up with mutual friend of my friend Cahir from home, Jake. He was a phenomenally gifted musician, and would take me to a house-party where everybody was supremely nice and also supremely drunk. They were all also very keen on getting this visiting Irishman as drunk as they were. The morning after, I was woken by a phone call from Jake who was outside in his car with his girlfriend and other friends waiting for me. Apparently I'd agreed to go on a day trip with them the night before to Cummins Falls National Park, an hour outside the city. I was glad that I did as there is no better hangover cure than walking half a mile in a freshwater stream to reach a beautiful waterfall to wash all the badness away. I heartily recommend it.

Most nights I would spend on the porch of Anita and Marks house getting to know one another better with each passing evening. One night I joined them for drinks at their favoured watering hole, Frans' Karaoke Bar, which was probably the most genuine Nashville bar I was in the whole time. One where I witnessed a beer bellied, vest wearing, mulleted and moustachioed, non-hipster, genuine article local perform the Elvis classic 'Suspicious Minds', complete with kung-fu moves.

All these people were so unflinchingly good to me, and the kindness and warmth they showed to me is something I will never forget. They helped me greatly in abating the loneliness and uncertainty that was threatening to consume me. For that, they will always hold a special place in my heart.

But before I move onto the next portion of my odyssey, which so far had introduced me to some beautiful souls and thrown me much fortune, whilst also delving into some of the dustiest back rooms of my own psyche, I must remind you, and myself, of the initial purpose of this trip. Meetings with my publisher, and Nashville was no different.

22

The meeting with my music publishers had been shifted around a few times, which I wasn't surprised or annoyed at since this is the busiest music city in the world. After all, this *is* Music City. The day before my appointment, my liaison, Sarah-Jane Jones, mailed me to apologise that she wasn't going to be able to make it, and that her associate, Elaine, would be meeting with me instead.

The meeting with them in New York had been in a skyscraper on the 11th floor in the heart of Times Square, amongst a great many other businesses and tourist trapping locations.

Whereas in Nashville, the offices were in the epicentre of Music Row, which is probably the most concentrated area of the music business and its affiliates, anywhere in the world.

Record companies, publishers, streaming services, and high-end recording studios populate this hub of everything relating or pertaining to music.

It's a formidable sight.

If you make the right connections here, you have the strongest and best chances of going on to greatness.

Or so it is told.

In contrast with the 11th floor NY offices, I was confronted with a detached, two storey building that could have been mistaken for a house, as my cab driver and I did initially.

Looks, as we know, can be deceiving, and some the biggest hits and most popular songs you can imagine are published from this quaint looking dwelling.

Getting out of my cab and approaching the building I suspected was my destination, I saw a gathering of people sitting outside the fire escape having a smoke. I looked up toward them and a lady inquisitively yelled, "Tony?" "Right!", I punned in response, with my mediocre joke going un-noticed. Again.

Elaine introduced me to her fellow smokers and then invited me into her office, offering me coffee. Once we both were settled, having talked a little about things not relating to music, I gave her the rehearsed spiel which I had given in the New York offices a fortnight before. Briefly mentioning the band, what had happened, tours I'd been on, releases, and how the last one, with my buddy David Lyttle, had been my most successful, charting at 19 in the UK and no.1

on Amazon. Elaine was cool and listened, but she didn't ask me any questions, nodding the whole time. Then, finally, she asked me a question, and probably the most pertinent one since she'd been asked to take this meeting at the last minute.

"Got any music with ya?"

I handed her two CDs, one was my first album, and the other was a CDR of my first two EPs, then I told her I would mail her the aforementioned smash hit collaboration with Mr Lyttle if Sarah-Jane hadn't sent it on. She hadn't. Elaine kept on nodding, and then put my first album on, and she put it on LOUD.

Generally, I don't like listening to my own stuff with other people, barring perhaps the producer or any other writers or musicians from the recordings. It makes me feel deeply uneasy, and I know I'm not alone in this, with many of my peers feeling the same way. This feeling of uneasiness is broadened even further when the person who is hearing it for the first time could – in theory – make or break you. However, having said this, we all love listening to it by ourselves and in a narcissistic manner, revelling in our supposed genius like a proverbial pig in shit.

She seemed to be into it, yelling her approval over the top of it from time to time. All in all we listened to three tracks, before she turned it off and told me that she liked what she heard. She said it wasn't the usual stuff that they get through this particular office, since it's not country. I again expressed my desire to work closer with them and perhaps other songwriters, telling her that there was a country song on that record, 'Help Myself', and that the whole purpose of VerseChorusVerse was to never be tied down to one genre and to constantly be working on and honing new styles. Elaine nodded some more. She was honest with me; telling me that it's hard to break into any of the established songwriting partnerships or existing cliques since everybody had worked so hard to get there, they don't let strangers or newcomers in too easily.

I told her that I understood and respected that, but that I had worked hard too, and given my background, I could help expose them to other music fans that may not ordinarily give that sort of thing a listen.

All of this was done in good nature, smiling and laughing along the way. We kept it light whilst reasoning from both corners. I'd been there about an hour and a half and didn't want to outstay my welcome, knowing how busy she must be.

As I thanked her for her time and expressed how I hoped we could make something work, she invited me to a writers night they were hosting in a few days with some of their associated writers and other publishers, suggesting that it would give me a better sense of Nashville and the styles that succeed here, as well as enabling me to meet her associate, Sarah-Jane. I gratefully accepted the invite and thanked her again for her time, after all, she hadn't really expected me. She was kind enough to drop me closer to civilisation and show me the joint that would be hosting the writers night. Which, I must add, had the wonderful name of "Pitch Please".

So it was puns that tickled Nashvilliains...noted.

I wandered around the periphery of Music Row, sweating in the heat. The irony not being lost on me for a second.

23

My final day in Nashville was the day of the "Pitch Please" writers night Elaine had kindly invited me to. I was told that there was no chance of me getting to play a song as it's booked up with the cream of the new writing talent for months in advance. This did not stop me from bringing my guitar.

It was upstairs in a pizza restaurant called Soul Shine, near Music Row, and the music would be happening on a roof top with a half veranda to provide some shade. When I got there it was practically empty. There was a girl with a guitar mulling near the stage where an engineer was setting up the microphones and providing seats for the musicians. It was going to be an in-the-round format, which is the standard for these writing nights, and from what Elaine had briefly said, there would be three rounds of three, with each songwriter getting the chance to play two of their songs in the hope that it would be pounced on by some of the music business people in attendance.

I got a pitcher of water, ordered some pizza, and took a seat at the back of the balcony, making sure to get in the shaded area. It was hot that day. It was hot most days.

It was probably the most considerate place for a smelly smoker such as myself to sit. No point in me sitting up front and choking the poor songbirds trying to catch a break, that would be cruel. Give 'em the best chance they can possibly have, it's frightening out there, as I knew only too well. The back was also a good vantage point to see where Elaine was when she arrived and to wave frantically, like a man possessed by a possessed man, to make my presence known.

The balcony started to fill up, and *nobody* dared come and sit at the table with the smelly smoker. That's not to say that others weren't smoking, but people seemed to look in my direction and then prefer the standing option. Fair enough, I thought, as I pulled another chair near me and put my feet up, exhaling skyward as if it was a Cuban cigar & not a rollie.

Soon the place was packed, with couples and solitary figures jostling for a vantage point, not a seat was to be had. Well, barring the four at my table that is. I scanned the floor for bird shit. Clean as a shit free whistle.

The first three songwriters had taken their seats onstage and were preparing to begin. Looking around, I couldn't see Elaine anywhere in the audience, so I sent her an email telling her where I was sitting. The first songwriter started, a young lady in her early twenties, and the audience got a little quieter, but there was still a level of murmuring that ought to be unacceptable at such an evening. This was not an easy plight to begin with for the performer and, coupled with the initially dreadful sound, I felt for her. Her voice was by no means a soprano, but had a tender quality that needed an attentive sound engineer to elevate above the chattering few. Unfortunately, the sound man was amongst the chattering few, lounging near the rail of the balcony, flirting with a girl. *Damn it man, do your job*, I thought. Wishing now – with hindsight – that I had said it.

Eventually he returned to the sound desk, tweaked a few sliders and knobs, and the singing was audible. Alas this was on the last line of the final chorus.

Regardless, the hitherto uninterested audience suddenly broke from their conversation and started cheering like they'd just heard Taylor Swift sing the American National Anthem. I felt glad for the poor girl, but at the same time rather confused by the reaction.

The second singer began, this time a youngish male, who had a more boisterous approach to his songwriting and performing style. His sound was on point from the beginning, and as a result the audience went a little quieter that they had been before. The songs' lyrical content contained many of the staples of country songwriting, at least *New* country anyway. He bellowed out well worn lyrical atrophies about his girl, his truck, and drinking beer. This was Nashville after all, and I, clearly, am a snob. The song had a pleasant rhythm to it and the melody was instantly memorable, because of its previous usage in hundreds of songs before it. Granted, there are only so many combinations of notes to use, and some are better liked than others, hence their repeated use. I'm sure I've been guilty of it in the past. He finished, and the crowd lost their collective minds. The gathered industry heads smelled a generic radio friendly smash when they heard one.

Still, I couldn't see Elaine anywhere, so I mailed again.

The third player started, another lady in her early to mid twenties, and another ballad. This time delivered with a little more gusto than the first. Lyrically, it wasn't a million miles from 'The Greatest Love of All'. She had a great voice and sang strongly but, for me, it was again formulaic and a little beige. Then again, that is probably why these young musicians are getting the opportunity to play for the gathered industry and possibly break into the big time, or at the very least the chance to make a sustainable career out of it, and why I am sitting alone at five seater table, with a space surrounding me like I just admitted to leprosy.

These songwriters were churning out songs for the machine, and more power to them, I guess. Personally, I've always preferred a little invention, or risk taking, be it musically or lyrically or even aesthetically. A little *artistry*.

This cycle seemed to repeat with each new round, and still, I couldn't see Elaine. The music was getting a bit much for me to really take, and I decided to get out of there. It wasn't an easy decision to come to, as I felt almost like I was admitting defeat and that I really didn't belong here.

That initial doubt fed into another. What the hell am I doing even being a musician? I love music and creating it, but look at me. I'm quite literally repelling people in the industry, no one will even dare sit at this table! I had been stood up first by Sarah-Jane Jones and then by Elaine who I had been passed onto at the last minute. I'm broke, lonely, thousands of miles from "home", and I use inverted commas because I don't have a home to speak of.

Something had to give.

Between music rounds, I picked up my guitar and got up to leave.

"Tony!" a voice called from behind me as I neared the exit.

It was Elaine, and she was motioning me towards their table near the stage. She introduced me to her wife and some of her workmates, and offered to buy me a beer. I accepted, asked whether she had received my emails (she hadn't), and sat down, telling myself I should stay for a little longer, if for no other reason to meet Sarah-Jane and find out if maybe...just maybe, she had listened to the music I had sent her months before, and to see if anybody out here connected to the company that I had signed my musical rights away to actually gave a damn about me, or at the very least, my music.

Elaine came back with a beer and asked me if I'd met Sarah-Jane. A lady a few feet in front of me, whom I'd seen come in earlier, turned towards us, smiling. Elaine introduced us and we shook hands, and she apologised that she hadn't been able to meet me before like we had planned. I asked whether she had listened to any of the music I had sent to her a couple of months before, and, of course, she hadn't.

Naturally, I smiled and said nothing.

She then told me how great it was to "Finally meet me", and that hopefully we would do it again soon, before turning back to the direction of the stage. Not even to talk to someone else, but just to look at a vacant stage. I'm sure you can gather I may have felt a tad insulted by this. So insulted in fact I was shocked into total silence, still wearing my dumb grin. I returned to my seat, sporting said dumb grin, and drank my beer quietly, but quickly.

Now I totally understand that people in the music industry get a lot of music to listen to, but when someone is traveling across the Atlantic Ocean, who has entrusted the rights of his music and livelihood to the wonderfully innovative company you work for, you'd think they could take a few minutes to play even one track.

It dawned on me that I hadn't seemed to have learnt a thing about the music industry in the twenty years I had been professionally affiliated with it.

I was throwing stones into an impenetrable frozen lake, and still expecting a ripple.

Without fuss, I thanked Elaine for the beer, said goodbye and made my exit, suppressing any visible sign of indignant disappointment as best as I could.

Arriving back in McGavock Pike, after a brief stop at the Discount Liquor Store on Gallatin, I had an email from Paul asking for some details to book my return flight from LA to San Francisco. This buoyed me slightly, and I replied with the information he was looking for. I told him that I would book a train for the outward leg of the journey. Despite it being a twelve hour train ride, I preferred the prospect of getting to see a little bit of Californian scenery, rather than spending another day sitting around an airport. My trip was entering its final stage, and I wanted some time to reflect on all that had happened, but also in what the future could possibly hold and how best to deal with it, moving forward.

Anita, Mark, and Ralphie were in their extensive back garden, tending to their vegetable patches, and I asked them whether they would like a Pale Ale from the Six Pack I had just bought. They were delighted to do so, and we made our way to the front porch to drink them and see the evening out. It was the best way I could imagine to finish off my strange time in their fair city and home. Nightmares, doubts, and epiphanies may have coloured my time here, but the people I had met made it worthwhile.

After a few drinks, they asked me if I could play them a few songs, and I was only too happy oblige. Finally, a Nashville gig! I played them a few, including a new song I had written a couple of evenings previously that nobody had yet heard.

It was a country song called, '(Its strange to be a) Stranger in Nashville'.

Every last cliché about Nashville,
Yeah they're sad & funny & true.
A million songwriters with one dream,
& a million waiting tables too.
Songs are farmed and sold just like cattle,
Some slaughtered to pay their dues.
Yeah it's strange to be a stranger in Nashville,
When you've walked in a million shoes.

I'll keep rolling on with you.

From Five Points down to Downtown,
Try to make it on Music Row.
You'll never hear talent quite like it,
Struggle to get a show.
Like moths to a bulb, we flock here,
Our hopes & wishes in tow.
Bloodied, sweaty & tearful,
Praying we reap what we sew.

I'll keep rolling on with you.

Part Four

24

I landed in Los Angeles around 10pm the next evening after the long flight from Tennessee. LAX was very busy, as I imagine it always is, but it seemed exceptionally so on that particular evening. I mentioned this to my cab driver on our way to my hotel, and he explained that Bernie Sanders, Hillary Clinton, and Donald Trump had all arrived in the city that day on their respective campaign trails.

Nearing our hotel, I asked him if he knew the area I was staying in, and whether he could recommend somewhere to get a bite to eat or something to drink.

"You're staying in Downtown, man. Get a cab if you're going someplace..." pausing before he added, "...you don't fuck around in Downtown."

Point taken.

The hotel seemed nice. It was the Mayfair Hotel, or, as they preferred to call it according to the sign in the lobby, the Historic Mayfair Hotel. The brochures on offer gave a little more detail...

Built during a period of opulence in the Roaring 20's, The Mayfair Hotel played host to rambunctious flapper girls and indulgent oil barons alike.

Fairly self-explanatory, I think you'll agree. That's not to say it wasn't a nice place, because it was. It stood out in the area much like Biff's Casino in *Back to the Future 2* when Marty visits his dystopian present. I really have made a lot of reference to those movies, haven't I? Anyway, the place was nice, and more than suited my needs for a one night stay. I got into bed and channel hopped for a while, amused by the weather man's 'name', Dallas Rains. Eventually I fell asleep watching Jimmy Kimmel, who was interviewing Trump. No nightmares, mercifully.

Union Station in Los Angeles is a sight to behold. More a Railway Palace Ballroom than a railway station, surrounded by palm trees on the outside, and opulent marble within. The place is immaculately clean, which is in marked difference to the outside and the railway line as you head north. Which is exactly what I was doing.

I was getting the romantically name "Coastal Starlight" train north to Emeryville, just outside of San Francisco, where I was meeting up with Gogol Bordello, crew and band, for a couple of gigs in Berkeley and Napa. The Coastal Starlight would take twelve hours for me to reach my destination, but the train would continue after that all along the western seaboard to Seattle, Washington.

American trains are huge snaking behemoths, often two storeys high, and each housing a separate snack shop, thankfully, as I craved some of that fine American coffee. Simply because they know not to burn the coffee beans, unlike most places in Ireland and the UK.

I took my seat – which had acres of space afforded to little ol' me – on coach 12. A young family were seated just ahead of me, and two beautiful Spanish speaking women adjacent to me, which further endeared me to this glorious beast of a train. We exchanged smiles and it made my day.

The carriage ahead was a viewing panorama of splendour, with windows above as well as beside us. Once we got out of central LA, the conductor would pipe up over the PA and tell us which particular Western movie had been shot in which particular bit of desert.

As we trundled out of the inner city, we passed by innumerable small movie lots, palm trees, strip clubs, general detritus, and the biggest used car lots you could ever imagine. You could sense the ghosts of Fante and Bukowski, the old LA that is as lost as the yesterdays that once held it.

Onward we rolled, past Burbank, Semi Valley and towards Santa Barbara.

Vineyards, tennis courts and olive groves began to fill the land. Water Sprinklers became more and more regular, for reasons most obvious in this yellow, brown and green landscape.

We careered alongside the North Lewis Road and the town of Camarillo, where kids played baseball and football, and then we were back amongst farmlands and sprinklers within moments.

The farmland, harbouring all manner of crops, poured on for miles and miles.

Next stop, Santa Barbara. My only knowledge of this place was a poor US soap opera of the same name from when I was very young, and off sick from school. I was growing more excited, as we neared the Pacific Ocean. Being from a coastal town and having been separate from any view of the sea for a while, well, it tends to affect me a little. You'd never have guessed.

Nothing can truly calm my unruly mind like a gaze into the unending blue of this planet's true physical master, and I began to catch my first glimpse of it on the vista to my left, peeking through the myriad palm trees. I was listening to Beethoven's 9th, and the blueness took my breath away. Musical and visual magnificence in near perfect unison.

The view was interrupted every so often by a motel or supermarket, but never enough to wipe the smile off of my face as I gazed out of the panoramic windows. One of the young Spanish ladies passed me on her way back from getting a coffee, and our smiles greeted each other once more.

Way beyond me, on the precipice of the horizon, I could spy a large freighter, and I imagined exaggerated adventures in their shipping life, my imagination working more richly and vividly than it had done in years.

A gathering of surfers danced with the waves. Huge RVs (or Motorhomes) lined the road alongside the coast, whilst the view on the right began to stretch upwards, as Los Padres National Forest started to reach towards the sky.

More and more piers appeared as we sidled up by Santa Barbara Avenue, with villages dotting the right hand side, propelling further north. All of this, and we were barely two hours outside Los Angeles. The second Spanish girl passed by me and flashed me another smile as our eyes met. Fantastic. Either side of us, campsites became more and more frequent, whilst on the right, the mountains became more and more magnificent.

The last little town before we reached Santa Barbara was appropriately had the most soap opera sounding name I have ever encountered (yep, even more so than the eponymous real one I mentioned earlier). *Ladies and Gentleman, I give you... Summerland.*

I half expected it to be an amusement park, and we passed by it in the blink of an eye.

We briefly stopped again, so I disembarked for leg stretching and smoking purposes. A large gentleman from Alabama by the name of James began ranting at me about having to go so far from the train to get a smoke.

"I mean man, back in Alabama we have smoking laws too, but here in California they're so far up their own ass they may as well be in Uranus!"

James was a friendly guy and advised me to go and see Yosemite Park if I had the time, which alas, I didn't. We would make minor chit-chat back on the train for the remainder of my trip.

We continued north, and the train was now pretty full. The panoramic carriage was now at capacity, and I returned to my allotted seat, where I overheard that one of the Spanish ladies had left her laptop at Union Station and she was understandably quite upset. I offered my best wishes, and they thanked me, still smiling, but I felt quite dreadful for them. My wishes were nothing but a gesture, and they were all I could really offer. Then a lady nearby offered up her prayers to the universe that it would get handed in by a kindly soul. I really hope it did.

Two National Park Guides had boarded the train, and proceeded to give an audio tour of the sights available to us.

"To your left, ladies and gentleman, you'll see a few ol' oil rigs. Oil was discovered here in the 1920s, and you may have heard of the spill that happened here a few years back. You can still see remnants o' the slick out there, regretfully... For those of you a little older you may remember back in 1942 a Japanese submarine attacked these coastlines to, of course, little effect. A pier was destroyed, and rumour has it that the resulting wood was sold to a local businessman, who built and opened a restaurant with the wreckage. To the very keen-eyed amongst you, you may spy a few whales out there in the Pacific as they migrate north, kinda like us..."

Though informative and pleasant, I returned to my seat to take in the sights for myself.

Northbound we sped.

The coastline that stretched out before me was nothing short of spectacular.

My view bathed in the seemingly infinite multi-hued blue expanse, and all the feelings of loneliness and worry that had been blighting me drifted away, as I began to tantalize my ears with Vivaldi's Four Seasons.

The last time I had been on the move in California, driving down Route 101 in the opposite direction, I had listened pretty much only to Woody Guthrie. This choice of classical soundtrack may have been alien to these shores, but its beauty synchronised with the unfolding, natural delights like water does to life, each twist and turn revealing yet more and more wonder.

Little Beach resorts peppered with para-gliders, bathers and dunes.

Lurching cliffs and rocky out-posts.

Sun scorched, water starved fields.

All watched over by a near cloudless and perfect sky.

More fauna and green started to appear as we crept north, colours familiar to my hometown of Portstewart on a good summer's day. A REALLY good summer's day. Then new, unfamiliar colours of pink, purple, and deepest orange introduced themselves. The land was now no longer arid, but bountiful in plant-life, and the contrasts with the greenish blues of the ocean were nothing short of remarkable. The sand was turning from mild yellow to white on the hilly dunes, and looked as fine as fairy dust.

We drifted further inland, the ocean still in sight, but it seemed like we were sailing through the mountains now. I was told that we were in a huge area of private property that the only way to gain passage through it, as a civilian, was onboard this very train.

Ride of the Valkyries came on my "Now That's What I Call Classical" level of playlist, it seemed very apt.

The scenery became a classic setting for a western.

We passed by what appeared to be a chicken farm and car dump hybrid. In the midst of all this barren beauty, it never ceases to astound me that humanity finds a way to survive, always accumulating junk along the way. We stopped at a red signal waiting for the go ahead from the dispatcher by the side of this farm breakers' yard. Chickens in makeshift coops of plywood and corrugated metal, with long rusted and stationary Volkswagens, vans, and defunct tractors taking up the remaining space.

A huge hawk circled overhead; this is not a place humans should really be. Green signal.

Onwards.

We went past a now defunct mine, quickly followed by a gigantic strawberry field and a huge cooling plant, used to keep the vast array of crops grown out on these lands ready for packaging out to the rest of the country. The sudden change in landscape from dry to lush was always astonishing, like skipping from Earth to Mars and back again.

We approached Pismo Beach, which until now I had thought only existed in Bugs Bunny and Daffy Duck cartoons as a destination they never reached or took a wrong turn at.

There was a bar called "The Great American Melodrama" on our right.

Edna Valley was soon met, a rich source of Nickel and Paragon, as well as a rich vineyard. What a combination, I thought. That wine must have a fairly unique sensation on the palate. All the classical music was clearly having an effect on my thought process.

The next stop was San Luis Obispo, where we were held slightly back from the station as our south travelling counterpart raced by us. This marked us nearing the end of the Santa Lucia Wilderness we'd been riding parallel to, and which we about to spectacularly cut through.

On the left as we departed the station, there was a practice Rodeo Ranch, where the cattle were loaded straight off the train into their pens.

The conductor made an announcement that if we looked out of windows to the right, from the back of the train we could see the front of the train as it took a slow but sharp right turn. What he didn't mention was the facility that came into view directly beneath the turn on the opposite side.

The California Men's Colony, a rather genteel name for a prison.

Apparently the jail is known as the garden spot of Californian prisons due to its "Wide variety of vocational, educational and psychological treatment programs".

Some notable, former inmates include Ike Turner, Timothy Leary, Suge Knight, Huey P. Newton, and Christian Brando, son of Marlon. It sent a shiver down my spine as a stark reminder of America's vast network of privately owned prisons. An old folk song, 'Down in the Valley (The Birmingham Jail)', leapt into my mind and I remembered the beautiful rendition sang in the Gene Wilder and Richard Pryor classic, *Stir Crazy*.

> *Down in the Valley,*
> *The Valley so low,*
> *Hang your head over,*
> *Hear the wind blow.*
>
> *Write me a letter,*
> *Send it by mail,*
> *Send it in care of,*
> *The Birmingham Jail.*
>
> *If you don't love me,*
> *Love who you please,*
> *Put your arms round me,*
> *Give my heart ease.*
>
> *Roses love sunshine,*
> *Violets love dew,*
> *Angels in Heaven,*
> *Know I love you.*

As we cut through the San Lucia Wilderness, through the centre of its mountains, I was distracted by another passenger, in the most pleasant way. One of the Spanish ladies (who were actually Costa Rican, I found out at this point) came back to her seat to gather her things. I politely asked whether they had any joy in the recovery of her friend's laptop, but no news had come through. Her name was Lori, and she had the brownest of eyes. She and her friend were on the way to a music festival. She asked me some details about myself and for my contact details, as they would be in San Francisco for a few days too, and since we were all strangers in a strange land, we should meet up. I thought, why not? Lori apologised for her English on a few occasions, to which I assured her she had no need, it was infinitely superior to my Spanish, and I resisted the temptation to exclaim, "Manchero! Cerveza por favor!" and, of course, "Su puta madre!"

We said our goodbyes after she had gathered her belongings, being sure not to repeat the unfortunate lapse of concentration that had perhaps cost her friend a laptop, and she returned to her on the viewing carriage. If I close my eyes I can still see her brown eyes, hoping that I'd see them again. I would not.

Barring the odd stop along the way, north we rode. Six and a half hours had passed since we'd set off from Los Angeles, and we were about thirty minutes over the halfway line.

Each stop introduced a new cast of characters to the train, as some of my fellow seasoned wayfarers departed to continue along on their own adventures.

Roughly thirty miles from the coast, the sky remained as blue and near-cloudless as ever. Birds of prey lingered above some unfortunate roadkill as we ran parallel with Route 101, coming closer to San Miguel.

We passed by some Mexican-looking churches, and the telegraph poles came to resemble huge crucifixes, springing up every 100ft like a never-ending Golgotha. To the right, the hills became less rugged looking, and the rockiness was replaced with soft, rounded curves.

Further on, starboard, an oil field began to totally dominate the land at the foot of the hills, huge mechanical drills and pullers going on for miles and miles and miles, gathering the fuel that keeps this nation lubricated and moving, for better or for worse.

After this expanse of man-made refinery, an orchard came into view, followed by a field of crops four times as big as the refinery and plant. Great to see it, but I was beginning to yearn for the Pacific once more. From my map checking and calculations, I reasoned that would be in another two and a half hours, closer to Salinas.

The flatlands meant that dust clouds were much more likely. Sure enough and true to form, they started to blow south against us, as we sat protected from them, nestled in our giant steel, railed capsule.

The mixture of the sun, six hours past its peak, and the distant mountain skyline silhouetted from the swirling dust cloud, really is quite beautiful. It made me rethink the landscape here.

Now listening to Rodriguez, the lines and the stark raw quality to the flatness shadowed from the mountain-scape is a beauty all onto itself. It may not have the glamour of a sea view or the majesty of a densely forested valley, but its very simplicity, almost like the music I was listening to was equally as spellbinding.

Beauty is very much in the eye, or the ear, of the beholder.

Then, in an instant, the blue skies surrendered to an all-encompassing and darkening cloud. A greyness swooped upon Salinas, mid-California, and all of a sudden the sunshine state looked not too dissimilar from any county on my native island. Only with more palm trees.

About 15 minutes outside of Salinas, as we neared Watsonville and the town of Freedom (I wondered if I could go there without any money?), the land became more Irish-looking in its greenery, and its wetlands resembled a bog. The sun continued its valiant effort to burst through the fortress of clouds that had engulfed overhead. I listened to David Bowie and smiled as a semi-drunk lady sitting adjacent to me talked to everybody that passed her by, generously offering a drink to anyone who listened. A few did. She was making her way to Seattle, and I admitted to myself that I was glad I was not.

Nine hours down, three to go, circumstance permitting.

The grasslands turned to green mountains on my left, then briefly to a mining facility of some sort, and I could've been passing near to Glenveagh National Park in County Donegal, barring the mine of course.

'When the Wind Blows' by Bowie played, followed by 'Moonlight Sonata'.

In the distance I could see a spot on the mountain face where the sun was winning its battle.

Pockets of blue sky were intercepting the gathered greyness, when suddenly we broke through into brilliant sunshine once more.

'Lawyers, Guns & Money' by Warren Zevon soundtracked this glorious moment, as the land opened up once more in perfect tandem with the dissipating and – for now – defeated clouds.

This was a victory party for the sun; I had to pull out the big guns.

Only Ms Martha Reeves and the Vandellas' 'Dancing in the Street' would suffice, and I contemplated getting a drink, despite my worry over the amount I'd consumed in the past 22 days. 'Nowhere To Run' came on.

Well, I thought, surely it would be rude not to?

The sun had sank further in the sky since its last appearance, and as we slowed to stop at a red signal outside the town of Morgan Hill, south of San Jose, it cast a beautiful sheen across the ubiquitous flat farming land, as the mountains flanked us in the distance on either side.

A tired stillness had settled both outside and within the train.

Finally, as we were pulling out of San Jose station, the sun had had enough, and she set, venturing off to give its life to another spot of the globe. As a parting gift, she lit the sky one last time in a soft orange and pink that had a tender, but fire-like quality, cushioning the final remnants of the blue that graciously accompanied us all for so long that day, as the sky grew darker, before finally turning to dusk.

It was the perfect accompaniment to my half bottle of Chardonnay and The Bobby Fuller Four, 'Let Her Dance'.

Emeryville was little over an hour away. It had been a beautiful day.

Now, just because the day was headed somewhere else, it in no way meant we weren't still in store for beauty along the way. Outside of the city, nearing Newark (the western one, unless we'd taken one hell of a detour and broken several laws of physics), wetlands graced us once more, and the reflection of the retreating day on the stiller-than-still water was dazzling. These reflections even rendered the rendering plants beautiful, despite spewing their poisons into the sky. The Dali-esque reflections in my Chardonnay-tinted glasses were a sight indeed.

Artistry in the contradictory symmetry.

Fittingly, as in keeping with my encroaching sozzledness-ness, 'You Can Call Me Al' by Paul Simon came on, and I started shifting weight in my seat, much to the bemusement of the nice elderly Latino lady who had shared a large portion of the journey with me.

Bass solo.

From there, on the final stretch, the journey took on a minimal beauty. Man-made light dotting the landscape.

Sometimes near, sometimes far.

Sometimes illuminating needfully, sometimes needlessly.

'Homeless', from the same album, *Graceland*, came on and I reflected on the time since I had become so.

I was on the west coast of America, playing a gig in a beautiful theatre the following night.

I had encountered great kindness and warmth from coast to coast.

Moonlight asleep on a midnight lake.

The cynical demon appeared on my shoulder warning me of a fall, I ignored him.

The wine helped no doubt, but for now, life was good, and I was enjoying the moment and learning to embrace just that – the moment.

Meanwhile, in the midst of my philosophical pondering, friendly drunk Seattle lady was now giving out free prescription drugs, like some sort of High Times, pilot light fish.

This is the 21st Century, people were biting.

Five minutes from Emeryville, my final stop, I jumped off at Oakland, home of the former Los Angeles Raiders (some 12 hours by train apart...to use an Americanism, go figure), for a smoke, just beside Jack London square.

The camaraderie and friendliness of my fellow passengers and JFK's fellow Americans touched me. Everybody helped everybody else out, one nation under a groove, and that groove was spellbinding. I hopped back on-board and gathered my things, saying a brief goodbye to the inebriated lady on her way to Seattle.

That had been one hell of a train journey.

Next time, I intend on doing it from North to South, the whole hog.

I took a short cab ride to the college town of Berkeley, where I was booked to stay at the Shattuck Plaza on Allston Way for the next few days, along with the band and crew of Gogol Bordello. When I arrived, Paolo greeted me enthusiastically and introduced me to Swax, merch guy extraordinaire, and all round great guy. Paolo and Swax were both excited that they had someone else to talk about football with. I was excited I had people to talk to.

I collected my key, took the elevator to the fifth floor, ditched my bags and guitar, then made my way back to the lobby. Another few members of the crew were now there: Kev, the stage manager, and Frankie the FOH (Front of House) engineer, and we made our way into town.

"What a whirlwind of a day," was the prevalent thing on my mind, as I enjoyed the company and jokes of my temporary associates and new friends.

25

The next morning was one of those days that I really should've had a hangover, but the nervous energy was enough to get me up, into the shower, and out of the hotel bedroom door. As I closed the door to my room, I discovered I was adjacent to the Presidential Suite.

Coincidence? Most certainly.

The lobby call in this beautiful hotel on this gorgeous Northern Californian day was at 12.30pm, and the venue we were headed to was The UC Theatre on University Avenue.

I reached the lobby with one minute to spare, quietly pleased with my timing, as I was intent on make a good impression. I noticed that there was some football on the television at the lobby bar, England were beating Australia 1-0 in an international friendly. A gentleman sat at the bar watching, and I noticed he had a tour laminate on. Buoyed and confident about the upcoming gigs, I introduced myself and told him I was so pleased to be joining them on the road for the next few days. To which I was greeted with a look of distinct confusion. I then noticed his laminate didn't say Gogol Bordello, but rather it had Above & Beyond emblazoned upon it. I quickly made my laughing apology, explained my mistake, and backed away, bravely.

The UC Theatre was quite literally just around the corner from The Shattuck Plaza Hotel.

We wandered in, accompanied by the local crew, via the rear doors. As everybody scuttled off to do their own particular jobs, I took in the surroundings.

The venue was beautiful, and bigger than anywhere I have played since going solo. Manchester and Brighton Cathedral were pretty big, but this had the highest capacity – 1450 to be precise – and it was sold out. "Not a bad spot for my first Californian gig", I thought.

Inspired by them and not wanting to walk around with a gaping jaw hanging open, I mirrored the professionalism of the crew and I took my guitar, found a quiet spot to clean it up and change the strings.

After I'd done what needed to be done, I set off in search of something cold, something that wasn't alcoholic or sugary. It was a hot day in Berkeley, and my stomach felt uncomfortably full due to the amount of beer I had drank in the past few weeks. I managed to pick up granola yoghurt with fresh strawberries that I'm sure aided me more than most things I had consumed in the past while.

The day before, as we had been going through nearby Oakland, I had been reminded of the legendary Californian writer, Jack London, as we passed by his eponymous square. For quite some time I'd been looking to pick up a copy of London's, *The Iron Heel*, which many saw as the precursor to such influential works as Aldous Huxley's *Brave New World*, HG Welles' *The Shape of Things To Come,* or indeed, George Orwell's 1984. This search had proved fruitless in bookshops the length and breadth of Ireland and the UK, but with a bit of luck, I reasoned, it shouldn't be the case in an area in which he is so celebrated. He was a San Francisco man, after all.

Today wasn't to be that day, as I investigated some truly magnificent bookshops, to no avail.

I pressed on with my meanderings, and found myself at the entrance to University College Berkeley, one of the world's great educational establishments.

As I strolled the grounds, it conjured up hitherto unknown perceptions of Ancient Rome, in the aesthetic, at the very least. Cautiously, I entered the University Library, not aware if visitors were permitted entry.

If anyone did ask, I was gonna try and use my Gogol Bordello AAA laminate to try and get myself out of any accidental trouble. Yep, I'm hilarious, but thankfully my humour wasn't called upon as nobody batted an extremely intelligent eyelid at me.

To the right-hand side as you enter, is a statue of that great American wit, Mark Twain. As you go through the doors to the ground floor library, you are greeted with a bust of Albert Einstein. I was in fine company. Those guys definitely shared a barber, at some stage at least.

There were a handful of people in that modestly sized, but most beautiful of libraries, and I didn't want to disturb anyone whatsoever, as I could have inadvertently botched a potential cancer cure or perpetual motion device, with one rogue sneeze. I'd hate to have that on my conscience.

Back into the sunshine I went, my brain feeling a little inadequate in this most high profile of educational facilities. It is only upon reflection that I see how true that last statement is. You see, after I left the library and made my way back to downtown Berkeley, the first stop I made was into a Comic Book store, looking for a copy of the alternate universe Superman tale, *Red Son*.

I expect UC Berkeley will be making their call with an offer of an honorary doctorate any day now...

Outside the UC Theatre, there was an extremely friendly security guard called

Bob with whom I had a brief, but entertaining conversation as I finished a cigarette.

"Welcome to the Executive Smoking section, my man," he opened with.

"Ha ha, it's very nice, thank you! My name is Tony, good to meet you."

"Tony, it's a pleasure. I'm Bob, great to have you here."

"Thanks Bob."

"Yeah, it's a palindrome, same both ways."

"It is indeed! Like racecar..."

"That's right! Like: A man, a plan, a canal: Panama."

"Huh?"

"A man, a plan, a canal: Panama."

"..."

"It's a palindrome kid! Well, sort of..."

"Wow, I'd never heard that one. That's a good one!"

"Sure is."

"You know, my name works out pretty cool backwards. I mean, it's not a palindrome, but it's a bit of advice I try to live by."

"Oh yeah, what's that?"

"...Y not?"

Bob erupted with laughter while I finished my cigarette, and then made my way back into the venue with a smile on my face after a friendly slap on his shoulder. This exchange with Bob helped to set me at ease about the night's impending gig. It chased off some of the niggling doubts that have a way of setting up camp within my subconscious before a performance. Some of these doubts are easily dealt with and dispelled before they even get a chance to pitch a tent, but there were some new ones that I hadn't experienced before.

I'm playing with a notoriously high energy, ten piece, gypsy punk rock band that have a dedicated following, to a sold out theatre in a city I've never played before, and its just little old me...yelling into a microphone and bashing my acoustic guitar...

The more I thought about it, the more I realised that I should forget it about it.

A paradox in itself, I know. Mercifully, the positive voice in my head – the little angel on my shoulder, if I may – was buoyed by the past month and how receptive I felt America had been to me, reminding myself on my own confidence in my ability, and how this isn't just what I do, it's also very much who I am, and that I had earned my chance, through circumstance admittedly, and that I could go out there and knock 'em dead. After all, my name spelt backwards was, "Y not".

Gogol soundchecked for just over two hours, and I watched from the back of the venue, enraptured by their musicianship, and by what a mesmerizing band leader the singer, Eugene Hutz was. Pointing the way and conducting each band member, whether it be beckoning new guitar player Boris forward, or getting accordion player Pasha to perform more pelvic thrusts, Eugene was in control.

The band themselves are made up of a glorious melting pot of cultures and nationalities, Ukrainian, Russian, Ethiopian, Ecuadorian, American, and Belarusian, mixing punk with gypsy with dub with rock, with even some jazz thrown in for good measure. Their soundcheck is more energetic than most bands' actual performances.

The sound man, Frankie (himself of Dutch and Thai descent) was doing an exquisite job in pulling the myriad frequencies into audible cohesion, and the lighting man, Gabe was getting the lighting rig all set, making the bulbs dance in glorious unison to the unfolding musical patchwork being expertly stitched together in front of my privileged ears.

All this and it was only the sound check, I couldn't wait for the actual battle.

After Gogol were done and had cleared the stage, I made my way up and introduced myself to the local crew who, were fantastically helpful. I set up my modest equipment, a guitar tuner and...well...my guitar.

In honesty, my soundcheck was done in about thirty seconds, but I needed to stay up there and play, if anything just to warm myself up, both vocally and dexterously. Besides, if I got off stage I'd more than likely be drinking beers and smoking to keep my idle hands and mind busy before the gig. So I stayed onstage and played my set, some songs once, some songs twice, and some songs that I wasn't planning on playing, but just for the vocal and guitar workout.

Doors opened at 8pm and the sold out crowd began to make their way in, straight towards the barrier at the front of the stage, despite the fact I wouldn't be on for an hour and Gogol, whom they were really waiting for, wouldn't be on for two.

My nerves were strangely absent, and I was somewhat calm.

About ten minutes before I was due to go on, I walked onstage to quickly fine tune my guitar. I kept my head down, and didn't once look at the gathered throng, and they largely ignored me.

I went backstage to grab a beer, a bottle of water, and to ditch my jacket and any money I had on my person (I always try to go on with no cash, or a lighter, in my pockets). The majority of Gogol Bordello had left the venue to either get something to eat, or to go back to the hotel around the corner. I was a little disappointed as I'd hoped they would hear my set, but I didn't let it bother me as I had a job to do, and I was intent on doing it well.

"Five minutes," said the venue stage manager, as he popped his smiling face around the door.

"You ready, man?" Paolo, our TM, enquired from his temporary workstation in the dressing room.

"Think so...Yeah, see you in 30 minutes or so," I replied. I then exited the dressing room to stand behind the curtain at the rear of the stage in the beautiful, cavernous venue.

The familiar sound of an audience murmuring permeated the venue, only a lot louder than I was generally used to, save for a few festival appearances with my old band, and the nerves began to creep. My stomach was awash with freshly awoken butterflies that had chosen a fine time to emerge from their pupae.

"Okay, I'll radio front of house to get the house lights dimmed then you're on. Cool, man?"

"Yep... yes... yeah, cool...thanks..." I replied whilst resorting to deep relaxing breaths to help quell the nerves.

"Cool, that's you man, you're on...good luck!"

Show time.

The house lights dimmed, and with that the illumination turned to the stage, and the audience murmur morphed to a building applause. I emerged from behind the curtain to rapturous roar from the assembled capacity crowd, and as they grew louder, the nerves in my gut retreated, a strange peace descending upon me. Everything slowed down as I told myself to savour this moment, and I raised my hand in appreciation and acknowledgement of their anticipation. My raised fist acted like a conductors baton, making the crowd cheer even louder as I strapped on my guitar.

"Good evening," I said, keeping it brief and simple before launching into my set.

The first track from my debut album, 'Our Truth Could Be Their Lie' was my chosen opener, as it has been many times before. Melodically, the bridge has a slight accidental resemblance to The Zombies' 'She's Not There', which seemed like a fitting opener. I started it with a mix of palm muted strumming interspersed with guitar licks that would hopefully set out my stall as not your average troubadour balladeering my way through life, which I'm sure some folk in the audience could have been wholly forgiving for thinking is what was about to unfold in front of them.

I wanted to make sure they knew this was a one man rock/blues/soul show.

My eyes remained open for the duration, giving the impression of staring down the crowd and showing no fear, when in reality I was looking between spaces, not making eye contact with anyone but from their point of view it looked like I was picking out adversaries amongst them and directing the venom suggested in some of the lyrics directly at them.

The same trick I had employed in New York. The same trick I employ at every gig.

During the middle eight, I began to "pedal on the G", as it's known, essentially just sitting on the chord of G minor, and slowly getting quieter whilst throwing in blues licks, hammer ons and hammer offs, at the end of each half or quarter bar. People started cheering.

I had them, and it felt really good. "*Savour this*", I said to myself again.

When I went about as soft as I could go, I hit them with a few lines from the blues standard 'Baby, Please Don't Go', which the crowd immediately responded to, so well is the song known, whether it be from Lightnin' Hopkins, Big Bill Broonzy, John Lee Hooker, or my fellow countrymen, Them. Momentarily returning me to Mikey's Dive Bar in Nashville. Cue the audience clapping along. "*Savour this...*" Building the volume up again, I segued back into the final bridge and chorus of my song with a final burst of dynamics and energy, before an abrupt stop, killing the last chord dead, not allowing it to reverberate or hang.

There was a millisecond of total silence in the room.

My heart stopped, and I momentarily couldn't breathe, as I philosophically thought, "*Oh fuck.*"

A million and one thoughts and feelings of terror surged through my spotlighted body, as I readied myself to make eye-contact with someone, anyone, in the front few rows.

The silence broke.

A unanimous roar of approval from suitably entertained and appreciative music fans rushed me like a tsunami of sound and emotion.

Top of the world, Ma. Top of the world.

But this was no time to soak in such moments and bask in them. I still had 25 minutes to get through and not drown. For now I was afloat and swimming, if I could ride this wave I'd be able to remember it for the rest of my life, and for all the right reasons.

I had a show to finish – these people needed entertaining, dammit! – and at this precise moment, in this precise location, onstage at the former Movie Theatre in Berkley Northern California, on Friday May 27th 2016, I was exactly the man for the job.

Before I started into my next song, I had to formerly introduce myself.

At a completely optimistic guess, I would say about 99.9% of the good people in attendance had no idea who I was. After all, I had been added to the bill only the week before, and I was not on the tickets or the advertising billings outside the venue.

"Hi, I'm VerseChorusVerse. Well, it's not my real name...my parents weren't that crazy. I'm Tony, but VerseChorusVerse is the name I use when...well...in these situations." I spoke slowly and enunciated carefully, ever aware that my accent is thousands of miles away from home, and the audience seemed to understand, reciprocating with laughter.

Praise be. Still swimming.

'Yet To Break', the final song from my most recent release, Say & Do (not that anyone here other than I would have known), was up next. An up-tempo folk stomper of a track, telling the tale of a protagonist wandering the earth, looking for somebody or something, and whether they could ever entice that special someone or something home to, in a sense, complete them. Sound familiar? The song's final verse laments and advises, "You must live your life as you must, my friends, you must live your life as you must..." It was the first time I'd sung that lyric and really felt the power I was trying to convey, as my trip across America seemed to make sense for a fleeting, glorious moment.

I don't know if it was the lyrics or the music, hopefully a combination of the two, that the audience connected to so much, but after the final strum of the song, once more the assembled peoples of the UC Theatre erupted into applause. "Savour it..." as I had thought so many times before in the past ten minutes lingered in my head as I held my hand to my chest and genuinely gasped for air, afloat on the wave.

"Okay, I used to be in an instrumental punk rock band, and I always had a whole bunch of effects pedals in front of me to, you know, manipulate the sounds and stuff. I don't have that anymore, just this guitar and my voice, but I'm gonna change my voice up a little here, like I used to with my guitar sounds way back then. I hope you like it, this is called, 'Have Some Soul.'"

This song was a bit of a gamble since it's such a slower tempo. The opening two songs had been folky, rock stomp-alongs, and this was very much a slow, bluesy soul number, that depends on a guttural yet soaring vocal. Think Tom Waits or Screamin' Jay Hawkins singing an Aretha Franklin song. Well, trying to sing an Aretha Franklin song.

The lyrics in this one shift swiftly from despair to survival, with a chorus refrain of, "Have some soul babe, it's all I know." The fourth time I sing the word "soul," the vocal lifts to a place where I feel my stomach rising into my ribcage and taking up residence between my lungs, then turning to a tonal whimper, before changing back to a bluesy rasp for the chorus' concluding line of, "...babe...it's all I know". Now, somewhere in the middle of the elongated fourth, "sooooooouuuuul", the audience let me know how much they enjoyed and appreciated my diaphragm gymnastics by cheering and screaming along with me.

"Duly noted", I thought. *"I'll have to go higher and hold it longer for the next and final chorus".*

As I reached the crest of the song, hitting that unhealthy, but oh-so satisfying 'soul' note, I could feel my diaphragm sending a message down into my once traumatised scrotum, despite and through the impenetrable metal gauze, telling my nuts, "C'mon fellas, we need you up here for a second," whilst my stomach brought my lungs level with my shoulder blades, and my Adam's Apple saw the stage lights for the first time in our co-existence.

The roar of approval from the audience grew swollen before peaking in frenzied cheers, the like of which I had been a part of, but never before on the receiving end for.

My balls, diaphragm, stomach, lungs, and Adam's Apple all hung in suspension as I held the note longer than I had ever managed before, willed on by the crowd, finally completing the line and song, as each piece of internal anatomy descended to its rightful position and home within me.

I am positive my face was as red as a supernova star, making my hair look blonde in comparison. The rush was incomparable. We had all hit that note together.

I didn't talk much, or offer an explanation about the next song (other than it was dedicated to fans of alliteration), 'Teddy Told A Tall Tale', for a couple of reasons.

1. I had talked quite a lot already and time was scarce if I planned on playing two more songs after this one.

2. "...had to high tail all the way to Moscow", is a lyric repeated in it a few times and there was a little bit of me that was worried it may offend some of the Russian members of Gogol Bordello.

The tune itself is a short, catchy little blues rocker, with a nice little breakdown in the middle that started the audience clapping along, impromptu, which is always the best way. Even better than that, they were in time with the song! Something which, I assure you, is not always a given.

As is more often than not the way with life, none of my above fears were realised, and the song went down a treat. My confidence was sky high, and so long as a meteor didn't crash into the venue, I felt as though it was plain sailing from here on in, and I should really, really enjoy myself.

My penultimate song, 'Shakedown Sally' is a real nod to American Rock n Roll, so I dedicated it to everyone in attendance. From the local crew to the bar staff to the security to the audience, and finally to Gogol and their crew, each group elicited a bigger cheer than before. As the cheering subdued slightly, I pulled my phone out from my back pocket and asked if the crew could turn the house lights on just for a second, much to the crowd's delight, as I backed away from the microphone to take a picture of them in their unified glory.

"Look how beautiful you all are!" I shouted from a distance toward the mic, as I tried to fit everyone in frame.

'Shakedown Sally' was written at a time when I was more consciously than ever before trying to get away from the standard singer-songwriter fare, and also at a time when I happened to be listening to way too much Gene Vincent.

Who am I kidding... it's not possible to listen to too much Gene Vincent.

The audience agreed in kind, clapping and stomping along with me. It was like having the world's biggest percussive section playing with me.

Glorious.

I didn't want it to end. Although, I knew it must and told myself again to remember all of this and how it looked, sounded, smelled, and felt.

"Guys, this...this...YOU... you have been amazing, thank you so, so, *so* much...I will never forget this...seriously...thank you..." I offered to them, not knowing if I've ever said a truer word. "This is my last song."

"Nooooo!" came the reply from a few hundred people. I couldn't quite believe it; that's not supposed to happen to unknown opening acts.

"Wow! Thank you! I'm afraid it is, but if you guys want, I'll come back sometime...if you'll have me?"

"Yeeeeeaaaahhhh!" came the unanimous response.

Truly humbled, I held my hand to my heart in acknowledgement and sincerest appreciation that they had enjoyed themselves. I led them on a few more cheers for Gogol Bordello, and introduced my last song.

"I'm gonna finish on a cover, if that's cool with you? You may actually be able to sing along, imagine that?! This is a fuckin' great song, a classic. I've changed it up a little bit by putting it in a minor key, LETS HEAR IT FOR THE MINOR KEY! This is an American classic, this was written in the forties by a songwriter called Merle Travis and made enormously popular by a singer called Tennessee Ernie Ford." Cheers began to ripple through the audience, some knowing from that clue what I was about to play. "Ladies and gentlemen, thank you one last time so very much. Ladies, gentlemen, this song is called 'Sixteen Tons'." There was that roar again.

Beautiful.

A healthy proportion of the crowd sang every word with me, and I knew I had to do a big finish. I had to do my best Robert Plant impression for my final note, holding it until breaking point before crashing down on the final chord. So I did just that.

If the long, pushed note on 'Have Some Soul' had been big, this one needed to be monumental. To borrow a sentiment from Richard Pryor; taking a deep breath, I reached deep, deep down into the South Pole, gained momentum in South America, swept up through Mexico before unleashing in California, a note so strong, and ordinarily beyond me, that I started seeing stars, and my left leg went weak. *"Enough is enough!"* my body told me, and I finished the song, just in time. Any longer and I would've passed out, I'm sure of it. This push of my physical limits hadn't gone un-noticed, and for one final surge, the audience showed me in kind, via their own volume, just how much they appreciated it.

And I bowed to them, so thankful that I had been given the chance to share in that communal experience with them. A few folk even called out for more. Unbelievable, are they trying to kill me?

In all seriousness though, I would have played for them all night, but then that wouldn't have been as special.

They had carried me and enabled me to swim.

To swim, until I couldn't see land.

After my performance, I returned to the backstage area were some of Gogol Bordello were gathered, readying themselves for their own show. The first of a long, wonderful summer of gigs across America, then Eastern Europe to the west.

Boris and Sergev immediately congratulated me and thanked me for my set, showering superlatives on me, and I was so honoured for my set to be recognised by them. Gabe, Kevin and Matt all patted me on the back on their way out of the dressing room as they prepared to get ready for the headliner's performance. I grabbed a beer and said thanks to everyone for the opportunity, and made my exit to give the band space to prepare themselves, ducking out the backstage door for a cigarette.

As I inhaled and exhaled, an unshakeable wave of euphoria was still washing itself over me. It had been the biggest gig of my solo career, the most people I had ever sang in front of, played acoustic guitar in front of, told stories and jokes in front of.

Just me, my guitar and my voice.

No light show, no high octane stage antics, no trickery, nobody even knew who I was. Only the songs in the barest and most stripped down form, and it had been a resounding success. It was one of the best cigarettes I've ever had. Post coital gig smoke. I had earned a whiskey. Or two.

Returning inside, I didn't want to intrude on Gogol's pre-gig prep, so I showed my pass to security ("I know who you are, great show man!") and made my way out to the audience to get a drink. The place was jam packed, and I'd have to squeeze past a lot of people if I was to get to the bar and get my well-earned whiskey.

Being a short guy, this is easier – if a little smellier – than it is for most, as I can battle through the fields of armpits almost un-noticed. Nearing the rear of the venue the crowd began to thin out a little as some of the audience had exited the building for a smoke or some air, and as the crowd thinned out, my passage was much easier, as people started to recognise this little red-headed Irish fellow who moments before had been roaring at them onstage.

"Dude! It's you! Hey Rob! Denise! Sarah! Look, its the guy who was just on! VerseChorusVerse! Dude you were great! Can we get a picture?"

We hustled together to take a picture, which was a little awkward as Rob, Denise, Sarah and (I regrettably forget the original fellows name...let's call him 'Rudiger') Rudiger were all healthy young Americans and at least a foot taller than me. But through sheer grit, determination, and resilience, we made it work, dammit. I thanked them again and turned to join the queue at the bar.

"Dude!" Rudiger called after me, as I was about to be served.

"Yes, dear Rudiger?" I turned, smiled and replied.

"Dude, do you wanna drink?" Rudiger sweetly enquired.

"Oh its fine, honestly, I couldn't possibly..." I lied: I could.

"Dude, no way, let us buy you a drink!" Rudiger insisted.

"Well, if you insist, Rudiger. That would be very kind, thank you."

"Pleasure is all ours, thank you for a great show! Whiskey?" he had read my stereotyped Irish mind.

"You read my stereotyped Irish mind!"

"Haha! No sweat, Rob...come up here! Five Jameson please!" he enthusiastically ordered before turning to me, "Jameson cool with you?" I smiled and reiterated that he had again read my stereotyped Irish mind. Denise and Sarah then joined us at the bar for our shots (I had wanted to actually drink and enjoy a whiskey, but I was not about to be so rude, nor idiotic, as to turn down a free Jameson). It was then that I asked who the fifth one was for?

"You, of course!" Rudiger responded, to much amusement from the others.

"Ah...obviously!" remembering with a smile, my stereotype.

"Cheers!" we all exclaimed, before I paused, keen to fully stereotype myself. "Or as we say back home, Slainte!"

"Slainte!" we chorused and promptly made the whiskey vanish. We all made the involuntary tick that necking a generous measure of whiskey can make one do, and then exhaled, happy to have kept it down.

I looked at the bottom of my glass, satisfied that it was drained, and made that weird noise that you also only do after imbibing such a tempting poison. My eyes raised from the glass and up toward my new friends, who were towering above me, smiling and staring down at their new willing whiskey disposal unit. Rudiger extended his hand forward, pushing the surplus, fifth Jameson toward me. Rob, Denise and Sarah all expectant smiles and eyes upon me, their focus darting between me and the full glass.

"Oh yeah! Um...I...haha..." I nervously laughed, perilously aware that all I had eaten that day was some yoghurt, granola, and strawberries, and my stomach was all giddy from the high of the gig. Still, these very nice people had bought me a drink, well, two drinks, and I was not going to be so rude as to turn them down and set an Irish stereotype back that has endured and tarnished our nation and its diaspora for centuries now.

"Slainte!", I shouted as I grabbed the drink from Rudiger, then opened my throat so as to not let it touch the sides, pouring it down briskly to a loud cheer from my three fresh cohorts. My eyes filled with whiskey tears and my stomach clenched like a nation's collective rectum in the midst of a penalty shoot-out during the World Cup.

"AHHHHHhhhhhh..." I exhaled, silently praying that my constitution was strong enough to hold it down, which thankfully, it was.

"Rob, Denise, Sarah and Rudiger...My *dear, dear* Rudiger...thank you so much for your generosity. I'm gonna go and get some air, but it was a pleasure to meet you and I'm so delighted you enjoyed yourselves, have a great night." And before I departed, I thought they may get a kick out of one more cliché, "Enjoy the b'jaesus outta Gogol!"

I gave each one of them hug and made my way out to the front of the venue to get a lungful of air and make sure I kept that second whiskey down.

The night air was warm and pleasant, as were the people. I was either greeted, high fived, back slapped or kissed on the cheek by almost everyone I passed. I sensed a glow of positivity and appreciation from these transatlantic strangers, and I repeated the mantra that I had done onstage, "...*savour this*..."

From inside, a cheer grew in volume and everybody outside finished their smokes or halted their conversations mid-sentence to hurry back in for the beginning of Gogol Bordello's set.

Everything went into slow motion and I reached into my inside pocket for my tobacco.

I rolled a cigarette, smiled to myself, and watched America happen all around me.

I felt in love.

26

The next day we were playing the Uptown Theatre in Napa, as an official after-show party from the BottleRock Music Festival that Gogol were due to play the following day.

These two days would prove to be a whirlwind, as I settled into the good company of the band and crew.

Lobby call the next morning was at 1230, and I just about made it. I had stayed up the previous night until about 4am, enjoying the company of people outside the hotel, exchanging stories, drinks, smokes, and laughs. Quietly and without any notice, I'd made my way to bed. I've been told in the past that this is known as an "Irish Goodbye", so I was perfectly qualified and justified in exercising it. I was riding in the band van, and I took my place in the far, back left corner, nestled away in an observation point. Everybody made their way into the van on time with the exception of Eugene. He was nearby in a diner and had just phoned Paolo, as he had no money on him and needed someone to settle the bill. No big deal. After the bill at the diner had been dealt with, he appeared and announced himself to us with a bombastic, "Alright Immigrants?! Are we ready to roll?"

Napa Valley, here we come.

Our hotel, the Marriott, was about 15 miles away from Napa in Vallejo, and right beside a Six Flags recreation park with a breakneck looking roller coaster, which the majority of us agreed we simply must check out. Paolo proceeded to get us checked in, and then told us that the crew had twenty minutes before they had to head into downtown Napa, and the band would be picked up again in three hours. Logistically, this was a bit of a nightmare for Paolo as the traffic was insane, due to the big music festival on. He would essentially have to drive in to connect with the promoter of both tonight's show and the following day's festival to collect passes, and then drive straight back to get the band to bring them in for soundcheck. Factoring in the two hours he had already driven from Berkeley to Napa AND the ninety plus degree heat, this was a long time to be in a van. Paolo being Paolo, a total pro, he didn't complain once. Anything to make the show that night the best possible show it could be. The band had to be comfortable, and that is what he was gonna guarantee.

At this stage, through no cause or action of anybody else, I felt like I would be overstepping a mark by travelling in with the band for soundcheck, they should have their own space. I was, after all, very much the new guy. So I opted to travel in for the crew call. Besides, why be trapped in a hotel room beside a freeway when I could go into Napa and check out the town? After I had changed my guitar strings, of course. I'm a professional, dammit.

The Uptown Theatre, inside and out, is a gorgeous Art Deco style building.
It first opened in 1937 – positively ancient in Californian terms – and closed in 2000 due to the big multiplexes luring attendees elsewhere, to bland and soulless cinema warehouses. It was purchased by a real estate developer in 2003, who put together a consortium of investors, including Francis Ford Coppola, to restore the building to its former glories and re-open it as a live entertainment venue. The Theatre finally reopened in 2010 and had played host to all manner of legends there, in the ensuing six years since.

From the legendary B.B. King to Dr John to Lyle Lovett to John Prine to Band of Horses to Cyndi Lauper to Willie Nelson to Merle Haggard to the one and only Emmylou Harris, they had all graced the stage in this palatial and beguiling entertainment edifice.

Thankfully, I knew nothing of this until after I had played, otherwise I may have felt more nervous than I was. My nerves weren't formidable, but they were still present, and I was worried that last night may have been a fluke.

Maybe the audience were all drunk? Maybe there were all higher than the sun? I mean, I had noticed a great deal of marijuana being smoked in around the city and venue, could they have been so stoned that a monkey with a make-shift shoebox guitar could have elicited the same reaction I had been so fortunately afforded?

I reasoned that I should try my best to ignore these pre-gig jitters by taking a walk and trying to find some ice cream and root beer. A noble quest, I'm sure you'll agree.

Strolling around Napa, it seemed that the "ghetto" which we were supposedly right beside, was probably nicer than most places I had rented in the 17 years since I left the nest. I am, of course, making judgements as an outsider looking in, and that may not be the reality, but it certainly looked a lot better than the projects I had seen in some US cities, and the estates and tower blocks I had experienced in the UK, Ireland, Europe, and Russia.

I observed a dearth of populace, forgetting that there was a music festival on just across the bridge. I also remember thinking that none of the buildings seemed to be more than four storeys high, which, given the San Andreas fault-line upon which California's fate lies, I figured was a pretty good bit of town planning.

Damn, it was hot here, down in the valley.

Finally, after circumnavigating several blocks, the shade very much determining my path, I found a chocolatier cafe that served ice cream and I indulged my fancy. I watched very little happen in the street in front of me, and had a race with my ice cream to see who would melt first.

The poor thing didn't stand a chance, so I put it out of its misery, and took myself back to the Uptown, where Gogol were beginning their in-depth soundcheck/rehearsal. I mulled around backstage, ate too many crisps, and drank enough water to be solely responsible for California's much discussed drought problems. Not that I didn't give back in abundance, and with greater frequency as both the years and I advance.

When sound-checks were done, I lingered around the stage, noodling on my guitar for a while. This will sound contrived and clichéd to the sceptics out there (congratulations on making it this far in the book by the way), but I let the my fingers do as they pleased, and they carved out a gorgeous melody as I sat alone in this gorgeous, cavernous auditorium.

A simple picked melody, and one I was sure I had never played or come across before.

One that danced between major and minor, conjuring feelings and unseen images of both hope and loss in an endless cycle.

The glory of creation and the melancholy of isolation.

Answers presenting themselves, only to be met with more questions, but as long as the chords looped, neither could be right nor wrong.

I hummed a counter melody over the top and added a few flourishes here and there to the original line on the guitar, all without thought, relying solely on musical instinct and where the music decided it should go next.

It was as if the theatre and all the wondrous music that had been performed there – the memory of it etched into the very walls, ceiling and floor – was willing my fingers and voice to compose for them. And it wasn't just the music that had been played there over the years; it was the feelings of the people.

The people that had witnessed the music AND the films.

After all, this had been a movie theatre far longer than it had been a live entertainment venue.

Who can possibly tell how many first kisses were had in this establishment?

How many first dates? How many last dates? Given how long ago it had first opened its doors, it's reasonable to assume that as some stage or another someone may have died whilst within these four walls. Conversely, on a slightly more positive note, chances are even higher that some couples left here, only to conceive new life.

Emotions will have swung from both extremes of the spectrum in here, be it from the tension and terror of a well executed thriller or horror film, to aching laughter from a masterly comedy, to uncontrollable tears from a devastating tragedy or a classic romance.

This building will have seen it all.

So I let that inform my playing.

I looked up after a little while of being lost within the music's otherworldly spell, only to notice Frankie, Gogol's wonderful mad scientist of a sound man, standing a few feet away from me, enraptured by the refrain.

I stopped to say hello.

"Hey, Frankie, you good?"

"Yes yes, but please, *please*, don't stop!" he answered, so I smiled in appreciation of his enjoyment, and played on as requested.

"Beautiful, just beautiful," he sighed, and I played on with my physical audience of one, and my ghostly audience of thousands, for another fifteen minutes.

Showtime approached, doors opened, and people started to make their way in.

I realised I had left my onstage tuner plugged in and, fearing that the battery may die mid-performance, emerged from behind the curtain to remove my guitar cable from the input.

"Tony! Hey Tony! Hey, VerseChorusVerse!" a voice called out from the thinly assembling audience. I looked up and there was a middle aged gentleman smiling and waving at me.

Pleasantly puzzled and not forgetting my manners, I jumped off the stage to go and say hello, having no idea who this friendly man was.

"Hey...um...man! I'm Tony," I awkwardly opened with, as I offered my hand in greeting.

"Dan, I'm Dan. I know who you are! Saw you last night in Berkeley, you killed it!"

I blushed, beholden.

"Really, I'm not kiddin'! So good, loved it. So did my son and his girlfriend. Josh! Laura! Over here, look!"

Dan's son Josh and his girlfriend Laura made their way over from their seats.

"Hey Josh, hey Laura! Didn't we meet last night?" extending my hands again, genuinely thrilled that I had made an impression.

"We sure did!" Laura and Josh responded in sweet, wide eyed stereo. "You were *Awesome!*" Laura continued. "Yeah you were! Can't believe you remember us!" Josh enthusiastically added.

Never being the best at accepting compliments, I felt I must take myself down a peg or two. "Well I hope you don't mind hearing all the same songs, stories, jokes and anecdotes tonight then?" I queried, half joking and half fearful, making a mental note that I had to change up some of the in-between song tales.

"Not at all!"

"Looking forward to 'em!"

"Can't wait!"

They all beamed at me and I was completely taken by their optimistic platitudes.

I thanked them again several times, and told them I hoped they enjoyed the show before saying my good byes, and returning to the intimate confines of our dressing room, shared with my fellow non-US nationals.

There was roughly 30 minutes until I was due on, so I had my first beer and chatted a little with the crew, and before I knew it I was onstage, once again to a packed house, and once again repeating to myself..."*Savour this*".

I finished, once again, with Sixteen Tons. Bellowing out the final screamed note, holding it for as long as I could without either passing out or doing irreparable damage.

Then, without warning, something remarkable happened. I crashed down on the parting A

Minor, took one step back, then bowed. Bringing my head back up, I was greeted with the vision of the audience, all 837 of them, risen from their seats, standing, applauding, and roaring for more.

My mantra of *"savour this..."* escaped me, and I regret I didn't acknowledge it more. My mind was more concerned that I may have ran over time, and not wanting to piss off the headliners, I should probably be getting off the stage.

That's not to say I didn't bow a few more times, hold my guitar in the air, place my hand on my heart and show my appreciation, but I sadly didn't drink it in and take a recording of it in my mind. Anyway, it's not the support act's place to bask in another band's audience, and I knew that.

It was only when I came offstage and the stage manager stopped me in my tracks, that it began to hit me.

"Buddy, I've worked in venues all over the States, and never in twenty years have I seen a support get a standing ovation..."

Paolo, the TM was making his way past me and put his hand on my shoulder. "Holy shit Tony", in his tamed Italian accent, "You fucking killed it, that was awesome! A fucking standing ovation, great job, man."

It was only then that it started to sink in. I could still hear the crowd cheering. I felt 100ft tall and made my way back to the dressing room, where I was going to come down to earth again.

Not with a crash, but a shot of reality was due, albeit a shot of weird, twisted, affluent California showbiz type reality. So, not reality at all, I guess?

Entering the dressing room, I was afforded the warmest of greetings from everyone. I felt like I had done my duty to the best of my ability. The crowd was fervently awaiting them now, hyped as could be.

"Excellent set, man. Great voice," a strange but familiar face told me. I thanked him and crossed over to the small outdoor section, trying to place where I knew his face from.

He was engaged in conversation with Eugene, and they were holding court. Clearly, they had known each other a long time as various old times were raised and finished with uproarious laughter rather than actual endings to the stories. Everybody was listening and laughing, whether they knew the end of the story or not. Laughter is infectious, to state the obvious.

Eugene reached for his phone and, as if part of due process and expectancy, he asked his friend, "Alright, shall we do this?" before putting his arm around him, and proceeding to take a picture of the two of them. His friend, this face that I knew from somewhere, contorted his features into a standard punk rock comedy grimace.

My memory pulled into alignment, just as his eyes, nose and mouth did the opposite.

The man in question was Tre Cool, drummer from Green Day.

I'd only ever seen him pulling stupid faces over the years in their music videos or photo shoots. So, fittingly; that was how I recognised him.

I'd grown up loving Green Day. They came into my life shortly after Kurt Cobain had exited his, and left a 'power trio rock' shaped hole in mine.

They offered a bit of levity from grunge, but still serving up big slices of radio friendly isolation and self-loathing, which was perfect for a thirteen year old coming to terms with their changing world and body.

I stood my distance and finished my cigarette feeling a little star struck, and it was at this point that Eugene broke off his conversation with his old friend, and came over to me with a huge smile, extending his hands toward me.

"Man! You did so great! Thank you for getting them ready! I was watching from side of stage. I am pumped!" He squeezed my shoulder again and turned away before I had a second to thank him, headed for the bathroom.

I just had to get a picture of Mr Green Day and I.

Instagram, Twitter, Facebook... they'd all love that. With retrospect, I'm really quite embarrassed by all of this. I've never once in my life thought it a good idea to intrude upon someone without having had a genuine conversation with them first, or perhaps to warn them they're about to be hit by a falling planet.

Knowing that my friend in New York, Gentleman Jesse, was best of friends with the singer from Green Day, Billie Joe Armstrong, I reasoned that Tre and him must be buddies too.

There was my 'in', a mutual acquaintance.

Tre was talking to Alfredo (former Beastie Boys drummer) and Tommy the bassist, chatting about old times and sharing a laugh. That was until 'Arsehole Candidate: Number One' (that's me, incase you've forgotten) sidles up to them.

"Hey!" I blurt out as soon as there is a dip in conversation, which naturally there was since some red headed buffoon had invited himself to join the three of them.

"Hey. Yeah great show man." Tre looked me up and down, justifiably enough wondering what I was doing, but probably suspicious enough of what was about to be asked.

"I...uh...I was just staying in New York with your friend Jesse Malin!" I offered with as little context as an idiot can muster.

"Oh. That's great." He turned to look at Tommy and Alfredo, who unfortunately for him had looked away thinking that their conversation was over and he was now talking to me.

He looked back at me and, bless him, tried to steer a conversation somewhere. "Staying with Jesse huh? Boy, that must've been somethin' for ya. Right in the heart of the village. Cool."

"Yeah, it was great. He's a fantastic guy. I...uh..." I'd already lost any interest the guy may have had, and was floundering badly. He looked away, so I figured I'd cut my losses and just ask for a picture.

"Cou...could I get a picture?"

He paused, and looked me up and down again. "Maybe later."

"S...sorry?" I spluttered.

"I said maybe later, y'know," as he subtly motioned to the rest of the room. "I'm just hangin' at the minute, haven't seen these guys in a while."

"I...yeah...of course...thanks...sorry...thanks..." I mumbled as I slinked off, crestfallen, shorn of my 100ft confidence, and reduced to the morale of a single cell organism that's just realised it's in a petri dish.

I had to get out of there, I was sure that everyone had heard every word of our encounter and were intent on pointing and laughing me out of the room. Although nothing could have been further from the truth. Who the hell cared?

Me, that's who, and me alone.

Grabbing a beer, I made my way downstairs to go to the smoking section outside, whilst quietly reflecting and fuming. The cocktail of emotions that went through my head in that ten second journey from backstage to outside was portentous. I was up and down again, quicker than a fiddler's elbow.

How rude! That's MY backstage! I performed! I don't care how many albums he's sold!

Actually, he's allowed an off night. How many people does he have asking that everyday over the last twenty years?

Yeah, but without fans he's nothing!

He was with friends and you interrupted.

Yeah, but...but...

But nothing. You asked him for the wrong reasons. Now grow up and remember how cool everything and everybody has been. Tre from Green Day thought you were great, as did Eugene and the rest of the band, and most importantly, you wilfully expectant gobshite, you got a standing ovation from the audience. You're in Napa Valley, California. Catch a grip and be thankful, for crying out loud.

Okay...you're right...you win...

Of course I'm right, now drink that beer, shut up and enjoy yourself.

27

The next morning I awoke bleary eyed and confused – as had become common – to the horrifying sound of hundreds of people screaming in terror. It took a second or two for it to register correctly, my mind blurring between being awake and asleep and not knowing whether I was in the midst of a night terror or a waking nightmare.

More screams. Dear, mercy.

I was most definitely awake. I sat bolt upright in my bed.

"Good god", I thought.

It was blood curdling.

What hell is unfolding outside my window?

An earthquake? A fire? Surely, an alarm would be sounding? Some sort of attack? Be it terrorist or worse yet, Godzilla? Sweet Jesus, what is happening? What abomination of events have I awoken to?

As the screaming dipped then intensified once more, I scrambled from my bed and pulled back my curtains, preparing myself for the undiluted awfulness I was about to witness.

Oh. That's right.

Our hotel was beside a huge Roller-coaster.

A more harrowing, but highly effective alarm system I've never known.

I was now more awake than I had been in several weeks. Feeling a heady mix of intense relief and bizarre disappointment that Godzilla wasn't mid attack, I showered and gathered a few bits and pieces for the day ahead.

Today was the final day of my Gogol Bordello adventure, but unfortunately I wasn't performing with them. Instead I was their guest at the BottleRock Music Festival back in the city of Napa, and I took solace in thanks of that.

Taking my notebook, my factor 50 sun block, a large bottle of water, my tobacco/papers/filters, and a little bit of home-grown Californian weed that had knocked me for six the previous night, I proceeded to join up with the band and crew in the lobby, and we made our way to the festival.

BottleRock was a relatively new festival, and played host to internationally known acts as well local bands. It was also a showcase for the great foods and wines available in the county. The headliners this year were Stevie Wonder, Florence and the Machine and the Red Hot Chili Peppers.

I noticed that SOAK – a fantastic songwriter from Derry – was on the bill for early that day too. Although, alas, she had already played by the time we arrived on site.

Soak had opened for me in Dublin's Workman's Club some four and a half years previously. She was sixteen then and the talk of the country thanks to her song, 'Sea Creatures'.

I was immensely happy for her and how far she had come, so I thought I would message her on Twitter to ask if she was still around, and if she wanted to meet up, all these miles from home and a few years since we had last seen each other. As I clicked on her profile I discovered that she had since un-followed me.

Being the ever mature individual, I reciprocated the sentiment. *"That'll show her"*, I thought. I am 35 years old.

Gogol Bordello were third from top on the bill, followed by The Lumineers and Red Hot Chili Peppers, so they were afforded a decent sized tent backstage. Well, it would be a decent size for most bands, but Gogol were a ten piece band, with a seven strong crew, and a haplessly handsome and modest red headed hanger on. Sensing that the right thing to do would be give them some space, I pinched a few beers from the fridge, announced that I was going walkabout, and set off on my merry way to investigate.

Taking leave of the artist's area, I sat underneath a tree and lathered up on the Factor 50 sun screen I had brought with me. I drank a beer and rolled a rollie with a peppering of marijuana for good measure. I tucked the exotic jazz cigarette behind my ear and then made my way towards the front of stage area. Before leaving the backstage enclave, I noticed a bar where nobody seemed to be exchanging currency for beverages. Intrigued and hopeful, I approached and asked for an IPA as well as a glass of prosecco, all they asked in return was some ID and my to see my wristband.

This seemed like a reasonable enough request so I duly obliged and they rewarded my obedience with said booze, free of charge. Marvellous.

Temperatures were sitting around 90 degrees – like a right angle – and the local populace were dressed fittingly for the heat: canvas shoes or sandals, shorts, bikini tops, vests, or topless. I defiantly strode around in a pair of heavy brown boots, thick denim jeans, and a tight black T-shirt, laden with drinks, attracting curious looks for my choice of attire, along with my reflective white skin. Bodies were strewn across the blanketed grass. Some people were creating their own make-shift tents out of blankets against the barrier to seek some temporary refuge from the unforgiving sun overhead. I kept myself to the sides and sought any natural shade I could, whilst observing all the beautiful people having a wonderful time of it, exchanging smiles all the while, as is only fitting on such a beautiful day, feasting on the music and the atmosphere.

The alcohol I'd brought disappeared much too quickly, and I made short work of the now lukewarm bottle of water I had in my leather hold-all. I found another entrance backstage – having circumnavigated the live arena – and ducked back to find another free bar, where I ordered another IPA, and smoked my diet joint.

Alcohol and weed, no matter how moderate the intake, will always intensify the other. This, coupled with the sunshine and my empty stomach, all proved to be a heady concoction as I wobbled and giggled my way back to the artist's area, knowing I could get my hands on some much needed food there.

When I returned to Gogol's tent, they had left already to prepare for their performance on the main stage. I joined a short queue to get a small pizza just outside of the catering tent, after which I felt a lot more human. Swax, from the crew appeared and after a brief conversation we both made our way to the side of the stage, just in time for the start of their set. I sat on a flight case beside Kev the stage manager, and watched a powerful performance in front of several thousand festival revellers, and again witnessed a masterful showcase of both musicianship and crowd entertaining.

It was, as it had been the past two nights, electrifying, and slowly but surely brought me round to feeling a lot more compos mentis once more.

When they had finished, I returned to the artist area on foot. Whilst walking back I bumped into Hilary and Dancy whom I had met the night before. We sat outside the tent and leisurely watched events unfold around us, whilst chatting and getting to know each other better. Gabe, Matt, and Frankie from the crew joined us, and soon Boris too. Hilary and Dancy said goodbye for now, Boris rolled another smoke, and we giggled the next hour away as The Lumineers began to play in the distance.

We collectively realised we hadn't been to see any other bands, and checked the line up to see who was on next and where. Husband and wife guitar duo Rodrigo Y Gabriela were just about to start so Boris, Frankie, and I managed to build up the will to take the walk and see them, despite our now stoned beyond compare state of being.

Boris had never heard them so Frankie and I excitedly filled him in on who they were and what they were all about. I believe we settled on describing them as a brilliant mix of flamenco and thrash metal, on acoustic guitars....dude.

A true stoned description, I'm sure you'll agree.

It turned out to be a very apt description however, as the last song they played was the Metallica classic, 'Master of Puppets', and to add the proverbial cherry on top, Metallica's bassist, Robert Trujillo, joined them onstage for a thrilling conclusion to a wonderful set.

The bus call was looming over our heads, so we walked back to the tent to see what was happening. Paolo told us we had just under an hour before we were due to hit the road, so Boris and I thought we may as well check out the Chili Peppers for a few minutes, who were beginning their headliner slot on the main stage.

As we headed there we bumped into Hilary and Dancy once again, who decided to join us. We grabbed a few beers from the complimentary bar, and exited the back stage confines to join the thousands of expectant music lovers out front. We battled our way through for a few minutes, but it was so packed we really only got about 30 feet from the exit/entrance. Dancy lit a fresh smoke and passed it round the three of us. This was by far the strongest of all the smokes I had partaken in during the day and, true to form, the alcohol combined with it to make me grinning, paranoid mess.

I'm never great in big crowds, never mind with a head full of weed and a belly full of booze, so I think I lasted all of about five minutes before I decided that the sound was awful (we were positioned in an awkward spot in fairness). I couldn't see anything but the backs of punters a lot taller than me and, to top it all off, the heat was too much. I mumbled this much to Boris and Dancy, and made my way back to the bus pick up point where I boarded the stationary vehicle, and barring the odd grunt, I sat silently the whole way back to our hotel, a stoned and drunk shadow of a man, spirits dropping a touch as I acknowledged I was nearing the end of my time with this wonderful and welcoming band of immigrants.

Rock & roll. Still, I was aware that the night was rather young, and if I could snap out of this, I'm sure there would be a little more partying to be done at the Marriott, or elsewhere.

28

Back at the hotel I had a quick shower to try and reanimate my mind, body, and soul.

There was a part of me that wanted to shut my eyes for twenty minutes, and hope that there was something happening after that. Probably not too unreasonable a request to make of one's self, but I was sure that a twenty minute nap would turn into a four or five hour slumber, and I perished the thought of missing any fun on my last night with the band and crew. Thankfully the shower did the trick, and I felt once again ready to re-join the human race.

Out front, Tommy, Boris, Frankie, Matt, and Pasha were sharing beers, wine, vodka, and laughs. As I joined them a few of them laughed and greeted me with, "Hey Tony! You're still alive! Haha! Smoke?" before putting a beer in one hand and a smoke in the other. Who was I to refuse such cross-global hospitality?

This continued for several hours with some people coming and some people going. After a while it dwindled down to just Boris and I, buying beers in turn, and comparing tales of our respective paths, and how we'd ended up outside the Marriott Hotel in Vallejo, California.

We'd been talking for an hour or so, and by this point it was nearing midnight. It rolled around again to being my round. I ducked back inside to get us a couple more beers. After I'd paid for them at the bar, I noticed Eugene was sitting on a seat right beside the entrance, apparently pre-occupied with his phone. Or so I thought.

"Hey Tony man, you wanna go to a party?" he asked with a mischievous smile.

"Sounds good, I'm in. You wanna beer?" I replied, reasserting to myself that this was my final few hours with the band, and that I should definitely make the most of them.

Eugene leapt from his seat with an even bigger smile, swiping the beer from my hand with an appreciative nod, before approaching the lady at reception. With the manners of a saint, he asked if she would be so kind to order a cab to take us back into Napa.

He started to stride towards the elevator and told me he would be down in a few minutes, so I bought another beer and reconvened with Boris outside for a cheers and a smoke. Neither of us had a clue as to where exactly we were going, but confident it would beat an early night in a hotel so far from any action.

A yellow taxi cab pulled up – the first I'd been in on my trip – and we piled in. Eugene took the front, leaving myself, Boris, and a new guy, John, to take the rear seats. John was another sound engineer that had toured with Gogol years ago when they supported Primus on a jaunt around the colonies.

"Yo Eugene, where we going, man?" Boris queried aloud what we were all thinking.

"You'll find out..." came the reply from the front as Eugene turned to smile that seemingly ever-present smile at us, having already told the driver the address before we got in. I could have taken it as ominous, not really knowing any of these guys, especially since I had smoked enough to justifiably be paranoid, but the truth was, I really wasn't. I trusted these guys that we wouldn't be going anywhere dangerous, and that wherever we ended up, it would be cool.

Napa was roughly 20 minutes away now the traffic had calmed after the festival, and as you may know from experience, if you have had a few, time can pass by in an instant. Before we knew it, we were there, 'there' being an entirely unremarkable little side alley. We had only dumpsters and rats for company, but this being Napa, I was sure the rats probably had healthier bank accounts than I did.

Eugene turned to us and said, "Okay guys, forty dollars, who has money?"

"Uuuuh..." came the collective reply.

"Come on guys, forty dollars, pay the man!" Eugene told us, still smiling, before getting out of the cab. I rummaged for my wallet, finding twenty dollars, offering to go to an ATM if necessary. John then grabbed it from my hand and paid the rest.

We said thanks to the driver, and got out. John, the saint, shoved a ten and a five into my hand, telling me he was sorry he didn't have more on him, and not to worry about, it wasn't even half of his Per Diem allowance.

A door opened behind me and a voice called out, "Eugene!" I turned round and Eugene walked forward to meet the man in a warm embrace. "This way!" the man said, beckoning us toward the door. Which we entered. Eugene, Boris, myself, and John, in that order.

We were in a narrow red corridor. We walked about ten feet before opening another door and climbing a flight of stairs, coming to another long red corridor, which led us around two equidistant corners. We repeated this cycle twice.

I remembered my dream from Nashville, and quickly shook the negative connotations from my mind. Right now I was in an upswing, and I wanted to stay that way, so I recalled the positive lessons I seemed to be in the midst of learning, and that I was sure my subconscious had tried to alert me to in that same dream. Jung had often spoke of "synchronicities", and I was trying to pay heed to them.

Forgetting that Boris had no idea either, I mirrored his earlier question from the taxi, only this time with added expletives.

"Boris...where the fuck are we and where the fuck are we going?"

"I have no idea dude," came the calm and expected answer.

"John?" hoping our new friend had some sense of what was happening.

"Nope!" came the jovial, excited reply.

Entering a door on the third floor, we finally came across some other human beings. A bluster of social activity could be seen unfolding, and in the distance I could hear the muffled, yet unmistakable sound of a band playing. We passed by what appeared to be a dressing room that was rammed with people, and had a lot of people standing outside.

"Excuse me..." a guy said as he squeezed by me.

"Of course, my apologies.." I offered as I pressed my back to the wall of the narrow red corridor.

"Dude," Boris whispered at me, "That was Jason Newsted." He looked at me, and I looked back a little puzzled. The name rang a bell, but my brain was too busy trying to figure out what exactly was going on. Boris stared at me then said, "Jason Newsted? Metallica? Metallica's old bass player?" "Oh yeeeeeaaaah", I slurred in realisation, marvelling at how much in common Metallica bass players appear to have with buses.

Eugene called out our names and entered the nearby, less busy dressing room, where we were introduced to the sharpest dressed man I'd seen in quite some time.

"Danny Clinch is the name fellas, Tangiers Blues Band is m'game." He was dressed exactly as someone cool enough to pull off that intro line should be; a fine, light brown three piece suit with the hat, shoes and rings to match. "You fellas help yourselves to any booze in here that you like, y'hear? Alright. Now if you'll excuse me, I'll catch y'all laters. Laters..." and off he walked with Eugene, leaving the three of us to damage our livers however we so pleased. We fixed some strong bourbons and put some beers in our pockets.

I noticed a guy walk by smoking a cigarette, and my eyes could not believe it. *Smoking? A cigarette? Indoors? In California? Not a joint? Where are the police?*

Boris, a New Yorker, was just as stunned, so we thought we would chance our luck and lit up a cigarette each. A security guard, right on cue, walked by.

Oh shit, rumbled.

"Evening fellas," the affable guard greeted us before walking on, leaving us to our questionable vices and life choices.

We all looked at each other, bewildered. We knew we were at some gig in Napa, but not quite sure of who was playing, other than the impeccably turned out Mr Danny Clinch and the Tangiers Blues Band and, possibly, Jason Newsted.

Leaving the spacious dressing room to investigate a little further – armed to the teeth with booze and smokes – we found ourselves back in the thin red corridor. On our right, Eugene came swaggering back toward us with his ever-present smile, and to our left a man with his back to us was playing bass, looking very much like he was warming up in preparation for going onstage. He had a familiar posture when he played. A stance I had seen on someone a hundred times before in the past but couldn't quite place it.

"Gentlemen! Here you go!" Eugene said as he thrust Access All Areas passes into our hands, motioning us to follow him up the stairs. I looked back over my shoulder, towards the bass player, when suddenly some drumsticks appeared from the doorway and proceed to march out a beat on the door frame, in tandem to whatever it was the bass player was playing. We went through another door, one last staircase and along one final corridor, the volume of the music growing with each step we took closer to the what was fast becoming apparent, a side entry to the stage.

Eugene flashed his pass and we followed suit, prompting a massive security guard to grant us access, opening the stage door. We parted a curtain, and all of a sudden we were side of stage in a beautiful venue, where a band was laying waste to an excited audience, mesmerized as the blonde frontman pulled all manner of rock frontman stances, borrowing moves from Mick Jagger, Steven Tyler, Robert Plant and Freddie Mercury. It was like he'd taken some sort of class in them.

Once more my mind started to rearrange the necessary pieces, like it had done with Tre Cool the night before. The languid, yet energetic floppy-haired blonde pedalling his musical wares on stage was none other than former Alanis Morissette sticksman, and current Foo Fighter, Taylor Hawkins, and his classic rock covers band, Chevy Metal.

"Riiiiiiight," I slurred in realisation.

They finished their song to a huge cheer from the crowd. I mean, they went *nuts*. Taylor started to talk, but I was too busy laughing with Boris and quaffing back bourbon to hear exactly what he was saying. Meanwhile, behind Boris, I observed that people were looking over their shoulders and clearing out of the way, making way for somebody.

"Please everybody," Mr Hawkins implored, "Make some noise for Mr Chad Smith and Flea of the Red Hot Chili Peppers!" And man oh man, did the audience reply in kind.

Flea and Chad made their way past us, all smiles and hellos like perfect gentlemen, and took the stage to replace their respective counterparts, to the loudest roar I'd heard all day. Regardless of what one may think of their parent band, they are one of the greatest rhythm sections ever in rock music.

Shortly after they had started playing, a few more people joined us at the side of the stage, four ladies who were all turned out for the occasion. They barged past everyone without warning, and yet seemed equally surprised and furious when I completely accidentally spilled a bit of my drink on what appeared to be the ring leader.

If looks could kill, they are lucky I wasn't wearing mirrored sunglasses, such was the contempt and venom their eyes fired at me.

I attempted to apologise but was greeted with an abrupt upright hand to my face, as they surveyed the damage they had both unwittingly and un-admittedly caused. Thankfully, after ten seconds or thereabouts, they realised life would indeed go on, and turned to enjoy the show. It was then that Taylor Hawkins walked towards the wings of the stage and planted a huge kiss on the lady whose dress my bourbon had become forever embroiled with.

Great. I've managed to piss off Taylor Hawkins wife.

That was why they had marched over so stridently, with unyielding entitlement, pushing us lowly 'fans' to one side. Still, a little humility never hurt anyone, and I didn't think about it for another second. Well, apart from the nasty looks I got every thirty seconds or so that I remained standing there. I mean, how dare I? How very bloody dare I?

Sensing that Mrs Hawkins and her elite team may, justifiably or not, turn at any moment and beat me to a bloody pulp, Boris and I left the stage area and returned downstairs to take of advantage of Mr Danny Clinch of the Tangiers Blues Band's kind offer of unlimited drink refills.

Entering the dressing room, we were met with none other than the same familiar face from the previous night, Mr Tre Cool.

It was like we were in some sort of elite rhythm section members club; no guitarists or front men allowed, excluding us. Which, given the stereotypical egos of some lead sections of some bands, could probably be a good thing.

Tre was also hijacking alcohol and was full of smiles, remembering my name as he thrust a beer into my hand and chatting amiably with Boris. I sheepishly smiled back but said little other than a near whispered, "Thanks..." still a little embarrassed from my self-supposed over stepping of the mark the night before.

As the three of us left the dressing room, a passer-by on the corridor noticed Tre and didn't hide his excitement a single iota.

"Holy shit! Tre Cool from Green Day! Oh man, I fuckin' love you guys!" he shouted at Mr Cool, before asking, "Could I get a picture?"

As his taken surname would suggest, and in stark contrast from my own picture request, Tre cooly responded casually with a smile, "Of course man, of course," putting his arm around the excited fellow and pulling one of those signature punk rock faces. I hurried away, stocked with drink, contemplating that there really *is* a time and a place for everything, and made my way back upstairs to catch the end of the set.

29

Once again, I was awoken by the aural terror of a hundred screams, and once again my mind raced through a thousand possible nightmare scenarios in a matter of milliseconds, before remembering the Roller-coaster located just outside of my window. I pulled myself together, showered, and packed my things, readying myself for the end of my Gogol Bordello adventure. I'd be lying if I said I wasn't a little saddened by this. I have never been a good purveyor or recipient of goodbyes.

Our two van motorcade made its way to San Francisco Airport, where they would then fly to Oklahoma to meet up with their support act for the remaining dates (Frank Turner and The Sleeping Souls) and I would depart into the city for a night, before my flight back to Los Angeles the following day.

Goodbyes, phone numbers, email addresses, and hugs were all exchanged. A few of the band and crew expressed their dismay that I wasn't joining them. I too shared in this dismay and, half jokingly, encouraged them to email their management to ask if there was any way I could stay on. To my amazement, some of them did, there and then in front of me. I optimistically held a slither of hope that I would get an email at some stage in the next week telling me to forget my flight back across the water, Gogol needed me back on the road! Right up until I boarded my flight the following week, I would periodically glance at my email on the off chance that I would receive such an email, finally accepting that wasn't to be the case this time when they closed the airplane doors.

Leaving my new friends – a solo traveller once more – I made my way to the taxi rank to get a cab to the San Francisco Hilton, where I was fortunate enough to be staying. I knew one person in the city; a young gent from Draperstown, County Derry, by the name of Mark McAllister, and we were due to meet for a beer.

After checking in at the Hilton, I revealed myself as the idiot I've always suspected myself to be. The hotel itself is so massive that I couldn't quite understand the co-ordinates (or as others may call them "Room number") I'd been given. There were three sky-scraping towers to the hotel. Three times I asked three different employees where on earth my room was. A forgivable question, I felt, as it seemed the hotel took up a sizeable portion of the earth.

Several birthdays and generations later, I eventually found my allotted dwelling space, where I dumped my things and took a walk towards the harbour, in the hope of finding a book shop that may be in possession of *The Iron Heel*, by Jack London. No such luck. The only bookshop I found denied its very existence to me, prompting me to show a wikipedia page proving its actuality, only to be reminded that anybody can create a wikipedia entry.

Beaten, but not defeated, I left the store assuring them it did exist, thanking them nonetheless.

Googling "Blues Bar", I was advised by the all-knowing oracle and advertising data collector to go to The Saloon bar, just off of Broadway. I told Mark I'd be there for the next while, and arranged to meet. The Saloon was a classic dive bar, but not in the Hipster sense. I was the youngest person in there by about twenty years, and it felt good. There was a two man band playing John Prine songs, and the toilet smelt exactly as bad as you would imagine. The beer was cold, and the people were friendly but didn't pry.

Mark arrived and we shared a beer and tales of our recent exploits. He had been over on a one year visa, a perk enjoyed by Irish nationals given our strong historical links with America. Ten months had passed, and he was lamenting that his time was nearing an end here.

"So, you made plans to skip your flight home and stay here then?" he asked with a smile, half joking, and at the same time very much serious.

We finished our beers and made our way to another bar. I'd explained about my quest to find this mythical Jack London novel, and he told me that if anywhere was going to have it, City Lights Bookstore, on the nexus of North Beach and Chinatown, would be the place. It also just so happened to be beside the bar we were going to, the preferred watering hole of Kerouac, Ginsberg, and Cassady, Vesuvio.

City Lights did not disappoint. They had one copy left of this book that I had been trying to locate for two years now (I'm aware I could have got a copy online somewhere; but where is the fun in that?). In celebration, we drank and we laughed for a good few hours in the historic imbibing emporium, Vesuvio, before sharing an Uber that dropped me off at my hotel and Mark continued on home. It had been nice to hear a familiar accent again, and to speak at our normal indecipherable rate.

Back in the Hilton, after having successfully found my room, I took a miniature bottle of wine from the fridge and remembered that I still had a little bit of weed in my wallet. I decided that it would be a criminal shame for me to retire at such an early hour, so I rolled a couple of enhanced cigarettes, and got a cab back to Broadway, where I smoked a few of my "secret agents" as I prowled the thoroughfare in an increasingly affected state of mind.

I found myself back at Vesuvio, but instead of going inside I noticed a busker in the alleyway (Jack Kerouac Alley) who had garnered a small tribe of listeners. Stumbling toward them, I was met warmly by the friendly gaggle, and we passed the guitar to one another, howling out numbers for the next few hours. Communal whiskey and joints were shared as freely as the music in the night air.

A memory, despite its haziness, I'll always cherish. Not to mention embellish.

I lurched along Broadway, feeling like the protagonist in a Tom Waits song, chatting with some of the friendliest police I've ever encountered, and laughing with the nice ladies who were trying to entice me into strip bars and lap dancing clubs. The only logical thing to do was go back to the hotel and sleep it all off, and logic isn't the easiest voice to listen to when you're three sheets to the wind in San Francisco.

My Waitsian evening the night before had left me deservedly hungover, out of pocket, and bothered by the thought of 8 hours to kill in an airport. Check out was midday and I wasn't about to risk a fine for flaunting it.

My mood was lifted somewhat though by a phone call from my oldest friend, Tiernan Welch. Tiernan and I had been best friends from the age of four, and although our lives had taken quite different routes, we remained very close, despite not seeing each other anywhere near enough. Tiernan and his wife Lauren had recently become parents for the first time to a beautiful baby girl, Penelope Wren Welch, and had elected to ask me if I would be her godfather. Naturally, I gratefully accepted and expressed my joy at them opting to ask me. Keen to make sure I wasn't too elated at being chosen from the many possible candidates, Tiernan stressed that they, "Needed a Catholic," which I am, "Whether you like it or not".

My hangover was banished by the good news, and the welcome sound of a life-long friend's voice in such fine spirits. I'm already a godfather to my gorgeous niece, Marisa Ursula Wright, so, in effect, I'll be the Godfather Part Two. Which is commonly and rightfully regarded as the best one. Whilst my id may disagree, my ego was in total accordance with these parallels.

30

The sky was overcast and the temperature moderate as I departed LAX. Not like the sunny, warm cloudless skies of Northern California I'd left two hours previously. I took an Uber to my rented apartment on Santa Monica Blvd and 7th, which was to be home for my final few days in America.

Being ever the organised soul, I'd only booked the accommodation two days before. I was lucky enough to find a one bedroom apartment close to Santa Monica beach, and at a huge discount due to the proprietors obviously preferring not to have an empty property on their hands. It worked out cheaper than a hotel, and I'd be able to cook and do my washing at no extra charge, so it seemed like an obvious choice.

En route, I got in touch with the property liaison agent, Brett, to tell him I would be there, as planned, in thirty minutes. An hour later Brett arrived, all apologies, to show me into my building. He talked the entire time about the other building that he'd been stuck at, saying sorry at every interlude he availed himself, with all the sincerity of a jobbing Politician.

We took the elevator to the fifth floor, where my apartment was. Brett had a fantastic habit of asking me questions without waiting for an answer and, as if he'd reminded himself of something else, and would move onto that topic before asking me another question, then repeating this cycle.

My apartment was number 501, like a pair of Levis, and this is how I would remember it.

Entering the apartment, Brett told me it was his favourite in the building, putting my bullshit detector into overdrive. This proving correct as only a second later, he expressed his surprise at it being a two bedroom when there was only one of me, at least last time I checked anyway.

Brett was a hoot. Albeit unwittingly.

He double checked that this was correct, and noticed an email saying that, for reasons unbeknownst to me (and Brett), I had been upgraded to a two bedroom. It was of no odds as far as I was concerned since I would only be needing one bed, but still I expressed my appreciation regardless.

Brett smiled, winked, and said, "Well you never know, you may get lucky and..."

"...And what? Invite a prospective partner in for a sleepover?"

Without a word, mercifully, he realised the absurdity of what he had just said, and went into business mode, telling me the rules, regulations and conditions, when I had to check out, no smoking etc, you know...all the fun stuff.

He wasn't a bad guy, and I was very lucky to have such a nice place so close to the beach. I thanked him for his help and he told me to call should I need anything, then he went on his way.

Not more than fifteen minutes had passed before I had to call my good buddy Brett.

"Hi Brett, its Tony,"

"Hey Tony, what's up? Everything okay?"

"Yeah, I was just wondering if you wanted to come over for a sleep-over?"

"I...uh...what? Oh...ha ha...I get it..." he answered, none too impressed.

"Couldn't resist. No, it's just that there seems to be some insects...I mean bugs...in this place."

"Really? What sorta bugs? How many? So you want out, huh?", he asked me all at once.

"I'll be right over, see you in five."

Thirty minutes later, my main man Brett knocked on the door to apartment 501.

"Hey Brett, I missed you..."

Brett nervously smiled, and I invited him in.

"Ok, so where are these little bastards?" he asked as his eyes began scanning the apartment.

"Just here, by the cupboard nearest the door. They're coming down along the wall, taking a detour by the knife block on the counter, then continuing their pilgrimage down the corner by the door. And there's some more over here on the other counter beside the table and the sink." I'd had a while to familiarise myself with my new flatmates.

"Uh-huh..." commented Brett, reaching for the cupboard beneath the sink and pulling out some sort of insect repellent spray, laying all the visible ones to waste.

"They're just babies, man," he remarked, like an unrepentant psychopath.

I felt kind of sorry for them all of a sudden. I felt responsible for this Formica infanticide, and was sure an ant of gargantuan proportions would come seeking vengeance from me at the earliest stage imaginable.

Shaking of this nightmarish vision of my future, I asked Brett how I could be sure there wouldn't be more?

"They seem to be coming from here," as he pointed toward a tiny hole, no bigger than a pin prick, on the kitchen wall. "I'll come by tomorrow with some of the proper repellent and lay it near the hole and on their trail, OR you can change apartment if you like, but you gotta remember Tony, this is California and we have ants!" he intelligibly and patronisingly reasoned.

Quelling the notion of my death from a grudge bearing, pissed off super-ant, and taking on board that dealing with ants may just be a thing people have to contend with here, I opted to stay, so long as Brett, my reluctant hero, would do as he promised the following day. Besides, I was shattered and wanted to relax.

Brett assured me he would be back the following day and that it was nothing to worry about.

I never saw Brett again.

Settling down for the evening, needing an early night, I watched the commercials telling me how I needed such and such medication that may also cause my heart to implode, interspersed with brief news bulletins. I said goodnight to the ants, and promptly fell asleep.

Rising the next morning around 9am, I was surprised at how overcast it still was, but having grown up on the coastline of the Pacific's second in command – the Atlantic – it made me feel strangely at home. After a shower, and exchanging brief morning pleasantries with my thousands of six legged roommates, I descended to street level to explore my final temporary home in these vast expansive lands.

Directly outside my building was the Santa Monica library. I was later told that it's heavily populated with homeless people on the city's hottest days, seeking air conditioned refuge. I walked south-west on the boulevard towards the water, figuring that all manner of possible breakfast stops would soon make themselves apparent. Foolishly assuming that the city would share this frequency of eatery with its north-eastern counterpart, NYC. It doesn't. After a while I began cursing myself that I hadn't stopped at Wexler's Deli, which was practically outside my front door.

Eventually, I ceased looking and grabbed some breakfast in a nondescript stall along Third Street Promenade, watching consumer after consumer pile in and out of the many high street chain stores that populate high streets the western capitalist world over. Apple Stores, H&M, Urban Outfitters, Starbucks (at least three in less than a quarter of a mile), Zara, Gap, and Victoria's Secret. I was in Los Angeles, but other than the accents and prices, there was little to differentiate this street from Dublin, London, Glasgow, Belfast, Cardiff, or indeed Paris, Rome, Berlin, Madrid, or Amsterdam.

Faced with the global market traders of today, and the over-riding reason why almost everybody who walked past me looked like identikit versions of one another, I felt that very few people actually stood out in any tangible way, including myself. I considered this for a while, and then I recalled the hipsters of Williamsburg, and how even a large proportion of them crafted their "individual" style on those that were suggested to them from an Urban Outfitters catalogue. I even began to ponder whether the public criticism of Hipsters was due to some sort of conspiracy to mock anyone who daren't conform to the by now ubiquitous uniform of preppy Hollister clothing I was surrounded by.

Good god, I had definitely been on my own too much...

I realised this was probably the longest I'd pondered fashion and aesthetics. I shook my head, and told myself that ancient truth, "Who gives a damn how someone else looks?" It was then that I remembered I should never take seriously any of the thoughts that I have before breakfast. Cynicism is possibly the only beast to thrive on an empty stomach.

Despite my regular morning cynicism being put to rest, I was a little sad that my American adventure was coming to an end. I tried, and mostly succeeded, to focus on the positives. I had five days left, and I'd enjoyed the most extraordinary time. The people I'd met had been nothing short of wonderful to me, and went out of their way to make me feel comfortable and at home, all these miles from my own. There was a large part of me that was holding onto the belief that, at any moment, I may receive a phone call from the Gogol Bordello people, telling me that I simply had to re-join the tour, and to cancel my plans of returning across the water...that there was a life over here for me, about to unfold, all the fantasies I'd ever had about cracking America were only moments away and, as a result, my purpose in this vast endless Universe was about to become apparent to all the dwellers of this perpetually spinning orb. The resolution was here upon me, finally!

I felt Titan, in both the Greek sense and, unfortunately, like a certain ship that was built back home. In America, I truly felt like I could be on the cusp of something great and life changing. I feared if I left, I could sink into the mire of missed opportunity and unfulfilled potential.

That evening, I was meeting up with a friend of a friend for drinks. He had cousins in my hometown back in County Derry, and our mutual friend, Tiernan, suggested over email that we liaise. We were due to meet in an English style pub at the end of the boulevard called, naturally, "Ye Olde Kings Head".

I arrived a little early, and awaited the arrival of someone whom I had no idea of what they looked like, but it was fine as he was in the same position. Besides, it wasn't the first time, on this journey or otherwise, that I'd been in this position.

Mike arrived a little after 7, and we figured out who each other was nearly instantaneously. It turned out that we had met before, when we were both around seventeen years old. He had been visiting his cousins in Ireland, and we all got monstrously pissed to make him feel welcome.

Even though it had been eighteen years since our last meeting, Mike was the easiest guy in the world to get on with, and we were soon laughing at each other's tales of how we had got to be who, and where, we are today.

He was a successful businessman, CEO of his own company, married to Anna, with young twin boys, Harry and James, and a big beautiful dog with a name to match his stark, handsome dog qualities: Tony.

Mike asked me about myself, what I was doing here, and how it was all going in general. I told him my past, about how I've been a musician for as long as I can really remember. I told him about my bands, how I found myself as a solo musician, much to my own surprise, how I've been trying to be a self-sufficient artist, and all the troubles that go along with that, and how I hoped this trip would hopefully provide me with some guidance as to what lay next in this path. How, whilst also a business trip to see my publishers, I felt slightly lost, scared, and alone, this feeling not helped by my perceptions that some of my publishers people weren't taking me seriously.

In honesty, I was probably too honest, and I probably said too much.

However, I did say most of this with a degree of levity. I didn't want to bum this nice man out with my own existential dread. We laughed throughout, which is highly recommended when detailing one's aforementioned existential dread. Although possibly not if you happen to either be in the company of a psychiatrist, a court of law or, worse yet, both.

At the end of our meal, Mike invited me to his home for dinner on the coming Saturday, my final night in America. He told me Anna's cousin, Jim, would be there, and that I should meet him, and that he works for a big music management company.

All of this sounded very familiar.

Mike then mentioned Jim's connection with Bruce Springsteen, and it was then that it hit me.

Jim, Anna's cousin, was the guy that Chris – from Nashville – had suggested I get Jesse – from New York – to ask to check me out. Jim and Jesse were good friends through Bruce – from New Jersey. Chris – from Nashville – had suggested a pincer movement through himself and Jesse – from New York – in order to get Jim's – Anna's cousin – attention. Remember now? Splendid.

I couldn't quite believe it, a coincidence that was strung from coast to coast across America?

No, surely this was something *more.*

As a foolhardy musician and wannabe poet, I sensed the touch of fate on my shoulder.

This was all part of a grand plan, surely?

Even if not, it was so boldly fortuitous that even the most cynical of realists would have to be made of stone not to delight in the magic of this apparent synchronicity.

Telling Mike of this, he laughed and told me that I had to tell Jim of this compelling twist of fate that would lead to us sharing dinner in a few nights time.

For the next hour or so, we told jokes and stories. Mike asked about other people he had met whilst in Portstewart, and what they were now up to. We talked about sports, finding that we shared a love of Liverpool FC. I mean, this guy, was the best.

After a little while, Mike had to split and I told him of how much I was looking forward to meeting up again. It had been a fateful evening, and I returned to my apartment to sing songs of freedom and redemption with my co-habiting ant friends, before a sound night's sleep.

Next on my small itinerary for the city of Los Angeles, was a meeting with an old college friend, Yoko. Yoko and I hadn't seen each other in twelve years, so it was a true pleasure and surprise to receive a mail from her suggesting we meet up whilst I was in California.

She picked me up outside my apartment, and we took a drive to pick up some coffees and catch up. We bought two ridiculously sized Americanos, and went for a walk along Santa Monica pier, stopping briefly to revel in the majesty of the Jesus/Johnny Cash singer. I daren't call him an impersonator, in case he's actually one of them.

Yoko, originally from Japan, had left her home when she was 18 to study music in Liverpool, where we met, and then moved to London, before ultimately settling in L.A.

She couldn't speak very much English when she first left Japan, but was now more than fluent and had a beautiful hybrid accent of English and American. Yoko told me how after years of trying to get some real music work, she was now writing the music for a successful American TV Show, and doors were now finally opening in all directions after an initially tough time.

She was getting married soon too, to a musician from Chicago who was also signed to my publishers. I was so delighted for her. It was heartening for the soul to see an old friend doing so well, and one that had taken such a plunge into the unknown all those years ago, which only reinforced my thinking that I needed to do something similar.

Yoko also told me of how well known my old band was in Japan, and how she bragged to friends back there how she went to college with me. This, I found conflictingly hilarious and upsetting. Mainly because I never made it to Japan; the band had only made it there for their first eastern tour after my departure, but I hid any disappointment from her. I was happy that music I had been part of was appreciated somewhere that I'd never been, but sad that knowledge of my involvement is probably not. Ego is a terrible thing.

She seemed to know a lot of what I had already been doing, and when someone tells you all of the things you have done, it can make you realise that maybe you've been doing better than you thought you have been doing all along.

I told her about my strange tale of coincidence with this fellow named Jim that I was due to meet, and being a musician also, she too ignored the chaotic nature of fate, and agreed that something bigger than mere chance must have been at play. After all, Musicians gotta muse...

Too soon, it was time to say goodbye. We made promises that it definitely wouldn't be another twelve years before our next meeting, and she told me that I always had a place to stay if I wanted to move to Los Angeles until I got my feet on the ground. An enormously generous offer that I thanked her for, and stowed it away, front and centre in the mental note area of my brain.

I strolled around the area, deep in thought, looking at the pavement as I searched the concrete for answers. It had been great to see Yoko and catch up, and it seemed that after an initially difficult time, opportunity had eventually caught up with her, giving her the lucky roll of the dice that she deserved, to reward both her patience and her hard work.

Was I on the cusp of that? Did I already have that, but I wasn't aware of it? How big in Japan was my old band? Did they know songs I had written? Had my chance been and gone? Are those *my* feet?

Such questioning can drive someone insane, so I tried to put it, as always, to the back of my mind, where hopefully they won't reorganize themselves as a stroke or a tumour. It was futile. I was on my own in this most alien of cities, and the black dog was on my tail again.

Anytime I was left to my own devices, it never seemed far away, manifesting itself in the form of paranoid regret and crippling self-doubt. I knew the bark of this hateful creature had only been amplified by the alcohol that I'd consumed on this trip, which was a great deal more than I had done in years, but the lonely confusion had been soothed by the drink, paradoxically.

I knew it was a perilous road, and it was not one that I cared to stumble too far down.

I had to face down this beast – as best as I could – and I had to do it dry. Eventually.

So, being a good boy, I returned to my apartment for the evening and did what I'm supposed to do, I played my guitar. I had my meeting with my publishers the next morning at 10am, and they were a long way across the city. I needed to be fresh.

31

It was my penultimate full day in the United States, and my fantasy phone call still hadn't come in from Gogol Bordello. Time was running out for that scenario, but other things were afoot. In a remarkable twist of fate, I was going to be having dinner with one of music's most successful managers the next day. But for now I had to get myself across the city to my scheduled appointment on Beverly Boulevard.

I decided that I'd get a bus in a last minute attempt to save some money, hoping that I'd still be able to eat for a few days when I got back across the water. It was a forty minute journey with two changes that gave me ample time to make it to the offices.

Running a little ahead of schedule, I stopped at a nearby cafe on a West 3rd Street called Toast. There was no point in me going into this meeting with an empty stomach, and letting the cynic in me take over and run amok. Eggs and coffee were required. It was a beautiful day and the people at the table next to me reflected this, humans so sculpted that it was like having breakfast in the midst of a troop of mobile mannequins. Upon leaving, I overheard a brief snippet of conversation that revealed they all worked in the porn industry, thus explaining the gargantuan, almost alien, efforts that they had taken to keep themselves looking so pristine.

My publishers offices were well air conditioned, thank god. I arrived bang on time at 10am, introduced myself to the receptionist, and was promptly offered coffee. So naturally, I asked for water. The nice lady on reception asked me to take a seat and informed me that Sarah-Jane – my A&R liaison – would be with me shortly.

After less than five minutes of waiting, the phone in the reception rang again for the twentieth time; it was my liaison, Sarah-Jane. It turned out that she wasn't actually in the building yet, and was wondering if we could meet at the nearby coffee shop a few buildings up. I made my way to the annoyingly cool coffee shop with the irritating name of Cup, ordered a coffee and awaited Sarah-Jane's arrival despite neither of us having a clue what each other looked like. I briefly entertained the thought that she may have looked me up online on their roster list that has a picture of me, before quickly laughing such a hopeful notion back out of my brain where it clearly had no place at this time.

Sarah-Jane arrived a few minutes later and, as it happened, we did pick each other out immediately. Being a much more astute LA dweller than I, she ordered an iced coffee. At this stage it was oppressively hot outside. I, however, resolutely stood by my ill choice of boiling hot black coffee.

She was very personable, brimming with smiles, positivity, and enthusiasm, keenly listening to what I had to say, and my pitch to work closer with the company. I felt it was all going rather well as she nodded at all the right points and laughed where I hoped she would throughout the conversation and pitch.

After about twenty minutes of this, she suggested we continue back at the office where I could also meet some of the team. Excellent, so far. We continued chatting and I continued selling myself as someone who was eager to maximise all possible ties with the company, for all of our futures. I used all the necessary bullshit music business lingo that I had accrued over the years. Essentially meaningless words, and I meant every one of them. So long as there is a sniff of a profit at the end, the business heads tend to lap it up. The commodification of art. Horrid, I know, but I had to do it if I was to continue doing it.

All of this mindless jibber-jabber see-sawed back and forth between us, and before I knew it I was in a small board room where I was quickly introduced to about seven other staff members, all seated around a circular table, and then, suddenly, I was outside the office facing the elevator.

It was the fastest 'Hello Goodbye' since the Beatles song of the same name was played at triple double quadruple speed onboard a Mach 3 Jet.

What the hell? Damn, they were good...

They had blinded me with so many introductions and flashy smiles that I didn't even realise I was being ushered out. Despite the fact I had travelled over 5,000 miles for this remarkable snubbing, I couldn't help but admire how expertly they had executed this dismissive manoeuvre.

"Hello! How Are You? Great To Meet You! Well, Until Next Time! Goodbye!" The door swung shut, closed behind me, ushered out into the sun-soaked swill with the other pigs once more.

I couldn't even remember a single person's name, but there's a persistent thought that tells me they were all called Sarah or Jane.

The heat outside was stifling, and I stuck to the shadows where possible. My meeting had obviously ended a lot quicker than expected, as it wasn't yet even 11am yet. Mike had arranged for me to meet with one of his associates, Tim, later that day, but that wasn't until 3pm. Determined not to get too disheartened at my treatment at the hands of my publishers, I wandered Beverly Boulevard for a little whilst trying to figure out what buses I needed to get to get me to Little Dom's on Hillhurst Avenue, dodging the sun when I could, but as high noon approached, that became increasingly difficult.

Little Dom's on Hillhurst Avenue is a cool little hidden gem. Well, that's not strictly true. It's a very popular place that everybody in LA knows about. But to me, given its distance from Northern Ireland, it's a hidden gem.

There's a few booths on the right upon entering, which were all occupied when I walked in, so I took a seat at the bar and waited for Tim to arrive. The bartender was a helpful young lady, and she took my order of a cranberry juice with plenty of ice.

Maybe it was the heat, maybe it was the exhaustion, maybe it was a combination of the two, or maybe it was just the honest truth, but given the distance I had travelled, I was pretty pissed off at the way I'd just been treated at my publishers offices. I reasoned with myself that I am a tiny entity on their roster, the least of their concerns and that I should, at the very least, be happy to be a part of that illustrious roster. Regardless of attempted appeasement, I couldn't shake my disappointment easily.

Attempting to take my mind off of it, I swung round on my bar stool to get better acquainted with my surroundings. It was your classic Italian Deli/Diner, the sort that I had seen in so many films, and for that reason, I instantly felt at ease in the place. To strengthen the feeling that it was straight out of a movie, I noticed that the British actor Tim Roth was sitting at one of the booths. He was staring straight at me when I noticed him. I can only presume it was because he heard my accent and recognised it as one from another trans-Atlantic compatriot, and hopefully not my potentially bright red face from too much sun.

I smiled and he continued with his conversation, flashing a brief grin back in recognition.

At least he wasn't recoiling in horror.

The last time I had seen him sitting in a booth was the opening scene of Pulp Fiction. It was all very meta, like much of Los Angeles.

Tim arrived and picked me out instantly, admittedly not a difficult task when I'm the only person in the place by themselves. He offered me a beer and, not breaking my new rule of never drinking alone, I graciously accepted. I pointed out Tim Roth, in the most casual way I could, and we raised a beer together.

We talked for a while about ourselves, getting to know one another, and then he started to tell me about his new business (this was a business meet, technically). It was a very cool new music start up, helping musicians grow their market, and it sounded genuinely exciting. I began to talk a little more about myself and why I was on this trip – the business side of it at least. I didn't think it would be fair or wise to go into too much detail about the inner quest that I was on in tandem. However, the more I began to talk about the business aims, the more I began to vent about how I had felt a little let down in Nashville and Los Angeles by my respective Sarah-Janes, but that I understood my expectations were probably too high.

Tim seemed genuinely concerned, and it was at the revealing of his concern that I then began to enthuse about all of the amazing things that had happened to me since I'd been on this vast expanse of land. All the while, trying my level best not to move into philosophy territory. For his sake and for mine.

Soon, we began talking about bands, and the various music genres that we were into. I mentioned my old band – he hadn't heard of us – which naturally segued us onto the topic of post-rock. At the mention of a few of these bands names (This Will Destroy You, God Is An Astronaut, etc), the bar tender chimed in saying how much she loved those bands. She named a few that I was familiar with, and a few I'd never heard of, mainly since I drifted away from listening to most instrumental rock when I left the band.

It was at this point that she put down two large whiskey glasses in front of Tim and I.

"You're Irish, right?"

"That is correct, what gave it away?" I asked, like the prize stereotype I had clearly become.

"Jameson, on the house, for you guys. You've got cool taste in music, *and* you're Irish," she replied, sensibly ignoring my rhetorical question, pouring us two huge whiskeys.

She then walked off to deal with another customer, possibly Mr Roth.

Tim couldn't quite believe our luck.

"Holy shit...this happen to you a lot?" he asked.

"Only over here Tim. Only over here..." raising my glass to him, smiling.

Tim, being the gentleman, then turned to our bar tender.

"Hey! You gotta have one too! C'mon, join us! If it's on the house you gotta have one too!"

"Yeah!" I interjected, remembering my bar manners, "Join us!"

Our kindly bar tender, having just finished with her other customer, looked at us. Her healthy complexion had turned a few shades paler.

"Oh god no..." her voice trembling, "I love that stuff too much...that's the crap that put me in AA".

She then turned and resumed cleaning the rear of the bar.

Tim and I looked at each other, our shoulders now slumped and our glasses, still full, returned to the bar. After a few seconds of awkwardness, I sheepishly raised my glass again then quietly, softly and almost inquisitively, spoke.

"Um...cheers?"

32

June 4th. My final full day in Barack Obama's United States of America.

I was looking forward to my dinner that evening at Mike's place with his family and the mysterious Jim whom, I felt, had somehow been woven into my destiny. If I could make a good impression on this guy, the repercussions from that encounter could alter the direction of my life, my fate.

Obviously this is not something that you want playing into your mind when going to dinner with good people. It's necessary to be aware of it, sure. But to let that be the presiding thought in your head throughout the day? A fool's folly, surely, and one that would condemn you to failure before a word has been spoken in earnest. I had to relax.

I wasn't due at Mikes place until later, so I took one last walk towards Santa Monica Pier.

Despite how alien the landscape was compared to what I was used to, amongst the Palm Trees and wide roads, there was something strangely homely about Santa Monica, to me at least. In the few days I had been resident there, the sky had been overcast, and therein lay the source of its comforting familiarity. It reminded me, quite literally, of a Hollywood version of my hometown and its neighbours (Portstewart, Portrush, and Coleraine) amalgamated into one. Like some future version of my former playgrounds, terraformed by The Jetsons, neither utopian nor dystopian, but an ambiguous middle ground with some of the pleasures and horrors of each.

Growing up by the sea affects one's mind in a peculiar way. To stare out to sea encourages dreaming, and thus, hopefully, ambition, purifying the lungs, eyes, and mind all at once. An invigorating feast, that's a fertile breeding ground for the imagination...what lies *out there?* What wonders lay out there on terra firma, and beyond that sub-aqua world from where we first crawled out of millennia ago, to conquer the lands and build sprawling conurbations such as this very one I stood upon, gazing back at our once and future home.

I walked once more to the end of the pier, and thought about I had started out at the Atlantic, man, to the Pacific lands, to be specific, man. And how soon I would be catapulted back that way, making a mental note to myself that no matter the outcome of tonight's dinner, I had to get back to America as soon as I could. As much as I would miss Ireland and my family, I had to take this plunge, and I had to remember to be brave enough to do so.

Whilst strolling around lower Santa Monica, killing time with no particular place to go, an older, snappily dressed gentleman approached me at a set of traffic lights as I was waiting to cross. He was wearing mostly beige – with a fedora and sunglasses to match – along with a pale tailored waistcoat, and sandals, mercifully without socks. He asked me if I knew where a certain restaurant was, and after I apologised that I didn't, and explained I was merely passing through, he made the by now familiar observation denoting my clearly apparent Irish heritage. Only he took it one further.

"Lemme guess...you're a musician right?"

"You are correct sir. Am I that obvious? Do I smell that bad?"

Not detecting the joke (unless I really *did* smell that bad), he ignored both questions.

"Irish musician, huh? I'm a poet. Lemme ask you this. You know the Duke? Peter? You know...The Duke? Duke Special? Peter...Duke Special? Peter Duke Special?"

I was astonished that, for the first time ever, an American had asked me if I knew someone that they did from Ireland, and I actually did.

"Wow, yes! Yes I do! Peter Wilson? Fantastic guy, I know him well, I've toured with him a few times. How do you know Peter?"

"Like I said, I'm a poet, I've worked with the guy, and you're right, fantastic guy. Stephen...Stephen is my name. Stephen Kalinich. Poet. Poet, Kalinich, Stephen. Stephen Kalinich. Poet."

I went on to introduce myself by my given name only, and walked with him for a few blocks. He reeled off a few other Irish musicians he'd worked with, such as Thomas Walsh of Pugwash.

A genuinely fascinating character, he was signed as a lyricist to the Beach Boys' label after relocating from New York to LA in 1966. He was a long-time collaborator with Brian Wilson, had written song lyrics for Paul McCartney, as well as Dennis Wilson, P.F. Sloan (The Mamas and the Papas), Randy Crawford, and Diana Ross. He then stunned me, when from out of nowhere – in the middle of a sentence – he stopped dead in his tracks, pointed at me and exclaimed, "Chorus Verse Chorus!"

Close enough.

I asked him how he knew, and he said, "I saw you online with Peter. I recognise your crazy hair." That was good enough for me.

After a little while we found his restaurant and, before I left him, we took a picture for posterity, which he asked me to send to Peter, along with his best wishes.

"You drop me a line when you're back in the city now Mr Chorus, you hear? I got a whole bunch of musicians that you just gotta meet." How can I refuse?

It was approaching 430pm, so I stopped by a liquor store and bought a bottle of wine to give Mike and his wife Anna. It was a bottle of red from Francis Ford Coppola's vineyard, which impressed me, but on reflection is probably not so impressive to residents of the state.

As had become the norm for me, I requested an Uber and keyed in my destination on the Pacific Palisades. My driver, Marvin, would be with me in five minutes.

Marvin's Toyota Prius arrived bang on time. He got out of the car, a six foot plus individual, immaculately coiffured facial hair, and with a bulky, sturdy frame. If I was American, I would have observed that he looked like a football player. But, I'm Irish, so I thought, "Size of yer man..."

"Michael? Michael Anthony?" Marvin began hollering whilst looking around him. His voice betrayed a man of his size; it was a higher pitch than you would expect from his appearance, but only made him more likeable.

I approached with my guitar (I was going to have to sing for my supper), smiling. I said hello and Marvin got very excited at the sight of the instrument.

"Oooooh BOY! You a guitar player Michael Anthony?"

"Yes. Yes I am, Marvin."

"That is BAD. ASS. I love getting musicians in my car Michael Anthony. Lemme take that for you and put it in the trunk...Get yo'self on in the car, I'll take care of this, Michael Anthony."

(People in this city seem to like saying people's names a lot. I liked it. Made feel at home and gave me that extra incentive to remember theirs, as I am most definitely a face person)

Marvin had the mannerisms of a chart friendly rapper, but more Vanilla Ice than Ice Cube.

"So..." straight back into conversation as we set off, "Pacific Palisades, huh? What takes you up there Michael Anthony? You a musician, huh? Where can I hear your stuff, Michael Anthony?"

"Um...one at a time please Marvin. Firstly, dinner at a friend's, yes I am, and search VerseChorusVerse online and you'll find me. All one word."

"Huh?"

"Verse. Chorus. Verse. Except it's all one word...you know...VerseChorusVerse."

"Uh-huh – I hear ya, I hear ya Michael Anthony. VerseChorusVerse... huh...I like that, Michael Anthony. Or should I say, Mr VerseChorusVerse? Ahhuhahuhahahuha!"

His laugh was somewhere between a quack and what I imagine a pterodactyl to sound like. No matter; it was infectious.

It was impossible not to like Marvin.

He spied a few ladies working out beside the road. They weren't overdressed.

"Oh shheeeeyyyiiiit, Michael Anthony! You see dat? Outside? On the left, on the left! I swear if..." mercifully, for all involved, he interrupted himself as a song came on the radio that he liked. Immediately, he cranked the volume up to distorting levels and then yelled over the top of it, flailing his right arm like he was winding down a periscope,

"SHEEEEYYYIIIT! BIG SHOUT OUT TO JAMIE XX MICHAEL ANTHONY, BIG. SHOUT. OUT!" And then he returned it to a normal volume.

It seemed Marvin had a wonderful habit of interrupting himself, this was how he ensured that conversation never tailed off; he was too busy having a rhetorical one with himself to ever let that happen with anyone else.

"Say, Michael Anthony, you like Jaime XX? Oooh man, look...look! To your right! Look at that Corvette!" he then rolled his righthand side window down. "Hey! HEY! MAN! HEEEEEY! THAT IS A SWEEEEEEET CORVETTE! Ahhuhahuhahahuha!"

He was not wrong, it was indeed a sweet corvette.

Seconds later, Marvin spotted another lady leaving a health food store.

She was in yoga pants, a vest and an unzipped hooded jacket, with her blonde hair tied back in a high pony tail. She was carrying what appeared to be a health shake that was a deep green colour.

"Lookie here, Michael Anthony, right here, this ladies body...damn...and look at that drink! Look at it! She'll be shitting for a week outta that pretty lil ass! I bet she's going to get fucked up tonight, or was fucked up last night, Michael Anthony. What you think Michael Anthony? Imma find out!" and good as his word, he rolled down his window and asked her.

"Hey! Hey baby! Say Girl!" She looked over and beamed a Californian white smile at us. "Say Girl! Why you drinking that green shit? Your fine ass body don't need that shit?"

Marvin was a poet.

She seemed to agree, as she replied laughing, "Why thank you, but I got all fucked up last night and I'm going out again tonight so I need it!"

"AH-HUHAHUHAHUHA! Okay baby! You have fun girl! Ahhuhahuhahahuha!"

As we drove on, she blew Marvin a kiss.

"See that house right there, Michael Anthony?" pointing to the left at a moderately sized house. "Three Million dollars...that one right there?" pointing to one a little further on, "Four million dollars...You must be a big deal if you're going for dinner up around here, Michael Anthony."

"Me? Oh, no. It's just dinner, I'm not..."

"Don't sell yourself so short, Michael Anthony! Yes you are! Yes. You. Are!" Marvin bellowed, hammering out the words on his steering wheel, and smiling at me in the rearview. There was a seconds silence as I tried to take on board his advice.

"Ooh, ooh that one? That's Chris Rocks house! BIG SHOUT OUT TO MY MAN CHRIS ROCK, MICHAEL ANTHONY! You like Chris Rock, Michael Anthony?"

"I do, Marvin. Yes..."

"Well...BIG SHOUT OUT!"

We swung down as close to the beach as I had been when not astride the pier. He pointed to a sea food restaurant on the left.

"Now, you see dat place, Michael Anthony? You see it?"

"I do..."

"I was in there two weeks ago, and motherfucking Rihanna was having a shellfish dinner with motherfucking Chris Martin! From motherfucking Coldplay, Michael Anthony! Coldplay! Rihanna! Shellfish!"

Just then, the song 'Breathe' by Blu Cantrell came on the radio.

Marvin exploded back into action.

"WELL HOE-LEE SHEEEYYYYIIITTT, MICHAEL ANTHONY! BIG. SHOUT. OUT. TO. MY. WOMAN. BLU CANTRELL!"

He cranked the volume on the stereo, and kept it up for a little while. I wasn't quite sure whether it was because he really loved the song, or he needed a second to catch his breath.

"Dat house...Andy Garcia...Five Million Dollars, baby..."

We arrived at Mike's place, and my face was aching from smiling. The perfect frame of mind to go into a dinner that my head had turned into an audition of some sort.

Marvin very kindly took my guitar out from the trunk, shook my hand and wished me luck.

"Alright Michael Anthony, good to meet you. I really enjoyed talking with you."

"I…"

"That's right, Michael Anthony. Or should I say, Mr VerseChorusVerse? Ah-huhahuhahahuha…"

As he got back in his car he beckoned me toward to his window,

"Now I'm gonna be downloading all your stuff, Mr Michael VerseChorus Anthony Verse…" he started the engine, turned and pointed at me. "…For free."

Then he sped off into the early evening, hopefully to make some other soul's night, too.

Mike's house was beautiful. Sitting astride a crest of a hill, it was the perfect Hollywood home.

I rang the doorbell, which played a pleasant descending three note melody. Mike answered the door with a hugely welcoming smile, and inviting me in.

The house was even more impressive on the inside. It had an almost TARDIS-like quality, seeming to expand from the interior.

We entered the kitchen, where he introduced me to the lady of the house, his good wife, Anna, whom I presented with my bottle of wine. They both told me that I shouldn't have, and thanked me for the gesture. Mike going as far to dispel my fears, telling me that the Coppola stuff is really good.

A huge dog burst into the room and came straight for me. He was excitedly and playfully barking as he jumped at me on his hind legs to give me a lick, a sniff, and generally say hello,

"Tony, meet Tony." I wasn't sure who was being introduced to whom. I proceeded to make a crappy joke about name confusion, if Tony were told to get off the furniture or stop sniffing crotches. Real classy of me, I'm sure you'll agree.

We then went into the adjacent living room, or den, where Mike and Anna's young twin boys were being entertained by their Uncle Jim. Mike introduced me to Jim who stood up to shake my hand. As he left his seat and straightened up, he revealed his height. Standing a good foot taller than me, and with a friendly smile, he gripped my hand firmly, and told me it was a pleasure. Mike and Anna's boys, Harry and James, sat laughing and strangely curious about my odd accent as I crouched down to say hello.

Our gracious host then put a beer in my hand and led us outside into his yard where his friend Tim, whom I had shared drinks with the previous day, was sitting. I shook his hand and we all took seats around the table outside, basking in the evening sunshine.

As we exchanged extended introductions, the doorbell rang, and Anna excused herself to answer it. We were then joined by the drummer in Mike's band, Carl, and his girlfriend Jill. Further intros were made, and we all drank merrily into the evening, telling stories and talking about the news then dominating current affairs, the unfortunate triumvirate of Bernie Sanders, Hillary Clinton, and Donald Trump.

It was all very grown up, which, for a gathering of people mostly thirty plus in age, is to be expected, I suppose.

The great Mohammed Ali had passed away the evening before, and we talked about what an incredible impact he had made, not only on innumerable other boxers, but on the world that we live in, and how his defiance had made the world a better a better place. As Mike and Anna were inside, putting the boys to bed, we watched a tribute to the great man from the comedian Billy Crystal. Mike then re-joined us only to reveal that, "Billy lives two doors up!"

Los Angeles, ladies and gentlemen.

Chat soon turned to the music industry, which was no surprise since we had five people around the table involved in it in some way. Thankfully, it was kept light.

There was no bullshit, mercenary industry talk going on, and mainly we just exchanged funny and strange stories of things that had happened to us throughout our respective time with music.

I recounted a story of my first time at Glastonbury Festival in 1998.

Arriving at the festival with no ticket, I paid a guy the princely sum of £5 to use his rope ladder to gain access to the main site. It was also, up until then, the muddiest Glastonbury on record.

Jim roared with laughter at this tale, and told me I'd have to tell that one when I'm, "on Conan O'Brien". I had to do my utter best to stifle the request for him to make that happen, and reason with myself internally that it was a throwaway remark and not an offer of a contract.

Dinner was about to be served, and we went back indoors to take our seats at the dining table.

Steak, potatoes, and salad was served up. It was easily the best meal I had in my entire time in the States, and I had eaten well. Nothing beats a home-cooked meal with good people. Camaraderie is thin on the ground when you're a solo musician.

We ate, drank, and laughed. Everybody got on famously, and the food was incredible. I felt incredibly lucky to be enjoying the company and the cuisine, and had an ever present voice in the back of my head telling me, *"Don't fuck this up"*.

After dinner and a few glasses of wine, Mike then told the table that there was a little after dinner entertainment. I sat forward, attentive and curious as to what our wonderful hosts now had up their sleeves... When it became clear that everyone was looking at me, I realised that the after-dinner entertainment was me.

"Of course!" I exclaimed, getting out of my seat to fetch my guitar.

Everybody went back to general after dinner chit-chat, whilst I tuned up my guitar.

Earlier in the day, assuming I would get to play three songs, I'd figured it was best to play the three that people have commented the most on to me.

The first song I was going play would be, 'Have Some Soul'.

I placed my capo on the 2nd fret, and played a few chords to make sure the intonation on the guitar was correct. Unfortunately, it was not. I rued my decision to not change strings earlier in the day, since these strings had now been on a week after the gig in Napa, and had dulled considerably in this time.

Mike enquired if I was ready to go, I bemoaned my strings and asked him I could possibly use his guitar. Being the superb and facilitating host that he is, he handed me a beautiful Taylor acoustic. It had fresh strings, it sounded, and played like a dream.

We were all seated around the table, I coughed for silence in an exaggerated manner, and got a few laughs before the room fell silent.

Here goes...

I struck the 3rd, 2nd, and 1st harmonics on the 14th fret, then hit the 6th string on that fret too – after a timely pause – then slid back to the open 2nd where the capo rested, and began the verse.

As I began singing, in the growling tone that this song demands, I saw everyone's eyes widen a little. It occurred to me that I probably should've told them before I started that I don't always sing this way, but soon pushed that thought out of my mind when I noticed feet tapping and fingers drumming on wineglasses as they locked in on the groove. I closed my eyes and did the same. Hitting every note clean as a whistle.

The song drew to a close, and my hosts and fellow diners clapped and cheered their approval.

"That's a pretty neat voice you got there," came the conclusion from Jim, accompanied by heads nodding in agreement around the table.

"Oh, I don't always sing that way, that's just to mix it up a little, keep people on their feet. Mainly mine. You wanna hear another?"

Thankfully they did.

Next up was 'Yet to Break', upping the tempo, as my voice returned to a more human timbre.

The song had been written nearly two years before, at a smaller dinner table back in County Antrim, so it felt perfectly suited to the environment. Everyone sat a little forward for the song's fourth and final verse, as I brought it down and added a softer touch on both my guitar and vocals. This is a requisite device of the song, it is also a great way to invoke reeling your listener in.

On the final chord, an enthusiastic response was afforded to me as my small audience clapped and cheered me on once more. I asked if they wanted to hear one more, and thank god – they did. That could have been hugely embarrassing otherwise.

Lastly, I opted to play 'Shakedown Sally'. I've played it as a set closer many times before, and it always went down well, so I thought it was a natural choice to end on this evening.

Introducing the song, I gave my usual spiel about Gene Vincent and classic rock 'n roll that I had given almost as many times as I had played the tune in question.

Within three seconds of playing, I could see feet tapping. Surely the surest sign that it's going well, that the music is being listened to at the very least. As the song ramped up a little, heads were nodding and Carl (a drummer, remember?) began lightly drumming on the table. Even better than all this, shoulders were moving and everyone, myself included, was *smiling*.

What more could a songwriter want?

Well, it would've been cool if everybody had leapt from their seats and broken into spontaneously choreographed dance. But still, this was pretty damn close. As close as reality can get anyway.

I hit the last chord and muted it immediately, and with that, everybody pushed back their seats and stood applauding. My third and final standing ovation on this American trip. It was so special.

So special in fact, that I jokingly told them shut up and sit down. Which they did shortly thereafter, obviously. It would have been weird if they didn't.

The after-dinner drinks continued to flow as we returned outside. We were all respectably lubricated by this point, and laughs were coming thick and fast. Eventually, I had built up enough Devil's Backbone to ask Jim if he enjoyed what he heard, and how much I'd love the opportunity to work with him. He nonchalantly replied, as if it was a given,

"Yeah, sure, the songs were great Tony, lets talk. Here's my card."

Wow. Was it that easy?

I thanked him profusely, and went on to tell him about the strange line of coincidence that had led for us to all meet. From my meeting with his (unbeknownst to me) employee Chris, and his suggestion that our mutual friend Jesse put us in touch, to actually sitting in the Hollywood hills together on the last night of my trip. I mean, you couldn't write this, it was all so fortuitous. It all had the distinct scent of fate about it, synchronicity in action. A domino effect of circumstance was even more far-fetched than this all being mere happy coincidence, surely? At least a modicum of destiny had to be at play here?

"Yeah, Mike told me about that. Pretty neat, huh?"

I could sense that the *huh* at the end of his reply was most definitely a rhetorical one, and that I should cease selling myself and the fortunate series of events that had brought us all to Mike and Anna's beautiful Hollywood home that evening.

The much better option, was to just enjoy myself.

A most sensational development, I'm sure you'll agree.

The night whiled away much too fast and before we knew it was 1am.

Carl and Jill ordered a cab and I followed suit, not wishing to be *that guy*, the houseguest that never leaves.

We said our goodbyes, and Mike and Anna told me to call them the following day if I had time to kill before going to the airport. Mike then told me that the next time I was in LA, I was staying with them. No questions asked. He left me with the eternally optimistic words, "The next trip, will be a *great* one."

Jim agreed with Mike, and then shook my hand, telling me he looked forward to us being in touch.

"*What did they mean?*" My drunken mind quizzed myself.

With a smile as wide as the Mariana Trench is deep, I thanked them and got in my cab, back to my luxurious, ant infested apartment in Santa Monica.

"*Everything, is going to work out just fine. Everything,*" My drunken – happy – mind told myself.

At my building, I took the elevator to the fifth floor and made my way to apartment 501.

I jumped over some cockroaches in the corridor that were as big as the grin on my face, even saying hello to a few of them, such was the buoyancy of my mood. When I unlocked my door, I greeted the hard at work ants that were still streaming from the cupboard with similar pleasantness, and remarked at how I admired their work ethic. These ants got things done.

Despite the fact that it was my last night in America, I felt an enormous sense of elation. I felt as if some sort of mission had been successfully accomplished. I thought all about all the incredible people I had met, not just over here but on all of my travels, solo tours as well as travails with the band, all of those people who had shown me such kindness and had made me feel at home in their company, going above, beyond, and out of their way to ensure this weary, song and dance man felt at ease so far from his family.

These people who had made their home, my home.

Their kindness reverberating, like a good gesture paid forward, and how I was possibly the luckiest man on earth as a result.

I was never as alone as I had ever thought.

Everything, is going to work out just fine.

I remembered the little bit of weed that had been given to me weeks before in New York, and rummaged through my bag to find it in an old tobacco packet lodged at the bottom. Enough for a small joint. It was now 2am, and the revelling drunken rebel in me slid back the balcony door to smoke it.

The night was warm, and the streets below were peaceful. I put my headphones in and, with one eye closed to help me focus, searched through the music on my phone for an appropriate sign off song. The end credits, if I may.

I was very close to putting on the excellent Joe Strummer and Johnny Cash cover of Bob Marley's 'Redemption Song'.

My finger hovered above the play button for a few seconds.

Hmmm, nah... too obvious.

Then it hit me.

I knew exactly what I wanted to hear.

I lit my smoke, cranked the volume and listened to 'Mannish Boy' by Muddy Waters.

Only this time, I kept my mouth shut, and my mind completely open.

"Maybe I'll try my hand at writing and acting too," I thought. "I mean...why not?"